Studies in the History of Medieval

C000226852

VOLUME IV

THE RULE OF THE TEMPLARS
The French Text of
the Rule of the Order of the Knights Templar

Studies in the History of Medieval Religion

ISSN 0955–2480

General Editor
Christopher Harper-Bill

THE RULE OF THE TEMPLARS

The French Text of
the Rule of the Order of
the Knights Templar

Translated and introduced by
J. M. UPTON-WARD

THE BOYDELL PRESS

First published 1992
The Boydell Press, Woodbridge
Reprinted in paperback 1997, 1999, 2001, 2005, 2008

Transferred to digital printing

ISBN 978-0-85115-701-6

The Boydell Press is an imprint of Boydell & Brewer Ltd
PO Box 9, Woodbridge, Suffolk IP12 3DF, UK
and of Boydell & Brewer Inc.
668 Mt Hope Avenue, Rochester, NY 14620, USA
website: www.boydellandbrewer.com

A catalogue record for this book is available
from the British Library

Library of Congress Catalog Card Number: 92-286

This publication is printed on acid-free paper

Printed in Great Britain by
Biddles Ltd, King's Lynn

Contents

Acknowledgements

Three members on the staff of Reading University have assisted in the preparation of this book:

My largest debt is to Professor Malcolm Barber of the History Department, who first suggested this project and supervised it as my MPhil dissertation. I cannot thank him enough for his continued support and encouragement, not to mention his expert advice.

I am also grateful to Dr Peter Noble of the Department of French Studies, who helped me with some more difficult points of the French, and Professor Brian Kemp, who assisted in the translation of the Latin passages.

This work has also benefited from the military expertise of Mr Matthew Bennett of the Royal Military Academy, Sandhurst, who shared this expertise with me and who receives my grateful thanks.

I thank my family and friends who have supported me, emotionally and financially, during the past few years.

I have taken the opportunity of this second printing to make a few revisions to the text. In this respect I am grateful particularly to Dr Denys Pringle, Dr Alan Forey and Professor Rudolf Hiestand for their comments.

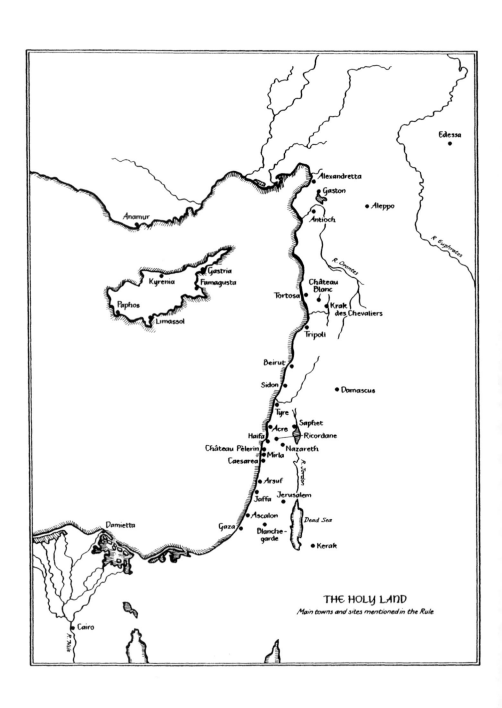

Edessa

Anamur

Alexandretta
Gaston
Aleppo
Antioch

R. Orontes

Gastria
Kyrenia
Famagusta
Château
Blanc
Tortosa
Krak
Paphos
des Chevaliers
Limassol
Tripoli

R. Euphrates

Beirut
Sidon
Damascus
Tyre
Saphet
Acre
Ricordane
Haifa
Château Pèlerin
Nazareth
Caesarea
Mirla
R. Jordan
Arsuf
Jaffa
Jerusalem
Damietta
Ascalon
Dead Sea
Gaza
Blanche-
garde
Kerak

R. Nile
Cairo

THE HOLY LAND
Main towns and sites mentioned in the Rule

Introduction

HISTORICAL BACKGROUND

The most authoritative chronicler of the Kingdom of Jerusalem in the twelfth century was William of Tyre. In his work *A History of Deeds Done Beyond the Sea*, which he compiled between 1167 and 1184, he places the foundation of the Templars in 1119/20, a date confirmed by charter evidence. Their original aim was to protect pilgrims from Moslem attacks as they travelled through Palestine to visit the Holy Places in Jerusalem and elsewhere.[1]

People had been making pilgrimages to the Holy Land for centuries, but the capture of Jerusalem in 1099 encouraged them to make the hazardous journey in greater numbers. Defence of the Christian-held lands was not easy, and man-power levels were such that the Franks were never able to muster sufficient trained men for both a large field army and an adequate garrison for their castles. Men could seldom be spared to patrol the pilgrim routes, nor to escort new arrivals from the ports. There are a number of accounts by pilgrims of the dangers they faced on their travels. They might be attacked by Moslem robbers and left dead by the roadside by their companions who were too afraid to stop to bury them;[2] or they might die of sunstroke or thirst, for the brigands allowed them no access to natural water sources. Pilgrim camps were easy targets, and people were advised not to travel without a large escort, which was not always easy to find. If one managed to escape these human dangers, there were the lions and other wild animals which lived in the Jordan valley.[3]

So it was that a small group of knights, led by Hugues de Payens, took pity on the plight of such pilgrims and vowed to devote themselves to their protection and to form a religious community for that purpose. The Order derived its title from the site of the former Jewish Temple, near to which Baldwin II, King of Jerusalem, gave them quarters in a wing of the royal palace. They took vows of poverty, chastity and obedience before the Patriarch of Jerusalem and were attached to the regular canons of the Holy Sepulchre who lived by the rule of St Augustine. The idea of protecting travellers was not new in the West. As part of

1   William of Tyre, 'Chronicon', ed. R.B.C. Huygens, in the *Corpus Christianorum*, vols. LXIII & LXIIIA (Brepols 1986), XII,7: 'Ordo militie Templi Ierosolimis instituitur', vol. LXIII, pp. 553–55. An English translation entitled *A History of Deeds Done Beyond the Sea* is available, tr. A.E. Babcock & A.C. Krey (New York 1976).
2   'Saewulf. A Reliable Account of the Situation of Jerusalem', in *Jerusalem Pilgrimage 1099–1185*, ed. J. Wilkinson, with J. Hill and W.F. Ryan, The Hakluyt Society, Series II, vol. 167, London 1988, p. 100.
3   'The Life and Journey of Daniel, Abbot of the Russian Land', in *Jerusalem Pilgrimage 1099–1185*, ed. J. Wilkinson, with J. Hill and W.F. Ryan, The Hakluyt Society, Series II, vol. 167, London 1988, p. 137.

a larger peace movement, which began in France towards the end of the tenth century, the Church had sought to use its power to forbid attacks upon pilgrims and travellers of all kinds. From the Synod of Charroux (c. 989) onwards, canons were enacted which demanded the cessation of warfare at certain times of the year and also the exemption of certain social groups, including pilgrims and travellers, from attack. Furthermore, at a Roman council of 1059 Pope Nicholas II adopted the policy of protecting both the persons and possessions of travellers, especially pilgrims to sacred shrines, as an obligation of the papacy.[4]

What was new, however, was the combination of monk and soldier as found in the brothers of the Temple. In the early Middle Ages the term 'knight of Christ' – miles Christi – referred to a member of one of the religious orders who fought evil with prayer and the mass, and is used in this sense in the rule of St Benedict. During the pontificate of Gregory VII (1073–1085), however, the term took on a new meaning. For Gregory, the 'warfare of Christ' came to mean armed clashes of feudal knights on the battlefields of Christendom, and the true milites Christi were those laymen who fought with material weapons in the interests of the Church. Until that time, laymen could hope for the absolution of their sins only by being founders or benefactors of a monastic order, or by taking the habit. Now the laity had a new means of salvation.[5] However, the religious vocation maintained its superior status over the call to arms. St Bernard states that it is permissible for these milites Christi to 'strike with the sword . . . provided they have not embraced a higher calling',[6] that is, provided they have not joined a monastic order. Moreover, monks were expressly forbidden to bear arms.

The Order seems to have attracted little interest during the early years, either in Palestine or in the West. By the time of the Council of Troyes in 1129,[7] William of Tyre puts the number of Templars at only nine. While this is probably an underestimate, they were obviously still few in number, and the insignificance of the Order at this time is indicated by the absence of any mention of the Templars by the historian Fulcher of Chartres, who was living and writing in Jerusalem up to about 1127.

Nevertheless, from the outset the Order attracted influential supporters. The

---

[4] J.A. Brundage, Medieval Canon Law and the Crusader (Madison 1969), p. 12.

[5] I.S. Robinson, 'Gregory VII and the Soldiers of Christ', History, 1973, vol. 58, No.193, pp. 169–92.

[6] Bernard of Clairvaux, 'Liber ad Milites Templi de laude Novae Militiae', Sancti Bernardi Opera, ed. J. Leclercq (Rome 1963), vol. III, III, 5, pp. 217–18. An English translation by C. Greenia can be found in Cistercian Fathers Series: 19 (Michigan 1977).

[7] It has long been accepted that the council was held in January 1128, and this, indeed, is the date given in the Rule itself. However, from the beginning of the twelfth century large areas of France began the year on 25 March; thus January 1128 would have been January 1129. Hiestand argues convincingly for January 1129 as the date of the council, basing his arguments principally on the movements of Matthew of Albano, who was present at the council. R. Hiestand, 'Kardinalbischof Matthäus von Albano, das Konzil von Troyes und die Entstehung des Templeordens', Zeitschrift für Kirchengeschichte, 1988, vol. 99, pp. 295–325.

king, the patriarch and various individuals supplied it with a number of benefices sufficient to feed and clothe its members. Fulk V, Count of Anjou (later Baldwin's successor to the throne of Jerusalem), lodged at the Temple while on pilgrimage in Jerusalem in 1120–21, and joined the Order as a lay associate. He also granted the Templars an annual subsidy of thirty *livres angevines* from his lands in Anjou. Hugh, Count of Champagne, with whom Hugues de Payens was closely connected – whether by blood or service is not certain – in 1125 ceded his lands to his nephew, Theobald, Count of Blois, and journeyed to the Holy Land, where he joined the new Order.[8]

It may well have been Count Hugh who first solicited support for the Order from Bernard of Clairvaux. The Count had been generous to religious houses and it is possible that he gave St Bernard the site for Clairvaux. The two were certainly on good terms, for after the Count had joined the Templars, Bernard wrote to congratulate him on giving himself to the service of God, although he wished it could have been with his own order, the Cistercians.[9] The Count was therefore in a position to influence Bernard and he may have prompted a letter which purports to be from Baldwin II to Bernard, commending to him two knights of the Temple, Andrew and Gondemar, and asking him to obtain approval of the Order from the pope. The rise of the Order is probably due to these influential friends, for otherwise the Templars may well not have been singled out from other small communities for recognition as a religious order with papal protection.

Despite this support, the Order seems to have been in difficulty by 1129. A letter,[10] the authorship of which is uncertain, but which may have been written by Hugues de Payens from the West at the time of the Council of Troyes, aimed to boost the morale of those brothers left in the East. With the brothers plagued by doubts, Hugues may have done well to keep the Order in being up to this point. His journey to the West may have been prompted by a fear that without more widespread support and recognition the Order might fail. The brothers lived in real poverty without any distinctive habit, and recruitment had been minimal. Besides spiritual doubts, there were practical difficulties. Perhaps their task seemed impossible given such small numbers, and the lack of growth of the Order may have given rise to doubts about God's approval for their mission.

Hugues, accompanied by five brothers, Godefroy de St Omer, Roland, Geoffroi Bisot, Payen de Montdidier and Archambaud de St Amand, put his case to the Council. He told of the humble beginnings of the Order and recounted its history.[11] The Council then deliberated upon its constitution and the Order was given its own Rule, based on that of the Cistercians. This Rule

8 M.C. Barber, 'The Origins of the Order of the Temple', *Studia Monastica*, 1970, vol. XII, p. 223. 'Chronica Albrici Monachi Trium Fontium', ed. Scheffer-Boichorst, *Monumenta Germaniae Historica*, XXIII, p. 826.

9 B.S. James, tr., *The Letters of St. Bernard of Clairvaux* (London 1953), p. 65.

10 J. Leclercq, 'Un Document sur les Débuts des Templiers', *Revue d'Histoire Ecclésiastique*, 1957, vol. 52, pp. 81–91.

11 Rule §7.

distinguished between knight brothers, who were to wear white mantles, and sergeants and squires, who were to wear black or brown ones.[12]

Hugues and his companions dispersed to their homelands in order to recruit new members and to found commanderies in Europe. In addition, while in the West Hugues was to recruit men for Baldwin II, who was planning an attack on Damascus. Indeed, Hugues' visit to the West may well have been financed by Baldwin.[13] Hugues first stayed in Champagne, then went to Anjou; the Anglo-Saxon Chronicle says that he visited Normandy, England and Scotland in 1128.[14] He then returned to the continent, and was back in the East by 1130. The trip had been a resounding success. Everywhere they went the brothers received grants of land and properties; gold and silver; and reliefs on fiefs, as well as men. The response in France was so great that Hugues appointed Payen de Montdidier to take care of the province. European expansion continued after Hugues' return to Jerusalem. Interest at this time was most marked in northern France, but the Order gained ground also in Portugal, Spain and Provence. Raymond-Berengar III, Count of Barcelona and Provence, joined the Order as an associate member on 14 July, 1130. The need for material support for the Holy Land had been recognised at the Council of Troyes, the Order's right to own land and collect tithes being expressly mentioned in the Primitive Rule,[15] and with donations of land, the Templars began to establish themselves as important landlords and thus undertook a new function.[16] During the rest of the twelfth century and the beginning of the thirteenth century, the fame and scale of the Order continued to grow beyond anything that Hugues and his co-founders could have imagined. With the many donations it received, it became extremely wealthy. The function of the houses in the West was to provide money, men and other provisions for the brothers fighting in the East. It was vital, therefore, that good communications existed between the two, and the principal method of transport was by sea. The Templars' main port was Acre and all the ships there were under the Commander of the Land of Jerusalem.[17]

The Council of Troyes was convened in 1129 with the main purpose of considering the claims of the Order for recognition. Bernard of Clairvaux was there and he played a major part in writing the Rule of the Order. Thereafter, he continued to give moral support and to promote the Order amongst his fellow churchmen. When Hugues asked St Bernard for a justification of his Order, this came in the form of the tract entitled *De laude Novae Militiae ad Milites Templi* written some time between 1129 and 1136, the probable date of Hugues' death. This exhortation is divided into thirteen chapters, only the first five of which deal directly with the Templars' dilemma, the rest being a description of the

---

[12] Rule §68.
[13] Barber, *op. cit.* p. 230.
[14] G.N. Garmondsway, tr. *The Anglo-Saxon Chronicle* (London 1953), p. 259, A.D. 1128.
[15] Rule §57–58.
[16] Barber, *op. cit.* p. 237.
[17] Rule §119.

major Holy Places and the biblical events which took place there. St Bernard treats several themes which echo both Hugues' letter and the Rule. It has been argued that St Bernard probably had Hugues' letter and the Rule in front of him as he wrote and, indeed, the manuscript of Hugues' letter was found between a copy of the Rule and the *De laude*.[18] The most important of the themes, in terms of justifying the new Order, is that of the soldier-monk, and for this St Bernard uses all the force of his eloquent language. Despite the initial opposition, with such whole-hearted approbation from a man of St Bernard's repute, the Templars could not fail to gain acceptance in the highest Church quarters.

Towards the end of the 1130s the Order emerged as a fully-fledged military order with a hierarchical structure, thanks largely to Hugues de Payens' successor as Grand Master, Robert de Craon, or Robert the Burgundian (1136–1149). Whereas Hugues had been above all a pious knight with determination and good leadership qualities, Robert was a great administrator. He saw that the Order could prosper only with the open support of the papacy and free of the local ecclesiastical authorities, some of whom were already jealous of the Order's success and were contesting its right to receive tithes and alms. In 1139 the Order received this support when Innocent II issued the bull *Omne datum optimum*, whose declared object was to create a new category of chaplain brothers for the Templars, to serve them in their now widespread houses. The chaplain brothers formed a separate group and had special privileges. The French Rule dictates that a chaplain brother was to be given the best robes and wear leather gloves.[19] The only other brothers permitted to wear gloves were the masons when they were working, to protect their hands.[20] A chaplain brother was to sit next to the Master at meal times, to be served first and given the best food.[21] If a chaplain brother sinned he was not expected to work with the slaves for his penance, but to say his psalter.[22] These chaplain brothers were full members of the Order and could hear confessions and absolve the brothers. In fact, according to the Rule, they had greater power to absolve on behalf of the pope than an archbishop.[23] However, according to the Rule, there were five faults which a chaplain brother could not absolve. These were the killing of a Christian man or woman; violently attacking another brother; attacking a member of another order or a priest; renouncing holy orders in order to be received as a brother; and entering the Order through simony.[24]

The introduction of chaplain brothers was indicative of the much wider significance of *Omne datum optimum*. By placing it directly under papal authority, Innocent gave the Order the autonomy which enabled it to act independently of the ecclesiastical and secular rulers in whose jurisdiction it

---

[18] Leclercq, 'Un Document', p. 91.
[19] Rule §268 and 325.
[20] Rule §325.
[21] Rule §268.
[22] Rule §270 and 637.
[23] Rule §269.
[24] Rule §272.

operated.[25] The Grand Master and chapter were given sole responsibility for the actions and conduct of the Order. Innocent II also exhorted the Templars to devote themselves to defending the Catholic Church against all enemies of the Cross. In this can be seen the formal recognition of the Order's much wider role as defenders of Christendom than the restricted function which Hugues and his companions originally undertook. However, they did not cease to act as the protectors of pilgrims. According to the Hierarchical Statutes, ten knights were assigned to this duty under the command of the Commander of the City of Jerusalem.[26] Nevertheless, by the end of 1139 the Order had adopted the form and function by which it was to be recognized throughout the rest of its history.

A logical extension of the Templars' role as protectors of pilgrims was as guardians of crusaders, whose mobile columns were almost as vulnerable as pilgrims. The Order's unique combination of monk and soldier made it invaluable to the crusading armies of the West, for the discipline of monastic life was applied to the battlefield. This is made clear in the French Rule, which sets out the discipline to be maintained on campaign. A brother was not allowed to charge without permission, except to rescue another Christian in distress,[27] and lost his habit if he did so. Leaving one's banner was considered desertion and resulted in expulsion from the Order.[28] If the Christians were defeated in battle and a brother returned to his garrison while there was still a Christian banner raised aloft, he was likewise expelled from the Order.[29] The Order's banner had both practical and symbolic significance to the brothers as a rallying point in battle. Up to ten knights were detailed to guard it.[30] A brother who carried the banner risked the loss of his habit if he charged without permission; he also lost the right to carry the banner again or to be a commander in battle. If harm came to the Christians because of his action he was put in irons.[31] The same penalty was given to a brother who lowered the banner.[32]

By the 1170s the number of Templar knights in the Kingdom of Jerusalem seems to have been approximately three hundred. With the Hospitallers they made up about half the effective fighting force of the kingdom and it is likely that they maintained comparable numbers in Antioch and Tripoli. Although the Templars and Hospitallers have frequently been portrayed as rivals, in fact instances of co-operation are more numerous than those of conflict. This relationship is built into the Rule. The two orders fought side by side in battle, and

---

[25] Practice may have been somewhat different from theory, however. Cf. J. Riley-Smith, 'The Templars and the Castle of Tortosa in Syria: An Unknown Document Concerning the Acquisition of the Fortress', *English Historical Review*, 1969, vol. 84, pp. 278–88.

[26] Rule §121.

[27] Rule §62, 243 and 613.

[28] Rule §524.

[29] Rule §168.

[30] Rule §164.

[31] Rule §242 and 612.

[32] Rule §241.

there are several passages in the Rule which express the special relationship which existed between them. For instance, brothers were not allowed to go to the lodgings of other religious without permission, except to the Hospitallers;[33] nor were they allowed to eat or drink wine outside their house, except with the Hospitallers.[34] In battle, if a brother could not rally round the Order's banner for any reason, he was to go to any other Christian banner, but especially to that of the Hospitallers.[35] A good deal of controversy arose when a Master ordered a group of brothers to retreat from Jerusalem to Jaffa because of the threat from invading Tartars (c. 1260), and the commander of the group refused to go without the Hospitallers who had joined them.[36]

Because of the continuity of their existence in the East, the Templars became a repository of military tradition and experience. No European crusading army could dispense with their advice for they knew the East and the strengths and weaknesses of the Moslem enemy. They were indispensable to the crusading effort and no major attack could take place without them. The Grand Masters of both the Hospital and the Temple would be present at councils convened when each new major contingent of crusaders arrived in the East, in order to determine a military objective compatible with the overall interests of the Latin states. As the crusaders gained victories, the Order was given castles to garrison and these formed a network of strongholds throughout the lands held by the Christians.

The Grand Master became involved in all important political decisions, for example in 1177 when the Count of Flanders was offered the Regency. His advice was respected and he could exert a moderating influence in the government of the kingdom because his men had to stay in the East and uphold the security of the Latin states, while the majority of crusaders eventually returned to the West. The Grand Master would also act as arbiter in local disputes which threatened to weaken the Latin states. In such cases he would not always be called upon directly, but an appeal would be made to the pope, who would refer the matter to the Master. His diplomatic skills were put to good use in dealings with the Eastern neighbours. For example, in 1147 Evrard de Barres helped to negotiate the passage of the Second Crusade through Constantinople with the Byzantine Emperor Manuel.

With their houses established all over Europe, the Templars inspired confidence because of their religious standing and their permanent presence in the Holy Land, and they added banking to their other functions. By the thirteenth century they were familiar figures among the fiscal advisers of Western royalty. They furnished both Louis VII and Louis IX with money in the crusades of 1148 and 1250. Indeed, from the time of Philip Augustus the treasure of the French

---

33 Rule §145.
34 Rule §320.
35 Rule §167/8 and 421.
36 Rule §576.

kings was kept at the Temple in Paris.[37] However, although the Order was renowned for its wealth, and its function as banker and landowner, it is interesting to note that there is very little reference to any of these in the Rule. Money is mentioned only when it is given to a brother in order for him to purchase a particular item or perform a specific task for the Order; and any sum left over had to be returned immediately. Failure to do so resulted in expulsion from the Order, and a brother who was found to have money on him when he died was not buried in consecrated ground, nor were the brothers required to pray for his soul.[38] The Rule even goes as far as to say that his body should be thrown to the dogs.[39] There are few direct references to land ownership. One example is that the Master was not allowed to give away or sell land without the permission of the chapter.[40] One of the historical examples of penances given implies land ownership and cultivation when it recounts that brothers from the garden lost their habits when they ate dinner with some brothers from the vineyard after they had been forbidden to do so.[41] *Casals*, farms or villages owned by the Order and dependent upon a major house or castle, are mentioned briefly, but there are no details of their activities. Such evidence is recorded in charters, but as the Templar archive is lost, it must be obtained indirectly from the charters of other institutions, such as the Hospitallers, with which the Templars made agreements. The lack of such evidence within the text suggests that the leaders and those who laid down the regulations were not concerned with such matters. Their priorities were fighting the enemies of Christendom and worshipping God through lives governed by their vows of poverty, chastity and obedience.

Meanwhile, they had the whole-hearted support of the papacy and the privileges granted to them and confirmed in successive bulls made them almost autonomous. However, the attitudes of the papacy and the local Church hierarchy were often diametrically opposed, for as long as Rome granted and confirmed the Order's privileges, the Church was denied jurisdiction over it and revenue from its lands. The privileges granted to the Templars in *Omne datum optimum* drew heavy criticism during the Third Lateran Council of 1179, when a flood of complaints demanded a stop to the progressive exemptions of the military orders. Some half-hearted attempts to limit them followed, but by then the major privileges had already been granted and they were not repealed. There was not necessarily conflict between these orders and the Church, however; early charters show mutual co-operation.

With the fall of Jerusalem in 1187, the importance of the military orders was increased. The Frankish knighthood was ruined; the monarchy had lost the greater part of its domain and its revenues; the resources of the Church had

[37] J.W. Baldwin, *The Government of Philip Augustus* (University of California Press 1986), p. 57.
[38] Rule §331.
[39] Rule §566.
[40] Rule §85.
[41] Rule §616/7.

dwindled, despite subsidies from the papacy; but the military orders, despite very heavy losses in manpower, had not suffered in the same way, for their main wealth lay in the West. Under these conditions, it was recognised that the Holy Land could not be defended without them. The Templars lost many of their original castles, but even so during the thirteenth century it became increasingly clear that only the military orders had the resources to maintain the defences of the crusader states on the necessary scale, and after about 1250 the Templars began to receive the guard of castles which their lords could no longer afford. The papacy continued to act as the Order's protector and towards the end of the thirteenth century the Master of the Temple was an important European figure in the eyes of the Moslems. Even so, the Latin settlements in Palestine and Syria were coming under ever greater pressure, and when Acre fell to the Mamluks in 1291, the Order lost its base and its *raison d'être*, unlike the other two major military orders. The Hospitallers continued their original purpose of caring for the sick on the islands of Rhodes (1309–1522) and later Malta (1530–1798), while the Teutonic Knights went to carry on the crusade against the pagan Slavs in eastern Europe. The Templars moved their headquarters to Cyprus, but had outlived their usefulness in the eyes of many. Shortly after the fall of Acre, the crusading theorists Raymond Lull and Pierre Dubois put forward the idea of an amalgamation of the military orders.[42] These authors were merely echoing a widely-held opinion, and the question of amalgamation was considered on a number of occasions in the late-thirteenth and early-fourteenth centuries by the ecclesiastical authorities. It was discussed at the Council of Lyon in 1274; and in 1291, a few months after the fall of Acre, Pope Nicholas IV ordered the summoning of provincial councils to consider the matter. A series of assemblies was convened in the latter part of 1291 and early in 1292, and all the conciliar recommendations on this issue which have survived – from England, France, Germany and Italy – were in favour of union. Nicholas died, however, in April 1292, before anything further could be done. The matter was taken up again by both Boniface VIII and Clement V, but when, in 1307, the Templars in France were suddenly arrested, there had still been no attempt to put the proposals into practice.

To ensure that the military orders pulled their weight in the crusading effort, it was suggested at the Council of Lyon that their properties should be assessed in order to discover how many knights could be maintained from their lands, and it was argued that the orders should be obliged to keep this number in the East. The implication was that a minimum number of knights should remain in the West and this opinion was stated in a letter from the French clergy to Nicholas IV.[43] The prelates at the Council of Reims, one of the provincial councils convened to discuss the matter, appear to have envisaged the confiscation of the

---

[42] A.J. Forey, 'The Military Orders in the Crusading Proposals of the Late-Thirteenth and Early-Fourteenth Centuries', *Traditio*, 1980, vol. 36, p. 320. Pierre Dubois, *The Recovery of the Holy Land*, tr. W.I. Brandt (New York 1956), I, 14, pp. 81–2.

[43] Forey, *op. cit.* p. 327.

military orders' property only if they were unwilling to provide an adequate force of troops for the Holy Land. Others, including the Norman lawyer, Pierre Dubois, were of the opinion that their property should be appropriated in any case and that they should subsist from their properties in the East. The members who were resident in the West, it was argued, should be made to join Cistercian monasteries.[44] In the main body of his work, Dubois' proposals refer to all the military orders, but in a postscript, probably written in the light of knowledge of their arrest, he attacks only the Templars and advocates the abolition of the Order.[45] In fact, the Templars had always been well aware of the vital need to maintain manpower levels in the East, and there were strict instructions governing the sending of brothers back to the West, either because they were ill or in order to carry out some task for the Order. A list of likely candidates had to be drawn up and given to the Master, and he could make alterations only with the advice of the Marshal, the Commander of the Land of Jerusalem, the Draper and the Commander of Acre, together with a group of the most respected brothers.[46]

When accusations of idolatry and immoral practices were brought to the attention of Philip IV of France, he seems to have seen an opportunity both to rid himself of an apparent threat of heresy and to augment governmental income. Those who lived in the East were suspected of having adopted Saracen ways and of having been contaminated by Islam.[47] In the accusations brought against them, great emphasis was also placed upon the fact that the Templars adopted absolute secrecy in all their internal activities, although this was normal practice among monastic orders, and was particularly important for the Templars, bearing in mind that military matters would be discussed and the security of the Holy Land was at stake. Nevertheless, suspicions were aroused and this assisted the French king in his plans. The Inquisition was brought in and many Templars confessed to heresy under torture. Despite failing to gain support from other European monarchs, Philip manipulated the pope, Clement V, and the Order was dissolved in 1312. The pope ruled that the Order's estates should pass into the hands of the Hospitallers. Two years later, the last Grand Master of the Order, Jacques de Molay, was burned at the stake as a relapsed heretic. Few besides Philip IV were convinced of the heretical charges brought against the Templars. Since, however, the pope had dissolved the Order, the monarchs of Europe found various means of coping with the situation. In England, Edward II pensioned them and they were mostly transferred to other monastic orders in small numbers. In Spain the Templars joined the other military orders of Montesa and Calatrava. The Portuguese king, Denis, maintained them as before and called them 'Knights of Christ'.[48]

---

[44] Dubois, *op. cit.* I, 15, pp. 82–3.
[45] *Ibid.* Appendix 3, p. 200 and Appendix 5, p. 201.
[46] Rule §93.
[47] See J. Riley-Smith, 'Peace Never Established: The Case of the Kingdom of Jerusalem', *Transactions of the Royal Historical Society*, 1978, vol. 28, pp. 87–102.
[48] G. Bordonove, *La Vie Quotidienne des Templiers au XIIIe Siècle* (Paris 1975), p. 213.

THE TEXT

The whole document is divided into seven main sections: the Primitive Rule, the Hierarchical Statutes, Penances, Conventual Life, the Holding of Ordinary Chapters, Further Details on Penances and, finally, Reception into the Order. It evolved over almost 150 years and is not, therefore, a homogeneous piece of work from the same period and by the same author. Its constituent texts were written one after another without revisions, giving rise to numerous repetitions.

There are no original manuscripts extant; these were probably destroyed at the time of the arrests in France. The three which Henri de Curzon used for his edition of 1886, from which this translation is taken, are those of Paris, Rome and Dijon. The manuscripts of Paris and Rome date from the end of the thirteenth century or the beginning of the fourteenth and are practically identical, indicating that they derive from the same source. That of Dijon dates from the beginning of the thirteenth century, but consists of only the Primitive Rule and the Hierarchical Statutes. There is one other French manuscript which was unknown at the time of de Curzon's edition. There are also several Latin manuscripts of the Primitive Rule,[49] while an incomplete Catalan version of the *retrais* is conserved in Barcelona. The small number of manuscripts is explained by the fact that they were limited during the existence of the Order and none were recorded at the time of the proceedings against the brothers. Evidence for the restriction of the distribution of the document is contained within the text itself.[50] It is interesting to note that in clause 326 a distinction is made between the Rule and the *retrais*. The Rule obviously refers to the Primitive Rule, while the *retrais* are the Hierarchical Statutes and the regulations governing conventual life. The Primitive Rule must have been widely available even outside the Order, but circulation of the *retrais*, containing information which could have been of interest to an enemy, was restricted to the higher officials of the Order.

The Primitive Rule
The Primitive Rule, originally written in Latin, is the result of the deliberations of the Council of Troyes, which opened on 13 January, 1129. In the debate concerning the 'authorship' of the Primitive Rule it must not be forgotten that the Order had been in existence for several years and had built up its own traditions and customs before Hugues de Payens' appearance at the Council of Troyes. To a considerable extent, then, the Primitive Rule is based upon existing practices. However, these practices must have been modified by the council

---

49 L. Daillez, *La Règle du Temple* (Nice 1977), claims to have found nine, although S.S. Rovik, *The Templars in the Holy Land during the Twelfth Century* (Oxford D.Phil. thesis 1986), p. 86 casts doubt on the existence of some of them. See S. Cerrini's survey of all the known manuscripts (six Latin, four French), S. Cerrini, 'La Tradition Manuscrite de la Règle du Temple', in *Autour de la Première Croisade. Actes du Colloque de la Society for the Study of the Crusades and the Latin East (Clement-Ferrand, 22–25 juin 1995)*, ed. M. Balard, Paris 1996 (Publications de la Sorbonne, Série Byzantina Sorbonensia, 14), pp. 203–19.

50 Rule §326.

because until that time the brothers had been following the rule of St Augustine. It is in these modifications that we see the influence of St Bernard in the Rule. The Cistercians were reformed Benedictines, and there are close similarities between the Rule of the Templars and the rule of St Benedict. Schnürer[51] lists 30 clauses which contain literal borrowings from the rule of St Benedict and which deal with monastic life.[52] In addition to these modifications, the Primitive Rule also contains a decision of the General Chapter[53] of the Order. Schnürer believed he could also identify amendments (24 new clauses and 12 modified) made by Etienne de Chartres, Patriarch of Jerusalem. However, Etienne would have had little time to rework the Rule between Hugues de Payens' return to the Holy Land in 1129 and his own death in 1130. It is more likely that the practices were influenced by Etienne's predecessor, Gormond, to whom Hugues and his companions made their first vows, and who continued to be associated with the Order until his death in 1127.

In his detailed analysis of the Primitive Rule, made at the beginning of this century, Schnürer attempted to distinguish between all these elements. However, the customs of the Order before the Council of Troyes are difficult to distinguish, as they are referred to in only a few cases;[54] sometimes their existence is merely implied.[55]

The Rule was translated into French some years after 1129, most probably during the mastership of Robert de Craon who was Master between 1136 and 1149. The translation was certainly made after the Council of Pisa which was held on 30 May 1135, because clauses 74 to 76, which appear in the French version, but not in the original Latin, list the fasts and feast days to be observed which were laid down at that Council. The most probable *terminus post quem* is 1139, the date of *Omne datum optimum*, when the Order was granted permission to have its own chaplains. This may be substantiated by the mention of chaplains in clause 64, but it is not clear from the text whether these chaplains are full members of the Order or serve for a fixed term like other associates. A *terminus ante quem* for the translation may well be 1147, when the knights were granted the right to wear a red cross on their white mantles, since there is no mention of this in the clauses devoted to the brothers' clothing. On the contrary, they are forbidden any decoration.[56] It seems unlikely that such an import-

---

[51] G. Schnürer, *Die Ursprüngliche Templeregel* (Freiburg 1903).

[52] *Ibid.* p. 57, note 3.

[53] Rule §65–67.

[54] For example:

§15: It has been made known to us . . . that immoderately and without restraint you hear the divine office whilst standing.

§62: We expressly forbid all other offerings which used to be made at will and without discretion by the Poor Knights of the Temple on the death of brothers, at the feast of Easter and at other feasts.

§70: Henceforth let not ladies be admitted as sisters into the house of the Temple.

§72: We forbid all brothers henceforth to dare to raise children over the font . . .

[55] Schnürer, *op. cit.*

[56] Rule §18.

ant innovation would go unmentioned in the translation if it had been introduced by that time, especially as there are other instances in which the French differs from the Latin when customs have changed. Two important examples of this concern a probationary period and contact with excommunicated people. In the first case, the Latin gives a probationary period after the postulant has made a formal request in chapter to join the Order, but the sentence is omitted entirely in the French.[57] In the second case the Latin Rule instructs the brothers to go wherever non-excommunicated knights may be, but the French advises the opposite.[58] Whilst the first example may be considered a scribal omission, the second is obviously deliberate, and both may be taken as evidence that the Order was widening its net and relaxing its requirements for entry. Given a date of between 1135 and 1147 for the translation of the Primitive Rule into French, this would appear to be a very early example of French prose. The reason for such an early translation must be seen in the fact that the Rule was to be used by men who knew no Latin. The brothers were not educated clerics, but soldiers who dedicated their lives to the defence of the Holy Places. Early in the history of the Order there was a practical need for a rule which they could understand.

The Hierarchical Statutes
The Hierarchical Statutes are generally dated to around 1165. Several clauses indicate that they were certainly written prior to 1187. Firstly, there is the office of the Commander of the City of Jerusalem, an office which became defunct in 1187 with the fall of that city. Secondly, there are instructions on guarding the True Cross, which was lost to the Saracens at the Battle of Hattin in July of the same year.[59] Circumstantial evidence would also date the Hierarchical Statutes to this period. As the Order grew rapidly in size and took on increased responsibilities, it would need a formal hierarchy.

This section sets out the hierarchy of the Order. It is also concerned in great detail with the conventual, military and religious life, clothing and equipment, duties and privileges of the officers and brothers of the Order. Although these regulations differ in some instances from the Primitive Rule, it is in this section that they take on their definitive form. Beginning with the Master and working down through the hierarchy to the sergeant brothers, the *retrais* itemise the number of horses, squires and other servants, as well as the equipment, to which each Templar was entitled. There follow detailed instructions on how to set up camp, how to behave on the move and what to do when the Marshal gives the order to charge.

---

[57] Rule §11. For a discussion of the novitiate in the military orders, see A.J. Forey, 'Novitiate and Instruction in the Military Orders during the Twelfth and Thirteenth Centuries', *Speculum*, 1986, vol. 61, part 1, pp. 1–17.
[58] Rule §12.
[59] Rule §122.

Some clauses, which appear to be wrongly placed, deal with meals,[60] while a separate section (clauses 198–223), which seems to be contemporary with the statutes, describes the procedure following the death of a Grand Master and the election of his successor.

Penances

This section, which briefly outlines the penances given within the Order, appears to be contemporary with the Hierarchical Statutes. It is less developed than the later sections which deal with the same subject. Firstly the nine infringements of discipline for which a brother could be expelled from the Order are listed, followed by thirty-one things which could lead to loss of the habit for a period of time judged fitting by chapter, depending on the gravity of the fault and the general conduct of the brother concerned. Two things – sleeping outside the house for two or more nights without permission, and returning the habit – automatically led to loss of the habit for a year and a day. There follows a list of the ten judgements which could be given, ranging from expulsion from the Order to acquittal. The section ends with details of the chaplain brothers' duties and how they should be treated within the Order, and the Latin formulae used at their profession.

Conventual Life

This section of the Rule deals with the regulations governing the daily life of the brothers: meals; getting up and going to bed; discipline within the house; relationships between brothers; religious offices; fasts; discipline and behaviour on campaign. Clause 326 may help in the dating of this section. It implies a pre-existent set of rules which had been written down and read before this section was composed. These rules were not necessarily the Hierarchical Statutes as they have come down to us. They may have been an earlier version containing information which could have been 'harmful to our Order'; that is, not details of esoteric practices as alleged in the accusations later brought against the Order, but military formations and plans.

In peacetime the daily life of the brothers was governed by the canonical hours and differed little from that of other monks.[61] The day started at about 4 a.m. with matins, after which the knights had to take care of their horses and were then allowed to return to bed.[62] Prime, terce and sext followed in the morning. The brothers then had their first meal of the day, which was eaten in silence while listening to a reading from Holy Scripture.[63] Nones was at 2.30 p.m. and vespers at 6 p.m., followed by supper. The day ended with compline,

---

[60] Rule §182–89.
[61] D. Knowles, *The Monastic Order in England* (Cambridge 1963), pp. 714–15.
[62] Rule §283.
[63] Rule §288.

after which silence was kept until after prime the next day. Orders were given after each office, except compline, when they were given before, so that silence would not be broken.[64]

When on campaign the brothers were to behave as nearly as possible as they did in the house. There are minute details on the procedures for the distribution of rations, and what should be done on hearing the alarm raised in the camp.

The Holding of Ordinary Chapters

In this section the Rule deals with the procedures to be adopted in the holding of ordinary chapters where the public accusations and confessions of violations of the Rule were heard, and with everything concerning the penal code of the Order.

The list of possible judgements given in the Penances section is repeated, with the ninth and tenth transposed. Nine things for which a brother could be expelled from the Order are given. This list differs somewhat from the one given in the Penances section, the most notable change being that sodomy is included. The fact that the list is revised and expanded suggests that this section post-dates what comes before, although it could still date from before 1187. Details were added as new situations arose and had to be dealt with. Other faults are classified and expounded according to the harshness of the penalty they attract, and there are minute details on how brothers are punished and absolved.

There is lengthy discussion on appropriate sentences, and on one occasion the writer ventures to give his own opinion.[65] There is also great emphasis on the opinion of the older men of the Order with regard to sentencing,[66] which suggests that this section of the Rule was constructed at least partly from established custom and memory. This reflects practice in the Latin Kingdom of Jerusalem as a whole. The barons consulted Baldwin III on difficult questions, such was his reputation for jurisprudence.[67] Also, the kingdom's thirteenth-century law books preserved the memories of experienced practitioners. After the fall of Jerusalem and the loss of the written laws of the kingdom, there are repeated references to and reliance upon the opinions of old men who remembered what had been done in the past, especially those living before 1187.[68]

The section ends with the procedure for closing the chapter.

[64] Rule §309.
[65] Rule §521.
[66] Rule §485.
[67] William of Tyre, op. cit., XVI, 2, vol. LXIIIA, p. 716.
[68] Philip of Novara, 'Livre de Forme de Plait', Recueil des Historiens des Croisades, Lois, vol. I, pp. 491, 525; John of Jaffa, 'Livre des Assises de la Haute Cour', Recueil des Historiens des Croisades, Lois, vol. I, p. 27. See also J. Riley-Smith, The Feudal Nobility and the Latin Kingdom of Jerusalem, 1174–1277 (London 1973).

Further Details on Penances

This section supplies us with solid historical evidence for its dating. It must surely have been written between the Tartar invasion of 1257, which is mentioned, and the loss of Gaston (Baghras) in 1268, which is not. This is indicated by the fact that the loss of Gaston is described at length in the Catalan Rule, which must therefore have been composed after 1268.[69] In the French Rule, it seems probable that this section was composed after that on the Holding of Ordinary Chapters, as it repeats and amplifies rules given there. It tells us how the application of the rules worked in practice.

The list of infringements of the regulations leading to expulsion from the Order is repeated, and actual examples are given. There follows a repetition of the thirty-one things for which a brother could lose the habit, again with historical examples. The ten judgements are then given, as in the Penances section.

Reception into the Order

This section appears to have no link with what goes before and is almost like an appendix. It has no introduction, but begins with a speech by the one in charge of the reception. Each step in the ceremony is explained: the questions to be put to the postulant; situations which would make him ineligible to join the Order; the promises he has to make. In order to be admitted as a knight brother, a man had to be the legitimate son[70] of a knight and of knightly lineage. He was asked if this were the case[71] and the punishment for lying, if it were proven otherwise later, was expulsion from the Order. If the brother showed great repentance he could be allowed to remain in the Order as a sergeant brother.[72] When the mantle had been placed round his shoulders, the postulant was told some of the customs of the Order and advised to learn the rest from other brothers.

[69] J. Delaville Le Roulx, 'Un Nouveau Manuscrit de la Règle du Temple', Annuaire-Bulletin de la Société de l'Histoire de France, 1889, vol. 26 (2), pp. 185–214, gives the passages in the Catalan Rule which have no equivalent in the French Rule. The author is at present working on a complete edition with translation. See also M. Melville, La Vie des Templiers (Paris 1951).

[70] Rule §337.

[71] Rule §673.

[72] Rule §436. The Rule relates the case of a knight brother who was found guilty of not being of knightly lineage. His white mantle was taken from him and he was given a brown one (§586).

SOME NOTES ON STYLE AND THE TRANSLATION

The style of the Primitive Rule is formal and contains a number of biblical quotations which illustrate the point being made.[73] We are fortunate that the scribe who wrote down the original Latin identifies himself.[74]

The later sections are written in a more informal style. The Templar who wrote them does not tell us his name, but he refers to the brothers in a familiar tone. Typical phrases which begin clauses are: 'All the brothers of the Temple should know that' and 'And also you should know that'. This was not an abstract document containing rulings promulgated by the Chapter General and removed from the daily life of the brothers. It discusses the penances, obviously everyday occurrences, in language which is almost slang. For example, phrases such as 'on the ground', 'on two days', 'on one day' are first used in clause 267 without any explanation. It is not until clauses 497 to 500 that they are discussed in detail and we are told that 'on the ground' means a brother had to eat his meals on the ground for a certain length of time; and that the phrases 'on one day' and 'on two days' denote the number of days per week that a brother had to fast.

I have thought it advisable to leave some words in the original, for various reasons. For example, a translation of the office of *bailli* into 'bailiff' would tend to be misleading, so I have kept this, and the area of his jurisdiction, the *baillie*.

It is difficult to find an accurate and concise rendering for *retrais*. In the past these have been referred to as the 'laws' and at first I translated them as 'duties and privileges'; but the French implies oral transmission, and this cannot effectively be conveyed in English.

Some of the games of chance which the brothers were allowed to play, for example *forbot*, have no direct equivalent.

I have been flexible in my treatment of personal names and place names. For example, I have translated the names of countries, and towns where there is a distinct English equivalent; also epithets, so that *Johan Bouche de lievre* becomes John Harelip[75] and *Roger l'Allemand* becomes Roger the German.[76] However, when place names form part of a person's name I have kept the whole in the original French, for example Hugues de Payens, Jacques de Ravane.

---

[73] E.g. Rule §39.
[74] Rule §5.
[75] Rule §617 and 619.
[76] Rule §569.

The Primitive Rule

Here begins the prologue to the Rule of the Temple

1. We speak firstly to all those who secretly despise their own will and desire with a pure heart to serve the sovereign king as a knight and with studious care desire to wear, and wear permanently, the very noble armour of obedience. And therefore we admonish you, you who until now have led the lives of secular knights, in which Jesus Christ was not the cause, but which you embraced for human favour only, to follow those whom God has chosen from the mass of perdition and whom he has ordered through his gracious mercy to defend the Holy Church, and that you hasten to join them forever.

2. Above all things, whosoever would be a knight of Christ, choosing such holy orders, you in your profession of faith must unite pure diligence and firm perseverence, which is so worthy and so holy, and is known to be so noble, that if it is preserved untainted for ever, you will deserve to keep company with the martyrs who gave their souls for Jesus Christ. In this religious order has flourished and is revitalised the order of knighthood. This knighthood despised the love of justice that constitutes its duties and did not do what it should, that is defend the poor, widows, orphans and churches, but strove to plunder, despoil and kill. God works well with us and our saviour Jesus Christ; He has sent his friends from the Holy City of Jerusalem to the marches of France and Burgundy, who for our salvation and the spread of the true faith do not cease to offer their souls to God, a welcome sacrifice.

3. Then we, in all joy and all brotherhood, at the request of Master Hugues de Payens,[1] by whom the aforementioned knighthood was founded by the grace of the Holy Spirit, assembled at Troyes from divers provinces beyond the mountains on the feast of my lord St Hilary,[2] in the year of the incarnation of Jesus Christ 1128, in the ninth year after the founding of the aforesaid knighthood. And the conduct and beginnings of the Order of Knighthood we heard in common chapter from the lips of the aforementioned Master, Brother Hugues de Payens; and according to the limitations of our understanding what seemed to us good and beneficial we praised, and what seemed wrong we eschewed.

4. And all that took place at that council cannot be told nor recounted; and so that it should not be taken lightly by us, but considered in wise prudence, we

3.1 Hugues de Payens was co-founder and first Grand Master of the Order. Payens is a village about eight miles north of Troyes, in the département of Aube. Hugues was connected in some way with the count of Champagne: if not a relative, then probably as one of his officers.
3.2 13 January.

left it to the discretion of both our honourable father lord Honorius[1] and of the noble patriarch of Jerusalem,[2] Stephen, who knew the affairs of the East and of the Poor Knights of Christ, by the advice of the common council we praised it unanimously. Although a great number of religious fathers who assembled at that council praised the authority of our words, nevertheless we should not pass over in silence the true sentences and judgements which they pronounced.

5. Therefore I, Jean Michel, to whom was entrusted and confided that divine office, by the grace of God served as the humble scribe of the present document by order of the council and of the venerable father Bernard, abbot of Clairvaux.

The Names of the Fathers who Attended the Council

6. First was Matthew,[1] bishop of Albano, by the grace of God legate of the Holy Church of Rome; R[enaud],[2] archbishop of Reims; H[enri],[3] archbishop of Sens; and then their suffragans:[4] G[ocelin],[5] bishop of Soissons; the bishop of Paris;[6] the bishop of Troyes;[7] the bishop of Orléans;[8] the bishop of Auxerre;[9] the bishop of Meaux;[10] the bishop of Châlons;[11] the bishop of Laon;[12] the bishop of Beauvais;[13] the abbot of Vézelay,[14] who was later made archbishop of Lyon and legate of the Church of Rome; the abbot of Cîteaux;[15] the abbot of Pontigny;[16] the abbot of Trois-Fontaines;[17] the abbot of St Denis de Reims;[18] the abbot of St-Etienne de Dijon;[19] the abbot of Molesmes;[20] the above-named B[ernard],[21]

4.1 Honorius II, pope from 15 December 1124 to 13 February 1130.
4.2 Stephen de la Ferté, patriarch from late summer 1128 to 1130. Formerly abbot of the Augustinian abbey of Saint-Jean-en-Vallée, Chartres.
6.1 Of the order of St Benedict. Bishop from 1125 to 1134.
6.2 Renaud de Martigné, ?1124 to 13 January 1138.
6.3 Henri Sanglier, archbishop from December 1122 to 10 January 1141.
6.4 The Latin text includes here Geoffroi de Lèves, archbishop of Chartres from 24 January ?1124 to 24 January 1149.
6.5 Gocelin de Vierzy, 1126 to 24 December 1152.
6.6 Etienne de Senlis, 1124 to 6 June 1142.
6.7 Hatton, 1123 to 1145, was a great benefactor of the Templars.
6.8 Jean II, 1096 to 1135.
6.9 Saint Hugues de Montaigu, 5 March 1116 to 10 August 1136.
6.10 Burcard, 1120 to 4 January 1134.
6.11 Erlebert, 1127 to 8 October 1130.
6.12 Barthélemi de Vir or de Jura, 1113 to 1151.
6.13 Pierre de Dammartin, 12 June 1114 to 8 November 1133.
6.14 Renaud de Saumur, sixteenth abbot of Vézelay. Named archbishop of Lyon in 1129.
6.15 Saint Stephen Harding, third abbot of Cîteaux.
6.16 Hugues, count of Mâcon, first abbot of the Cistercian abbey of Pontigny in 1114; bishop of Auxerre in 1136.
6.17 Gui, second abbot of the Cistercian abbey of Trois-Fontaines.
6.18 Ursion, second abbot of the Benedictine abbey of St Denis de Reims.
6.19 Herbert, sixteenth abbot of the Augustinian abbey of St-Etienne de Dijon.
6.20 Gui, third abbot of the Benedictine abbey of Molesmes.
6.21 Saint Bernard, first abbot of the Cistercian abbey of Clairvaux.

abbot of Clairvaux: whose words the aforementioned praised liberally. Also present were master Aubri de Reims; master Fulcher and several others whom it would be tedious to record. And of the others who have not been listed it seems profitable to furnish guarantees in this matter, that they are lovers of truth: they are count Theobald;[22] the count of Nevers;[23] André de Baudemant. These were at the council and acted in such a manner that by perfect, studious care they sought out that which was fine and disapproved that which did not seem right.

7. And also present was Brother Hugues de Payens, Master of the Knighthood, with some of his brothers whom he had brought with him. They were Brother Roland, Brother Godefroy, and Brother Geoffroi Bisot, Brother Payen de Montdidier, Brother Archambaut de Saint-Amand.[1] The same Master Hugues with his followers related to the above-named fathers the customs and observances of their humble beginnings and of the one who said: *Ego principium qui et loquor vobis*, that is to say: 'I who speak to you am the beginning,' according to one's memory.

8. It pleased the common council that the deliberations which were made there and the consideration of the Holy Scriptures which were diligently examined with the wisdom of my lord H[onorius], pope of the Holy Church of Rome, and of the patriarch of Jerusalem and with the assent of the chapter, together with the agreement of the Poor Knights of Christ of the Temple which is in Jerusalem, should be put in writing and not forgotten, steadfastly kept so that by an upright life one may come to his creator; the compassion of which Lord [is sweeter] than honey when compared with God; whose mercy resembles *oine*,[1] and permits us to come to Him whom they desire to serve. *Per infinita seculorum secula*. Amen.

Here Begins the Rule of the Poor Knighthood of the Temple

9. You who renounce your own wills, and you others serving the sovereign king with horses and arms, for the salvation of your souls, for a fixed term, strive everywhere with pure desire to hear matins and the entire service according to canonical law and the customs of the regular masters of the Holy City of

6.22 Theobald IV, seventh count of Blois and eighth count of Champagne, succeeded his father in 1102 to the counties of Blois, Chartres and Brie, and added the county of Champagne in 1125, when his uncle Hugh left for the East and joined the new Order. Hugh made his original vow in the presence of the patriarch, Gormond.

6.23 Guillaume II, count of Auxerre, Nevers and Tonnerre, 1089 to 1147.

7.1 There is little information on these first companions of the founder of the Order. However, we do know that Godefroy de St-Omer persuaded his father or brother, Guillaume, castellan of St-Omer, to give to the new Order the churches of Slypes and Leffinghe in Belgium. Payen de Montdidier abandoned his wealth, notably the land of Fontaines-sous-Montdidier. Archambaut de St-Amand should not be confused with Eudes or Odo de St-Amand who became Grand Master in 1171 and died in 1179.

8.1 I have not been able to find a meaning for this word. It may be connected with the verb *oindre*, to oil or rub with oil; or with *oing*, grease or lard.

Jerusalem.[1] O you venerable brothers, similarly God is with you, if you promise to despise the deceitful world in perpetual love of God, and scorn the temptations of your body: sustained by the food of God and watered and instructed in the commandments of Our Lord, at the end of the divine office, none should fear to go into battle if he henceforth wears the crown.

10. But if any brother is sent through the work of the house and of Christianity in the East – something we believe will happen often – and cannot hear the divine office, he should say instead of matins thirteen paternosters; seven for each hour and nine for vespers. And together we all order him to do so. But those who are sent for such a reason and cannot come at the hours set to hear the divine office, if possible the set hours should not be omitted, in order to render to God his due.

The Manner in which Brothers should be Received

11. If any secular knight, or any other man, wishes to leave the mass of perdition and abandon that secular life and choose your communal life, do not consent to receive him immediately, for thus said my lord St Paul: *Probate spiritus si ex Deo sunt.* That is to say: 'Test the soul to see if it comes from God.' Rather, if the company of the brothers is to be granted to him, let the Rule be read to him, and if he wishes to studiously obey the commandments of the Rule, and if it pleases the Master and the brothers to receive him, let him reveal his wish and desire before all the brothers assembled in chapter and let him make his request with a pure heart.[1]

On Excommunicated Knights

12. Where you know excommunicated knights to be gathered, there we command you to go;[1] and if anyone there wishes to join the order of knighthood from regions overseas, you should not consider worldly gain so much as the eternal salvation of his soul. We order him to be received on condition that he come before the bishop of that province and make his intention known to him. And when the bishop has heard and absolved him, he should send him to the Master and brothers of the Temple, and if his life is honest and worthy of their company, if he seems good to the Master and brothers, let him be mercifully received; and if he should die in the meanwhile, through the anguish and

9.1 The canons of the Holy Sepulchre, who followed the customs of the abbey of St Victor in Paris, whose rule and habit had been given by Godfrey de Bouillon when he founded the community for the guarding of Christ's tomb.

11.1 The Latin text has an additional sentence here which mentions a term of probation. The fact that this sentence was not translated into French suggests that this custom had been discontinued by the time of the translation.

12.1 This is in direct opposition to the meaning of the Latin text which has 'non-excommunicated knights'. See Introduction for a discussion of the possible reasons for this.

torment he has suffered, let him be given all the benefits of the brotherhood due to one of the Poor Knights of the Temple.

13. Under no other circumstances should the brothers of the Temple share the company of an obviously-excommunicated man, nor take his things; and this we prohibit strongly because it would be a fearful thing if they were excommunicated like him. But if he is only forbidden to hear the divine office, it is certainly possible to keep company with him and take his property for charity with the permission of their commander.

On Not Receiving Children

14. Although the rule of the holy fathers allows the receiving of children into a religious life,[1] we do not advise you to do this. For he who wishes to give his child eternally to the order of knighthood should bring him up until such time as he is able to bear arms with vigour,[2] and rid the land of the enemies of Jesus Christ. Then let the mother and father lead him to the house and make his request known to the brothers; and it is much better if he does not take the vow when he is a child, but when he is older, and it is better if he does not regret it than if he regrets it. And henceforth let him be put to the test according to the wisdom of the Master and brothers and according to the honesty of the life of the one who asks to be admitted to the brotherhood.

On Brothers who Stand Too Long in Chapel

15. It has been made known to us and we heard it from true witnesses that immoderately and without restraint you hear the divine service whilst standing. We do not ordain that you behave in this manner, on the contrary we disapprove of it. But we command that the strong as well as the weak, to avoid a fuss, once the psalm which is called *Venite*, with the invitatory[1] and the hymn have been sung, should sit down, and say their prayers in silence, softly and not loudly, so that the proclaimer does not disturb the prayers of the other brothers.

16. But at the end of the psalms, when the *Gloria patri* is sung, through reverence for the Holy Trinity, you will rise and bow towards the altar, while the weak and ill will incline their heads. So we command; and when the explanation of the Gospels is read, and the *Te deum laudamus* is sung,[1] and while all the lauds are sung, and the matins are finished, you will be on your feet. In such a manner we command you likewise to be on your feet at matins and at all the hours of Our Lady.[2]

14.1 Most founders of monastic orders authorised the reception of children. The Cistercians and other reformers gradually came to oppose it.

14.2 The Templars had no training programme. Brothers were expected to already be skilled in the art of warfare.

15.1 The first psalm of the office of matins, always Psalm 94.

16.1 These are the last two parts of the office of matins.

16.2 It was the custom in certain monastic orders to recite the hours of the Virgin

On the Brothers' Dress

17. We command that all the brothers' habits should always be of one col-our,[1] that is white or black or brown.[2] And we grant to all knight brothers in winter and in summer if possible, white cloaks; and no-one who does not belong to the aforementioned Knights of Christ is allowed to have a white cloak, so that those who have abandoned the life of darkness will recognise each other as being reconciled to their creator by the sign of the white habits: which signifies purity and complete chastity. Chastity is certitude of heart and healthiness of body. For if any brother does not take the vow of chastity he cannot come to eternal rest nor see God, by the promise of the apostle who said: *Pacem sectamini cum omnibus et castimoniam sine qua nemo Deum videbit.* That is to say: 'Strive to bring peace to all, keep chaste, without which no-one can see God.'

18. But these robes should be without any finery and without any show of pride.[1] And so we ordain that no brother will have a piece of fur[2] on his clothes, nor anything else which belongs to the usages of the body, not even a blanket unless it is of lamb's wool or sheep's wool. We command all to have the same, so that each can dress and undress, and put on and take off his boots easily.[3] And the Draper or the one who is in his place should studiously reflect and take care to have the reward of God in all the above-mentioned things, so that the eyes of the envious and evil-tongued cannot observe that the robes are too long or too short; but he should distribute them so that they fit those who must wear them, according to the size of each one.

19. And if any brother out of a feeling of pride or arrogance wishes to have as his due a better and finer habit, let him be given the worst. And those who receive new robes must immediately return the old ones, to be given to the squires and sergeants and often to the poor, according to what seems good to the one who holds that office.

On Shirts

20. Among the other things, we mercifully rule that, because of the great intensity of the heat which exists in the East, from Easter to All Saints, through

---

Mary before the hours of the day. During matins, this was said between the *Te Deum* and the lauds of the Virgin preceding the lauds of the day. The lauds always followed matins.

17.1 William of Tyre informs us that the brothers had previously worn secular cloth-ing: 'They wore such garments as the people, for the salvation of their souls, bestowed upon them.' A *History of Deeds done Beyond the Sea*, tr. A.E. Babcock & A.C. Krey (New York 1976), XII, 7, vol. I, pp. 524–7.

17.2 The French text has *bure*, a mixture of grey and russet.

18.1 *Cf.* St Bernard's comments in *De laude Novae Militiae ad Milites Templi*, discussed in the Introduction.

18.2 I have taken the reading of the Dijon manuscript here.

18.3 This was so that they could ready themselves in an emergency with the mini-mum of delay.

compassion and in no way as a right, a linen shirt shall be given to any brother who wishes to wear it.

On Bed Linen

21. We command by common consent that each man shall have clothes and bed linen according to the discretion of the Master. It is our intention that apart from a mattress, one bolster and one blanket should be sufficient for each; and he who lacks one of these may have a rug, and he may use a linen blanket at all times, that is to say with a soft pile. And they will at all times sleep dressed in shirt and breeches and shoes and belts, and where they sleep shall be lit until morning.[1] And the Draper should ensure that the brothers' hair is so well cut that they may be examined from the front and from behind; and we command you to firmly adhere to this same conduct with respect to beards and moustaches, so that no excess may be noted on their bodies.

On Pointed Shoes[1] and Shoe-Laces

22. We prohibit pointed shoes and shoe-laces and forbid any brother to wear them; nor do we permit them to those who serve the house for a fixed term; rather we forbid them to have shoes with points or laces under any circumstances. For it is manifest and well known that these abominable things belong to pagans. Nor should they wear their hair or their habits too long. For those who serve the sovereign creator must of necessity be born within and without through the promise of God himself who said: *Estote mundi quia ego mundus sum.* That is to say: 'Be born as I am born.'

How They Should Eat

23. In the palace,[1] or what should rather be called the refectory, they should eat together. But if you are in need of anything because you are not accustomed to the signs used by other men of religion,[2] quietly and privately you should ask for what you need at table, with all humility and submission. For the apostle said: *Manduca panem tuum cum silentio.* That is to say: 'Eat your bread in silence.' And the psalmist: *Posui ori meo custodiam.* That is to say: 'I held my tongue.' That is, 'I thought my tongue would fail me.' That is, 'I held my tongue so that I should speak no ill.'

21.1 The Rule of St Benedict (Chapter 22) required a light to burn in the dormitory all night and this became the custom in all religious communities.

22.1 Fashionable among the nobility during the early twelfth century.

23.1 Al-Aqsa mosque or Solomon's Temple.

23.2 Melville cites Udalric of Cluny who gives about thirty signs used in his monastery. A circle made with two fingers and the thumb denoted bread; sucking the little finger was a request for milk; licking the finger for honey; a swimming movement with the hands for fish, etc. *La Vie des Templiers* (Paris 1951), p. 45.

On the Reading of the Lesson

24. Always, at the convent's[1] dinner and supper, let the Holy Scripture be read, if possible. If we love God and all His holy words and His holy commandments, we should desire to listen attentively; the reader of the lesson will tell you to keep silent before he begins to read.

On Bowls and Drinking Vessels

25. Because of the shortage of bowls, the brothers will eat in pairs, so that one may study the other more closely, and so that neither austerity nor secret abstinence is introduced into the communal meal. And it seems just to us that each brother should have the same ration of wine in his cup.

On the Eating of Meat

26. It should be sufficient for you to eat meat three times a week, except at Christmas,[1] All Saints,[2] the Assumption[3] and the feast of the twelve apostles.[4] For it is understood that the custom of eating flesh corrupts the body.[5] But if a fast when meat must be forgone falls on a Tuesday, the next day let it be given to the brothers in plenty. And on Sundays all the brothers of the Temple, the chaplains and the clerks shall be given two meat meals in honour of the holy resurrection of Jesus Christ. And the rest of the household, that is to say the squires and sergeants, shall be content with one meal and shall be thankful to God for it.

On Weekday Meals

27. On the other days of the week, that is Mondays, Wednesdays and even Saturdays, the brothers shall have two or three meals of vegetables or other dishes eaten with bread; and we intend that this should be sufficient and command that it should be adhered to. For he who does not eat one meal shall eat the other.

On Friday Meals

28. On Fridays, let lenten food be given communally to the whole congregation, out of reverence for the passion of Jesus Christ; and you will fast from All Saints until Easter, except for Christmas Day, the Assumption and the feast of the twelve apostles. But weak and sick brothers shall not be kept to this. From Easter to All Saints they may eat twice, as long as there is no general fast.

24.1 The convent consisted of the brothers who made up the fighting force of the Order, i.e. the knight and sergeant brothers.
26.1 The Latin text has Easter in addition.
26.2 1 November.
26.3 15 August.
26.4 1 May.
26.5 The Cistercians held that rich food increases sexual appetite.

On Saying Grace

29. Always after every dinner and supper all the brothers should give thanks to God in silence, if the church is near to the palace where they eat, and if it is not nearby, in the place itself. With a humble heart they should give thanks to Jesus Christ who is the Lord Provider. Let the remains of the broken bread be given to the poor and whole loaves be kept. Although the reward of the poor, which is the kingdom of heaven, should be given to the poor without hesitation, and the Christian faith doubtless recognises you among them,[1] we ordain that a tenth part of the bread be given to your Almoner.

On Taking Collation

30. When daylight fades and night falls listen to the signal of the bell or the call to prayers, according to the customs of the country,[1] and all go to compline. But we command you first to take collation; although we place this light meal under the arbitration and discretion of the Master. When he wants water and when he orders, out of mercy, diluted wine, let it be given sensibly. Truly, it should not be taken to excess, but in moderation. For Solomon said: *Quia vinum facit apostatare sapientes.* That is to say that wine corrupts the wise.

On Keeping Silence

31. When the brothers come out of compline they have no permission to speak openly except in an emergency. But let each go to his bed quietly and in silence, and if he needs to speak to his squire, he should say what he has to say softly and quietly. But if by chance, as they come out of compline, the knighthood or the house has a serious problem which must be solved before morning, we intend that the Master or a party of elder brothers who govern the Order under the Master, may speak appropriately. And for this reason we command that it should be done in such a manner.

32. For it is written: *In multiloquio non effugies peccatum.* That is to say that to talk too much is not without sin. And elsewhere: *Mors et vita in manibus lingue.* That is to say: 'Life and death are in the power of the tongue.' And during that conversation we altogether prohibit idle words and wicked bursts of laughter. And if anything is said during that conversation that should not be said, when you go to bed we command you to say the paternoster prayer in all humility and pure devotion.

29.1 St Bernard believed that the kingdom of heaven rightly belongs to those who are voluntarily poor, i.e. those who have taken the vow of poverty and who were known as 'the poor in Christ'.

30.1 This is relevant to commanderies situated in the region of Palestine under Orthodox jurisdiction. In Orthodox countries a piece of wood was struck with a mallet as a sign to go to prayers.

On Ailing Brothers

33. Brothers who suffer illness through the work of the house need not rise at matins with the agreement and permission of the Master or of those who are charged with that office. But they should say instead of matins thirteen pater-nosters, as is established above, in such a manner that the words reflect the heart. Thus said David: *Psallite sapienter.* That is to say: 'Sing wisely.' And elsewhere the same David said: *In conspectu Angelorum psallam tibi.* That is to say: 'I will sing to you before the angels.' And let this thing be at all times at the discretion of the Master or of those who are charged with that office.[1]

On the Communal Life

34. One reads in the Holy Scriptures: *Dividebatur singulis prout cuique opus erat.* That is to say that to each was given according to his need. For this reason we say that no-one should be elevated among you, but all should take care of the sick; and he who is less ill should thank God and not be troubled; and let whoever is worse humble himself through his infirmity and not become proud through pity. In this way all members will live in peace. And we forbid anyone to embrace excessive abstinence; but firmly keep the communal life.

On the Master

35. The Master may give to whomsoever he pleases the horse and armour and whatever he likes of another brother, and the brother to whom the given thing belongs should not become vexed or angry: for be certain that if he becomes angry he will go against God.

On Giving Counsel

36. Let only those brothers whom the Master knows will give wise and beneficial advice be called to the council; for this we command, and by no means everyone should be chosen. For when it happens that they wish to treat serious matters like the giving of communal land, or to speak of the affairs of the house, or receive a brother, then if the Master wishes, it is appropriate to assemble the entire congregation to hear the advice of the whole chapter; and what seems to the Master best and most beneficial, let him do it.

On Brothers Sent Overseas

37. Brothers who are sent throughout divers countries of the world should endeavour to keep the commandments of the Rule according to their ability and live without reproach with regard to meat and wine, etc. so that they may receive a good report from outsiders and not sully by deed or word the precepts of the Order, and so that they may set an example of good works and wisdom;

33.1 In all monasteries a brother was chosen to wake the other brothers for both matins and prime. Among the Templars it was usually the Chaplain brother.

above all so that those with whom they associate and those in whose inns they lodge may be bestowed with honour. And if possible, the house where they sleep and take lodging should not be without light at night, so that shadowy enemies may not lead them to wickedness, which God forbids them.

On Keeping the Peace

38. Each brother should ensure that he does not incite another brother to wrath or anger, for the sovereign mercy of God holds the strong and weak brother equal, in the name of charity.

How the Brothers Should Go About

39. In order to carry out their holy duties and gain the glory of the Lord's joy and to escape the fear of hell-fire, it is fitting that all brothers who are professed strictly obey their Master. For nothing is dearer to Jesus Christ than obedience. For as soon as something is commanded by the Master or by him to whom the Master has given the authority, it should be done without delay as though Christ himself had commanded it. For thus said Jesus Christ through the mouth of David, and it is true: *Ob auditu auris obedivit mihi*. That is to say: 'He obeyed me as soon as he heard me.'

40. For this reason we pray and firmly command the knight brothers who have abandoned their own wills and all the others who serve for a fixed term not to presume to go out into the town or city without the permission of the Master or of the one who is given that office; except at night to the Sepulchre[1] and the places of prayer which lie within the walls of the city of Jerusalem.

41. There, brothers may go in pairs, but otherwise may not go out by day or night; and when they have stopped at an inn, neither brother nor squire nor sergeant may go to another's lodging to see or speak to him without permission, as is said above. We command by common consent that in this Order which is ruled by God, no brother should fight or rest according to his own will, but according to the orders of the Master, to whom all should submit, that they may follow this pronouncement of Jesus Christ who said: *Non veni facere voluntatem meam, sed ejus que misit me, patris*. That is to say: 'I did not come to do my own will, but the will of my father who sent me.'

How they should Effect an Exchange

42. Without permission from the Master or from the one who holds that office, let no brother exchange one thing for another, nor ask to, unless it is a small or petty thing.

40.1 The church of the Holy Sepulchre in Jerusalem.

On Locks

43. Without permission from the Master or from the one who holds that office, let no brother have a lockable purse or bag; but commanders of houses or provinces and Masters shall not be held to this. Without the consent of the Master or of his commander, let no brother have letters from his relatives or any other person; but if he has permission, and if it please the Master or the commander, the letters may be read to him.

On Secular Gifts

44. If anything which cannot be conserved, like meat, is given to any brother by a secular person in thanks, he should present it to the Master or the Commander of Victuals. But if it happens that any of his friends or relatives has something that they wish to give only to him, let him not take it without the permission of the Master or of the one who holds that office. Moreover, if the brother is sent any other thing by his relatives, let him not take it without the permission of the Master or of the one who holds that office. We do not wish the commanders or *baillis*,[1] who are especially charged to carry out this office, to be held to this aforementioned rule.

On Faults

45. If any brother, in speaking or soldiering, or in any other way commits a slight sin, he himself should willingly make known the fault to the Master, to make amends with a pure heart. And if he does not usually fail in this way let him be given a light penance, but if the fault is very serious let him go apart from the company of the brothers so that he does not eat or drink at any table with them, but all alone; and he should submit to the mercy and judgement of the Master and brothers, that he may be saved on the Day of Judgement.

On Serious Faults

46. Above all things, we should ensure that no brother, powerful or not powerful, strong or weak, who wishes to promote himself gradually and become proud and defend his crime, remain unpunished. But if he does not wish to atone for it let him be given a harsher punishment. And if by pious counsel prayers are said to God for him, and he does not wish to make amends, but wishes to boast more and more of it, let him be uprooted from the pious flock; according to the apostle who says: *Auferte malum ex vobis.* That is to say: 'Remove the wicked from among you.' It is necessary for you to remove the wicked sheep from the company of faithful brothers.

47. Moreover the Master, who should hold in his hand the staff and rod – the staff with which to sustain the weaknesses and strengths of others; the rod with which to beat the vices of those who sin – for love of justice by counsel of the

44.1 Provincial commanders, who could be knight brothers or sergeant brothers.

patriarch, should take care to do this. But also, as my lord St Maxime[1] said: 'May the leniency be no greater than the fault; nor excessive punishment cause the sinner to return to evil deeds.'

On Rumour

48. We command you by divine counsel to avoid a plague: envy, rumour, spite, slander. So each one should zealously guard against what the apostle said: *Ne sis criminator et susurro in populo*. That is to say: 'Do not accuse or malign the people of God.' But when a brother knows for certain that his fellow brother has sinned, quietly and with fraternal mercy let him be chastised privately between the two of them, and if he does not wish to listen, another brother should be called, and if he scorns them both he should recant openly before the whole chapter. Those who disparage others suffer from a terrible blindness and many are full of great sorrow that they do not guard against harbouring envy towards others; by which they shall be plunged into the ancient wickedness of the devil.

Let None Take Pride in his Faults

49. Although all idle words are generally known to be sinful, they will be spoken by those who take pride in their own sin before the strict judge Jesus Christ; which is demonstrated by what David said: *Obmutui et silui a bonis*. That is to say that one should refrain from speaking even good, and observe silence. Likewise one should guard against speaking evil, in order to escape the penalty of sin. We prohibit and firmly forbid any brother to recount to another brother nor to anyone else the brave deeds he has done in secular life, which should rather be called follies committed in the performance of knightly duties, and the pleasures of the flesh that he has had with immoral women; and if it happens that he hears them being told by another brother, he should immediately silence him; and if he cannot do this, he should straightaway leave that place and not give his heart's ear to the pedlar of filth.

Let None Ask

50. This custom among the others we command you to adhere to strictly and firmly: that no brother should explicitly ask for the horse or armour of another. It will therefore be done in this manner: if the infirmity of the brother or the frailty of his animals or his armour is known to be such that the brother cannot go out to do the work of the house without harm, let him go to the Master, or to the one who is in his place in that office after the Master, and make the situation known to him in pure faith and true fraternity, and henceforth remain at the disposal of the Master or of the one who holds that office.

47.1 Bishop of Turin, who died in 423, having written a great number of such homilies. His feast day is 15 June.

On Animals and Squires

51. Each knight brother may have three horses and no more without the permission of the Master, because of the great poverty which exists at the present time in the house of God and of the Temple of Solomon. To each knight brother we grant three horses and one squire, and if that squire willingly serves charity, the brother should not beat him for any sin he commits.

That No Brother May Have an Ornate Bridle[1]

52. We utterly forbid any brother to have gold or silver on his bridle, nor on his stirrups, nor on his spurs. That is, if he buys them; but if it happens that a harness is given to him in charity which is so old that the gold or silver is tarnished, that the resplendent beauty is not seen by others nor pride taken in them: then he may have them. But if he is given new equipment let the Master deal with it as he sees fit.

On Lance Covers

53. Let no brother have a cover on his shield or his lance, for it is no advantage, on the contrary we understand that it would be very harmful.[1]

On Food Bags

54. This command which is established by us it is beneficial for all to keep and for this reason we ordain that it be kept henceforth, and that no brother may make a food bag of linen or wool, principally, or anything else except a *profinel*.[1]

On Hunting

55. We collectively forbid any brother to hunt a bird with another bird.[1] It is not fitting for a man of religion to succumb to pleasures, but to hear willingly the commandments of God, to be often at prayer and each day to confess tearfully to God in his prayers the sins he has committed. No brother may presume to go particularly with a man who hunts one bird with another. Rather it is fitting for every religious man to go simply and humbly without laughing or talking too much, but reasonably and without raising his voice and for this reason we

---

52.1 It was the custom for knights to decorate their bridles with small metal plaques, a custom which St Bernard vehemently denounced in *De laude*.

53.1 The Teutonic Knights, however, were commanded to keep the tips of their lances covered in order to maintain the polish and keep them sharp. They disregarded several commandments of the Rule of the Templars which they had been given, but in 1244 were absolved and obtained from pope Innocent IV the right for their Master to make any changes he thought necessary.

54.1 It is difficult to be certain of the meaning of this word. It is probably a sort of bag made of mail or cord.

55.1 I.e. falconry was forbidden.

command especially all brothers not to go in the woods with longbow or crossbow to hunt animals or to accompany anyone who would do so, except out of love to save him from faithless pagans. Nor should you go after dogs, nor shout or chatter, nor spur on a horse out of a desire to capture a wild beast.

On the Lion

56. It is the truth that you especially are charged with the duty of giving your souls for your brothers, as did Jesus Christ, and of defending the land from the unbelieving pagans who are the enemies of the son of the Virgin Mary. This above-mentioned prohibition of hunting is by no means intended to include the lion, for he comes encircling and searching for what he can devour, his hands against every man and every man's hand against him.

How They May Have Lands and Men

57. This kind of new order we believe was born out of the Holy Scriptures and divine providence in the Holy Land of the East. That is to say that this armed company of knights may kill the enemies of the cross without sinning. For this reason we judge you to be rightly called knights of the Temple, with the double merit and beauty of probity, and that you may have lands and keep men, villeins and fields and govern them justly, and take your right to them as it is specifically established.

On Tithes

58. You who have abandoned the pleasant riches of this world, we believe you to have willingly subjected yourselves to poverty; therefore we are resolved that you who live the communal life may receive tithes. If the bishop of the place, to whom the tithe should be rendered by right, wishes to give it to you out of charity, with the consent of his chapter he may give those tithes which the Church possesses. Moreover, if any layman keeps the tithes of his patrimony, to his detriment and against the Church, and wishes to leave them to you, he may do so with the permission of the prelate and his chapter.

On Giving Judgement

59. We know, because we have seen it, that persecutors and people who like quarrels and endeavour to cruelly torment those faithful to the Holy Church and their friends, are without number. By the clear judgement of our council, we command that if there is anyone in the parties of the East or anywhere else who asks anything of you, for faithful men and love of truth you should judge the thing, if the other party wishes to allow it. This same commandment should be kept at all times when something is stolen from you.

On Elderly Brothers

60. We command by pious counsel that ageing and weak brothers be honoured with diligence and given consideration according to their frailty; and, kept well by the authority of the Rule in those things which are necessary to their physical welfare, should in no way be in distress.

On Sick Brothers

61. Let sick brothers be given consideration and care and be served according to the saying of the evangelist and Jesus Christ: *Infirmus fui et visitastis me*. That is to say: 'I was sick and you visited me'; and let this not be forgotten. For those brothers who are wretched should be treated quietly and with care, for which service, carried out without hesitation, you will gain the kingdom of heaven.

Therefore we command the Infirmarer to studiously and faithfully provide those things which are necessary to the various sick brothers, such as meat, flesh, birds and all other foods which bring good health, according to the means and the ability of the house.

On Deceased Brothers

62. When any brother passes from life to death, a thing from which no one is exempt, we command you to sing mass for his soul with a pure heart, and have the divine office performed by the priests who serve the sovereign king and you who serve charity for a fixed term and all the brothers who are present where the body lies and serve for a fixed term should say one hundred paternosters during the next seven days. And all the brothers who are under the command of that house where the brother has passed away should say the hundred paternosters, as is said above, after the death of the brother is known, by God's mercy. Also we pray and command by pastoral authority that a pauper be fed with meat and wine for forty days in memory of the dead brother, just as if he were alive. We expressly forbid all other offerings which used to be made at will and without discretion by the Poor Knights of the Temple on the death of brothers, at the feast of Easter and at other feasts.

63. Moreover, you should profess your faith with a pure heart night and day that you may be compared in this respect to the wisest of all the prophets, who said: *Calicem salutaris accipiam*. That is to say: 'I will take the cup of salvation.' Which means: 'I will avenge the death of Jesus Christ by my death. For just as Jesus Christ gave his body for me, I am prepared in the same way to give my soul for my brothers.' This is a suitable offering; a living sacrifice and very pleasing to God.

On the Priests and Clerks Who Serve Charity

64. The whole of the common council commands you to render all offerings and all kinds of alms in whatever manner they may be given, to the chaplains and clerks and to others who remain in charity for a fixed term. According to the

authority of the Lord God, the servants of the Church may have only food and clothing, and may not presume to have anything else unless the Master wishes to give them anything willingly out of charity.

On Secular Knights

65. Those who serve out of pity and remain with you for a fixed term are knights of the house of God and of the Temple of Solomon; therefore out of pity we pray and finally command that if during his stay the power of God takes any one of them, for love of God and out of brotherly mercy, one pauper be fed for seven days for the sake of his soul, and each brother in that house should say thirty paternosters.

On Secular Knights Who Serve for a Fixed Term

66. We command all secular knights who desire with a pure heart to serve Jesus Christ and the house of the Temple of Solomon for a fixed term to faithfully buy a suitable horse and arms, and everything that will be necessary for such work. Furthermore, we command both parties to put a price on the horse and to put the price in writing so that it is not forgotten; and let everything that the knight, his squire and horse need, even horseshoes, be given out of fraternal charity according to the means of the house. If, during the fixed term, it happens by chance that the horse dies in the service of the house, if the house can afford to, the Master should replace it. If, at the end of his tenure, the knight wishes to return to his own country, he should leave to the house, out of charity, half the price of the horse, and the other half he may, if he wishes, receive from the alms of the house.

On the Commitment of Sergeants

67. As the squires and sergeants who wish to serve charity in the house of the Temple for the salvation of their souls and for a fixed term come from divers regions, it seems to us beneficial that their promises be received, so that the envious enemy does not put it in their hearts to repent of or renounce their good intentions.

On White Mantles

68. By common counsel of all the chapter we forbid and order expulsion, for common vice, of anyone who without discretion was in the house of God and of the knights of the Temple; also that the sergeants and squires should not have white habits, from which custom great harm used to come to the house; for in the regions beyond the mountains false brothers, married men and others who said they were brothers of the Temple used to be sworn in; while they were of the world. They brought so much shame to us and harm to the Order of Knighthood that even their squires boasted of it; for this reason numerous scandals arose. Therefore let them assiduously be given black robes; but if these cannot be

found, they should be given what is available in that province; or what is the least expensive, that is *burell*.[1]

On Married Brothers

69. If married men ask to be admitted to the fraternity, benefice and devotions of the house, we permit you to receive them on the following conditions: that after their death they leave you a part of their estate and all that they have obtained henceforth. Meanwhile, they should lead honest lives and endeavour to act well towards the brothers. But they should not wear white habits or cloaks; moreover, if the lord should die before his lady, the brothers should take part of his estate and let the lady have the rest to support her during her lifetime; for it does not seem right to us that such *confrères*[1] should live in a house with brothers who have promised chastity to God.

On Sisters

70. The company of women is a dangerous thing, for by it the old devil has led many from the straight path to Paradise. Henceforth, let not ladies be admitted as sisters into the house of the Temple;[1] that is why, very dear brothers, henceforth it is not fitting to follow this custom, that the flower of chastity is always maintained among you.

Let Them Not Have Familiarity with Women

71. We believe it to be a dangerous thing for any religious to look too much upon the face of woman. For this reason none of you may presume to kiss a woman, be it widow, young girl, mother, sister, aunt or any other; and henceforth the Knighthood of Jesus Christ should avoid at all costs the embraces of women, by which men have perished many times, so that they may remain eternally before the face of God with a pure conscience and sure life.

On Not Being Godfathers

72. We forbid all brothers henceforth to dare to raise children over the font and none should be ashamed to refuse to be godfathers or godmothers; this shame brings more glory than sin.

68.1 A coarse woollen cloth.

69.1 An associate brother who served in the Order for a short time and did not take the monastic vows.

70.1 This implies that women were previously involved in the Order, not just as associates. However, this precept seems not always to have been kept. Forey gives examples of women who took the normal monastic vows and were accepted into the Order. 'Women and the Military Orders in the Twelfth and Thirteenth Centuries', *Studia Monastica*, 1987, pp. 65–6.

On the Commandments

73. All the commandments which are mentioned and written above in this present Rule are at the discretion and judgement of the Master.

These are the Feast Days and Fasts that all the Brothers should Celebrate and Observe

74. Let it be known to all present and future brothers of the Temple that they should fast at the vigils of the twelve apostles. That is to say: St Peter and St Paul;[1] St Andrew;[2] St James[3] and St Philip; St Thomas;[4] St Bartholomew;[5] Sts. Simon and Jude;[6] St James;[7] St Matthew.[8] The vigil of St John the Baptist;[9] the vigil of the Ascension[10] and the two days before, the rogation days; the vigil of Pentecost;[11] the ember days;[12] the vigil of St Laurence;[13] the vigil of Our Lady in mid-August;[14] the vigil of All Saints;[15] the vigil of Epiphany.[16] And they should fast on all the above-mentioned days according to the commandments of Pope Innocent at the council which took place in the city of Pisa.[17] And if any of the above-mentioned feast days fall on a Monday, they should fast on the preceding Saturday. If the nativity of Our Lord[18] falls on a Friday, the brothers should eat meat in honour of the festival. But they should fast on the feast day of St Mark[19] because of the Litany: for it is established by Rome for the mortality of men. However, if it falls during the octave of Easter, they should not fast.

74.1 28 June.
74.2 29 November.
74.3 St James the Less, 30 April.
74.4 20 December.
74.5 23 August.
74.6 27 October.
74.7 St James the Great, 24 July.
74.8 20 September.
74.9 23 June.
74.10 Varying between 29 April and 2 June.
74.11 Varying between 9 May and 12 June.
74.12 Any of four groups of three days of prayer and fasting – Wednesday, Friday, Saturday – occurring after (i) the first Sunday in Lent; (ii) Whit Sunday; (iii) Holy Cross Day (14 September); (iv) St Lucia's Day (13 December).
74.13 9 August.
74.14 14 August.
74.15 31 October.
74.16 5 January. The term used in the French text, Baptism, is rare and usually found only in the Armenian church.
74.17 30 May 1135. A council of all the western bishops was convened by Innocent II. St Bernard attended.
74.18 Christmas, 25 December.
74.19 25 April.

These are the Feast Days which should be Observed in the House of the Temple

75. The nativity of Our Lord; the feast of St Stephen;[1] St John the Evangelist;[2] the Holy Innocents;[3] the eighth day of Christmas, which is New Year's Day; Epiphany; St Mary Candlemas;[4] St Mathias the Apostle; the Annunciation of Our Lady in March;[5] Easter and the three days following; St George;[6] Sts Philip and James, two apostles; the finding of the Holy Cross;[7] the Ascension of Our Lord; Pentecost and the two days following; St John the Baptist;[8] St Peter and St Paul, two apostles;[9] St Mary Magdalene;[10] St James the Apostle; St Laurence;[11] the Assumption of Our Lady;[12] the nativity of Our Lady;[13] the Exaltation of the Holy Cross;[14] St Matthew the Apostle; St Michael;[15] Sts Simon and Jude; the feast of All Saints; St Martin in winter;[16] St Catherine in winter;[17] St Andrew; St Nicholas in winter;[18] St Thomas the Apostle.

76. None of the lesser feasts should be kept by the house of the Temple. And we wish and advise that this be strictly kept and adhered to: that all the brothers of the Temple should fast from the Sunday before St Martin's to the nativity of Our Lord, unless illness prevents them. And if it happens that the feast of St Martin falls on a Sunday, the brothers should go without meat on the preceding Sunday.

75.1 26 December.
75.2 27 December.
75.3 28 December.
75.4 2 February.
75.5 25 March.
75.6 23 April.
75.7 3 May. This commemorates the finding of the True Cross by Helena, mother of the Roman emperor, Constantine, in 335 during excavations for the foundations of Constantine's basilica of the Holy Sepulchre on Mount Calvary.
75.8 24 June.
75.9 29 June.
75.10 22 July.
75.11 10 August.
75.12 15 August.
75.13 8 September.
75.14 14 September.
75.15 29 September.
75.16 Martin of Tours, 11 November.
75.17 Catherine of Alexandria, 25 November.
75.18 6 December. Patron saint of Russia, bishop of Myra (now Muğla in south-west Turkey) under Constantine. Died around 342.

The Hierarchical Statutes

Here Begin the Retrais and Establishments of the House of the Temple

Retrais of the Master

77. The Master should have four horses, and one chaplain brother, one clerk with three horses, one sergeant brother with two horses, and one gentleman valet with one horse, to carry his shield and lance; and when he has served for a time, the Master may make him a knight brother if he wishes; but he should not do this too often. Also he should have a farrier, and Saracen scribe,[1] a turcopole[2] and a cook, and may have two foot soldiers and one turcoman[3] which should be kept in the caravan. And when the Master rides from one place to another, the turcoman should be led by a squire and by a horse from the caravan; when the Master returns it should be placed in the caravan, and in war he may keep it in his string.[4]

78. And when the Master rides from one place to another, he may take two pack animals. And when he is in camp or in pasture he may keep them in his string. And when he rides from one place to another where there is war, he may take four pack animals; or when he crosses the river Jordan or the Dog Pass.[1] And when he returns to the house where he is staying, the pack animals should return to the stables and work in the service of the house.

79. The Master should have two knight brothers as companions, who should be such worthy men that they are not excluded from any council of five or six brothers, and should have the same ration of barley as the Master. And when the brothers of the convent take rations for twelve horses, those of the Master count for ten. And when there is war and the brothers ride out, the provisions should be communal and should not be increased or decreased except by order of the chapter. Likewise with the oil and wine. But the Master may decrease the amount of barley as long as the pasture lasts. But when the grass runs out, the provisions should be as they were before.

77.1 To act as interpreter.
77.2 Turcopoles were of native Middle Eastern or mixed race, light cavalrymen with special skills in Saracen fighting techniques.
77.3 An élite riding horse.
77.4 I.e. together with his other horses.
78.1 A narrow gorge on the Dog river at Beirut. William of Tyre describes it as 'a very dangerous passage between a tempestuous sea and high mountains, where the steep ascent and rugged cliffs render the road almost impassible' (*op. cit.* X, 5, vol. I, p. 422).

80. If God summons any of the Master's companions, he may take for himself what he pleases of the man's equipment. And he should return the rest to the Marshal in the caravan.

81. The Master should not hold the lock or key to the treasury. But he may have in the treasury a lockable strong-box in which to keep his valuables; and if items are presented to the Master they should be put in the strong-room.

82. The Master may lend the assets of the house, up to one thousand besants, with the consent of a group of the worthy men of the house; and if the Master wishes to lend a large sum, he may do so with the consent of a large group of the worthy men of the house. And the Master may give one hundred besants or one horse to a noble friend of the house; also a gold or silver goblet, a squirrel-hair robe or other valuable items, worth one hundred besants or less, for the benefit of the house; and the Master should do this only with the consent of his companions and the worthy men of the house where he is; and this should be done for the benefit of the house. And all arms may be given, except sword, lance and coats of mail: these may not be given away.

83. When assets come from overseas, they should be placed in the treasury, by order of the Commander of the Kingdom of Jerusalem, and no-one may take or remove any of them until the Master has seen them and given his permission.

84. When horses arrive from overseas[1] they should be placed in the Marshal's caravan, and the Marshal should not give away or remove any of them until the Master has seen them; and if the Master wishes to take any for himself, he may do so; also he may keep one or two horses in the caravan to give to worthy, secular men who are friends of the house. And if horses are presented to him, he may give them to any brother he chooses. And the Master may ask for and take any horse he wishes, from any of the brothers, to give to a rich, secular man, for the increase of the house, or to ride himself, and the brother should agree to it. And the Master may give the brother one hundred besants if he wishes, in order to buy another, provided he has taken good care of the horse; and if not, the Master should ask the Marshal to give the brother another horse in compensation; and the Marshal should carry out the order if he has one.

85. The Master may not give away or sell land, nor take castles in the march lands,[1] without the permission of the chapter, nor should he relax or widen the scope of any order made by him or by the convent, except with his and the convent's consent.

Nor should he start a war or make a truce on land or in a castle where the house holds the seigniory, without the consent of the convent; but if it happens that truces are broken, the Master may extend them with the advice of the brothers who are in that country.

84.1 I.e. from the West.
85.1 The border regions, which were particularly vulnerable to enemy attack.

86. When the Master returns from riding, he may eat in his room, either if he is wounded or if he has invited knights or other secular men. And when he is ill he may lie in his room, and his companions should eat in the palace with the other brothers; and when he has recovered he should eat at one of the tables in the infirmary, and this should be better for all the brothers in the infirmary, for love of him.

87. The Master may not place commanders in the houses of the kingdoms without the consent of the chapter: such as the Seneshal, the Marshal, the Commander of the Kingdom of Jerusalem, the Commander of the city of Jerusalem; the Commander of Acre,[1] the Draper, the Commanders of the lands of Tripoli[2] and Antioch,[3] those of France and England,[4] of Poitiers, Aragon, Portugal, Apulia and Hungary. And the said commanders of the West should not come to the East unless under the instructions of the Master and chapter. And the placing of the other commanders of lands and baillis, because of the poverty of the land, is at the discretion of the Master with the consent of the chapter or, in the absence of the chapter, with the advice of a group of worthy men of the house; and if he cannot place them with the consent of the chapter, he may remove them without the chapter with the counsel of a group of worthy men of the house.

88. And if a Visitor or commander appointed by the Chapter General is recalled by the Master and the convent, and he remains for any reason whatsoever, he is dismissed and should send the seal[1] and treasury to the Master and the convent; and from then on the Visitor should not take part in the visitation, nor the commander of the baillie;[2] nor should the brothers obey them, but should put a worthy brother in place of the commander, and inform the Master and the convent, and await their instructions. And this should be understood by the baillis who are appointed with the advice of the Master.

89. When the Master wishes to go to the land of Tripoli or Antioch, he may take from the treasury three thousand besants or more if necessary, to help the

87.1 A coastal city now in northern Israel.
87.2 Established as a county by the crusaders in 1109, now in northern Lebanon.
87.3 A Frankish principality, now in southern Turkey.
87.4 It is not clear from the text if there were separate commanders for France and England in the early years. De Curzon gives, as the only example known to him to substantiate the theory that the two countries were under one commander, the case of Gaufridus de Vicherio, who bore the title visitator generalis domorum militie Templi in regnis Francie et Anglie ('Visitor General of the houses of the Knights of the Temple in the kingdoms of France and England'). Certainly by the thirteenth century, however, England, Scotland and Ireland formed a separate province under a grand preceptor whose usual title was Magister Militiae Templi in Anglia ('Master of the Knights of the Temple in England'). T.W. Parker, The Knights Templars in England (Tucson, Arizona 1963), pp. 17–18.
88.1 The seal was of lead or silver (see §234). It was kept locked by three keys which were entrusted to the Master and two high officials.
88.2 The territory under the command of a bailli.

houses there. But he should not take them without the permission of the Commander of the Kingdom of Jerusalem, who is Treasurer of the convent and who should keep and guard the keys of the treasury; and he should deliver the besants to the Master. But if it happens that the houses can manage without them, the Master should return the besants to the Commander; and the Commander should place them in the treasury.

90. When the Master rides from one place to another, he will look for and study the castles and houses; if he wishes, he may make one house help another if necessary. And if he wishes to take from the commanders anything which is under their authority it is from them that he should take it; this should be the case in all the *baillies*, from the greatest to the smallest.

91. If the Master or commanders ask the commanders under them to show them the things of the house, they should show them all; and if any should lie or keep anything back, and is found guilty of it, he could be expelled from the house.[1]

If items are given to the house, and the Master receives them, he should deliver them into the hands of the Commander of the Kingdom of Jerusalem who should place them in the common treasury.

92. When the Master leaves the Kingdom of Jerusalem he may leave the Commander of the Land or another brother in his place, and the one who remains in his place does not have increased authority except to advise on anything that may happen in the land and for which the Master cannot come, and to hold chapter and take up arms: for all are under his command.

The Master should not send any brother to the lands of Tripoli or Antioch in his place, over the commanders who are there, except for anything which arises in that land, to advise, or to see the castles' garrisons; and they should obey him in these things.

If the Master wishes to send one of the worthy men of the house overseas in his place to carry out the work of the house, he should do so with the consent of the chapter, and he may exclude all the *baillis* without remission, except the Seneschal.

93. When we hold Chapter General, if the Master wishes to send brothers overseas because of their illness or to carry out the work of the house, he should call the Marshal, the Commander of the Land, the Draper, the Commander of Acre, and three or four worthy men of the house, and should say to them, 'Go and see the brothers, to decide which it would be beneficial to send overseas'; and they should go to see the brothers in the infirmary and elsewhere. They should put in writing the names of those whom it seems most reasonable to send abroad and then return to the Master and show him what they have written; and if there are any alterations to be made they should be made with their advice.

94. If any valuables are presented to the house of the Temple as alms, the Master may take them and give them to whomsoever he chooses, or put them in his strong-box with his other valuables.

91.1 An example of this is given in §556.

Compline wine is at the discretion of the Master, whether to withhold it or give it; also the fourth horse, the second squire of the knight brothers, the second horse of the sergeant brothers, if they do not have them by the decision of the chapter, are at the discretion of the Master.

Every day that the Master is in the house of the Temple five paupers should eat in the house because of him, of the same food that the brothers eat.

95. Of all the brothers who are given a penance in the presence of the Master, none may rise from the floor unless he is raised by him; and the brothers may pardon them from manual labour and fasting, but may not raise them from the floor[1] and Friday fasting.

None may give permission to let blood, nor to race horses, bathe or joust in the place where the Master is, unless the Master gives it.

When the Master rides out, and any brother meets him or joins him on his way, he should not leave him without his permission.

When the Master eats at the convent's table, he may give from his bowl to whomsoever he wishes, and no brother may do this except the Master.

96. After Easter, when the houses have large expenditures to make out of the profits, and the commanders tell the Master that they do not have much meat, the Master may inform the brothers and ask their advice; and if the brothers agree to forgo meat on Tuesdays, they will abstain. But when the wheat is cut it [the meat] should be restored.

For everything that the Master does with the advice of the convent, he should seek the counsel of the brothers communally, and do what the majority of the brothers and the Master agree.

If any secular man or brother, here or overseas, sends a present to a brother of the Temple who has died, the gift should go into the hands of the Master.

97. The Master should not admit brothers without the consent of the chapter, but if he goes anywhere where he cannot find a chapter, and is beseeched by a worthy man to make him a brother for love of God, because he is so ill that it is believed he cannot escape death, then, with the consent of the brothers present, he may make him a brother providing he sees that he may rightly be a brother; and if God restores his health, as soon as he is in our house he should make his profession of faith before all the brothers and learn what a brother should do.

All the clothes and bed linen that the Master puts aside should be given for love of God to the lepers, or where he sees they will be best used. And if the Master gives any of his robes to a brother, he should give another in its place, for love of God, either to the lepers or where he sees it will be best used.

98. Wherever the Master is on Maundy Thursday,[1] he should wash the feet of thirteen paupers, and should give to each of them shirt and breeches, two loaves of bread, two deniers and a pair of shoes. And if he is in a place where he does

95.1 This refers to the punishment of eating on the floor, instead of at the table, for a set number of days per week.
98.1 Traditionally the day when Christ washed the feet of the Apostles.

not have them, when he comes to the first house of the Temple where he has them, he should give them, for love of God.

When it happens in time of war that the brothers are under arms in the field, the Master may take six or eight or up to ten knight brothers to accompany him.

All the brothers of the Temple should obey the Master, and the Master should obey his house.

Here Begin the Retrais of the Seneschal

99. The Seneschal may have four mounts and in place of a mule may have a palfrey; he should have two squires; and one knight brother as a companion, who should also have four horses and two squires; a sergeant brother with two horses; one deacon scribe to say his hours, one turcopole with one horse, and a Saracen scribe with one horse; he may also have two foot soldiers; and he may take all these with him. He should carry the same seal (bolle) as the Master.

The Seneschal carries the piebald banner[1] and a round tent like the Master and everywhere where the Master is absent, he takes his place. And when he rides his horses they should have the same rations as those of the Master. And everywhere where the Master is absent, all the equipment of the lands and houses, and all the houses and food are under the command of the Seneschal.

100. When the Seneschal is in one of the lands without the Master, he will study it and take from it what he likes, and make one house help another; and if he wishes brothers to move from one land to another he can make them, except to the land where the Master is.

The Seneschal may give to a worthy friend of the house one palfrey, one mule of either sex, a war-saddle,[1] a fine silver goblet, a robe of squirrel fur or scarlet,[2] or anything of less value. But all these gifts should be made with the advice of the brothers who are in that place, for the benefit of the house.

Here Begin the Retrais of the Marshal of the Convent of the Temple

101. The Marshal should have four horses and two squires, and in place of a mule he may have one fine turcoman, and if any brother asks him for it, he need not give it to him if he does not wish. And if he has an ungelded roncin[1] and he asks him for it, he should give it to him. He should also have a sergeant brother with one horse, and he may lend him another horse from the caravan if he wishes; he should have a turcopole with one horse, and a pavilion with four flaps, three poles and two pegs; and a tent for his squires and equipment; he should have the same equipment as the brothers of the convent and the same rations as the convent. And when he rides out into the countryside or elsewhere

99.1 The Templars' banner was a two-pointed pennant divided horizontally with white above and black below.
100.1 In the Middle Ages, this was a high, box-like saddle.
100.2 A cloth of superior quality in a variety of colours.
101.1 An entire horse, little better than a pack animal.

with the convent, he should make the Commander's baggage train carry his pavilion, his barley and cauldron wherever he happens to be.

102. The Marshal should have at his command all the arms of the house: those bought to give to the brothers of the convent as gifts, alms or booty. And all the spoils which are treated as arms or are auctioned should also be given to the Marshal. Also, all the equipment treated as arms belonging to the brothers who have died; except crossbows, which should be given to the Commander of the Land, and Turkish arms which the commanders buy to give to the craftsman sergeant brothers who are under their command. And the Marshal should give the brothers orders and deploy them wherever he happens to be, and he should not appoint a brother in his place unless he leaves the land or is ill.

103. When the war-cry is raised the commanders of the houses should gather their horses and when they are assembled they should all join the Marshal's squadron and then should not leave it without permission. And all the sergeant brothers should go to the Turcopolier and should not leave without permission. And all the knight brothers, all the sergeant brothers and the men at arms are under the command of the Marshal while they are under arms.

The Marshal may buy horses or mules of both sexes in whichever land he happens to be. But he should inform the Master if he is there. And the Master should give him besants if he sees that he needs them.

The Marshal may give to a secular nobleman a used or donated saddle and may also give small items of equipment, but he should not do it too often; and he should do nothing without the consent of the Master.

104. When the Marshal is in the land of Tripoli or Antioch the Commander may give him the marshalcy of that land if he wishes. But he need not if he does not wish to. And if the Marshal wishes he may accept, and he need not if he does not wish to. And if the Commander gives him the office and he takes it, he may give the brothers what they need; and if he does not, the Marshal of the convent will be in charge of the small items of equipment. And if there is a marshal in the land, the Marshal of the convent has no power in the marshalcy of the land, except for the commandments of the house, which he should carry out wherever he is, and also with regard to small items of equipment. But if he asks for a horse which is in the caravan to give to a brother living in that land, the marshal of the land must obey him.

105. And if the Marshal of the convent asks him to give it to a brother not resident in the land, he may refuse if he wishes; but if there is war in the land, and brothers who must ride out are without horses or mules, the Marshal of the convent may go to the caravan and see what is there; and he may order the marshal of the land to provide a brother with a particular horse, and the marshal must obey him. And when the brothers return they should return the horses to the caravan. And if there are two squadrons of knights, the marshal of the land should have one of them; and if there is no marshal, the Commander of the Land should have one squadron if he wishes or he may do without.

106. The Marshal of the convent may appoint the Under-Marshal and Standard Bearer if he wishes, with advice. And if the Marshal wishes to send equipment from the marshalcy from one house to another to be carried by the army either when at war or resting, the Commander of the Land should arrange for all that the Marshal gives him to be carried by the pack animals.

In whichever land the Marshal of the convent may be, the commander of that land may not make a baggage train of the convent's horses without speaking to him.

All that is said about the Marshal of the convent in the land of Tripoli also applies to the land of Antioch.

The Marshal of the convent should call the brothers to arms and give them orders wherever the Master is, or another in his place, and there where he is, for he is the *bailli* of the convent. The Marshal should hold chapter in the land of Jerusalem in the absence of the Master, Seneschal, or another who is in the Master's place.

107. When horses come from overseas they should be kept in the caravan until the Master has seen them. And the Master may take from them for his own use if necessary, as is mentioned above, one or two horses, to give away; but he should have them kept in the caravan until he has given them, and then the Marshal may share out the other horses to the brothers wherever he sees there is need.

And if any brother passes from this world who was resident in the land, or was sent to another land without his equipment, the equipment should remain in the marshalcy of the land and the equipment of the other brothers of the convent should come into the convent's marshalcy.

108. When the brothers are dispersed among the houses, the Marshal may not move them except to exchange one for another. And the Marshal of the convent may not take any brother resident in the land to place him in the convent, nor to send him out of the land; nor may the Marshal of the convent leave any brother in the land without the Master's consent. When the Master or brothers exclude brothers from the chapter in order to appoint commanders this side of the sea,[1] the Marshal may not be excluded unless the convent has first thanked him for his tenure of office; except the Seneschal only all the commanders this side of the sea may be excluded from the chapter to appoint marshals without being thanked for their tenure of office except the Seneschal and the Commander of the Kingdom of Jerusalem.

109. The Marshal may not send his companion of rank from one land to another to live, but he may send him only for a fortnight, for porterage and for the squadron.

The Marshal and the Commander of the Land should provide all that is necessary in the marshalcy except steel and Burgundy wire.[1]

108.1 I.e. in the East.
109.1 Presumably the steel was needed for making swords, and the wire for mail coats.

Here Begin the Retrais of the Commander of the Land of Jerusalem and of the Kingdom

110. The Commander of the Kingdom of Jerusalem should have four horses and in place of a mule may have a palfrey; and two squires; one sergeant brother with two mounts and a deacon who knows how to write; and one turcopole with one horse; and a Saracen scribe with one horse; and two foot soldiers like the Seneschal; and one tent for his squires and a pavilion like the Marshal. Moreover, the Draper should be his companion.

111. The Commander of the Land is Treasurer of the convent, and all the belongings of the house, wherever they may be brought from, here or overseas, should be given and delivered into the hands of the Commander of the Land; and he should put them in the treasury, and should not touch or remove anything until the Master has seen and counted them; and when he has seen them, they should be put in writing and the Commander should keep them in the treasury and use them according to the needs of the house. And if the Master or a party of worthy men of the house wishes to hear the list, he should give it to them.

112. The Commander of the Land should furnish the drapery with everything that is necessary, and may take what he wishes with the advice of the Draper; and the Draper must obey him.

The Commander of the Land may give one palfrey, a mule of either sex, a silver goblet, a robe of squirrel-fur or *brunete*,[1] a piece of squirrel or Reims cloth to friends who have given large donations to the house. And all the robes of squirrel and scarlet, and all the cloth which is not made up and which comes to the house through gifts or alms, belongs to the Commander of the Land; and the other made-up robes should go into the drapery.

113. The Commander of the Land should have purchases and legacies of one hundred besants and over which are made to the houses under his command.

But if the legacy comes to more than one hundred besants, it should be put in the strong-room, and if less than one hundred besants, it should go to the commander of the house where the alms are given; and if a bequest, large or small, is made to the house at sea, it should go into the strong-room.

If a slave buys his freedom, which is in the hands of the Commander, for one thousand besants or more, the money should go into the strong-room; and if the ransom is less than one thousand besants it should go into the hands of the Commander; and if the slave is from the marshalcy and the ransom comes to less than one thousand besants, it should go into the hands of the Marshal; and if the ransom comes to more than one thousand besants it should be placed in the strong-room.

114. The Commander may give to the brothers one or two mules from his string or one of his pack animals; but he should not do it too often. Moreover,

112.1 A fine woollen cloth worn by men of rank.

the Commander should not keep in his string the animal which the brother has exchanged; this should go to the stables if the Marshal has not given the brother permission to change it.

If the Commander has the brothers under his command feed the foals and any brother of the convent asks for one as his horse, if he is in agreement he may give him one or two. But he should not do it too often.

115. If the Commander needs horses for the brothers from his stables and pack trains and he asks the Marshal for them, he should help him if he can, and he may lend him foals or horses. But when he wishes he may take them back in order to equip the brothers of the convent, and the Commander should return them to him when they are needed. And if any brother asks the Marshal for a horse which he has borrowed from the stables, he may give it to him, for they should return all the animals which leave the stables; but if the Commander buys foals and gives them or any other animals to the brothers to feed, the Marshal may not take any of these without the permission of the Commander or the Master. And if the Marshal does not have the means with which to buy them, and he informs the Master or Commander, he should make him accept the animals that the brothers under his command have fed, those with which he can pay the brothers of the convent. And the Master may not take any of them without himself informing the Commander; and the Commander must obey him. The Commander may buy pack animals, camels and any other animals that he needs for his work.

116. All the booty, all the animals with packsaddles, all the slaves and all the livestock that the houses of the Kingdom of Jerusalem gain through warfare, should be under the command of the Commander of the Land, except the saddled horses, armour and arms, which go to the marshalcy.

If the Commander of the Kingdom of Jerusalem wishes to ride through the land and he carries goods with him, he may ask the Marshal for brothers for as long as he needs them to accompany him, and the Marshal should give them to him.

117. If the Commander's horses are tired and worn out, and he needs other horses in order to carry out the work of the house, he should ask them of the Marshal or the one who is in his place, and he should let him have them; and the Commander should place his own horses in the caravan. And when he comes back, he should take his own horses and return those he has borrowed.

If the Commander wants a saddle made in the marshalcy, either for himself or for any friend of the house, he may do so; but he should not do it too often.

118. Nor may the Commander of the Land send any brother out of his *baillie* to live in another land unless he is sent there by the Master.

All the houses and *casals*[1] of the Kingdom of Jerusalem, and all the brothers in them, are under the command of the Commander of the Land.

118.1 The *casal* was a farm or village dependent upon a house or castle.

Nor may the Commander offer an invitation or make gifts to secular people or to knights wherever the Master happens to be, except to friends of the house, privately. But if the Master is not there, he may do so.

119. If the Commander needs expenses he should inform the Master, and should take what he takes with his consent.

All the ships which belong to the house at Acre are under the command of the Commander of the Land. And the commander of the shipyard at Acre[1] and all the brothers who are there under him, are under his command, and all the things which the ships carry should be given to the Commander of the Land. But if a particular thing is sent there either to the Master or to another brother, that thing should be given to whomsoever it is sent.

When it comes to sharing out the brothers of the convent among the houses, the Commander may say to the Marshal, 'Place so many in this house and so many in the other.' And the Marshal should do it, and he should not place more or fewer there.

Here Begin the Retrais of the Commander of the City of Jerusalem

120. The Commander of the City of Jerusalem should have four horses, and in place of a mule he may have a turcoman or a fine *roncin*, two squires, a sergeant brother with two horses, a Saracen scribe with one horse and a turcopole with one horse; he should have the same rations as the Master and, in the city of Jerusalem, should have under him the Commander of the Knights.

121. The Commander of the City of Jerusalem should have ten knight brothers under his command to lead and guard the pilgrims who come to the river Jordan;[1] and he should carry a round tent and the piebald banner or flag, for as long as his authority lasts.

For this reason, when he is camping, if he finds a nobleman in need he should take him to his tent and serve him with the alms of the Order; and for this reason he should carry a round tent and food, and lead pack animals and bring back pilgrims on the animals if necessary.

122. When the True Cross[1] is transported by horse, the Commander of Jerusalem and the ten knights should guard it day and night, and should camp as

119.1 Acre was taken by the Franks in 1104 under the command of king Baldwin I. It was recaptured by Saladin in 1187 and fell to the Christians again in 1191, after a siege lasting two years. It was finally taken by the Saracens in 1291. It was the principal port of the Templars and their headquarters after the loss of Jerusalem. They had several establishments there. The one mentioned here as the vault consisted of the keep and buildings of the Master and knights which were situated on the coast. Because of the importance of the town, the commander, although only a sergeant brother, was one of the principal officers of the Order (see §143).

121.1 Pilgrimage to the river Jordan dates back to earliest Christian times. In the Middle Ages pilgrims went there to purify themselves in its waters and carry out various acts of devotion.

122.1 The part of the True Cross which the Order had in its possession was captured

near to the True Cross as they can for as long as the journey lasts; and each night two brothers should keep watch over the True Cross; and if it happens that camp is established, everyone should lodge with the convent.

123. The Commander of Jerusalem may give to the brothers wherever he is horses and mules of both sexes, and a Turkish saddle to a secular man if it is presented to him. And of all the booty gained through warfare beyond the river Jordan, which belongs to the Commander of the Kingdom of Jerusalem, the Commander of the City of Jerusalem should have half; and of all the booty gained this side of the river he may take nothing; rather, those things which befit him belong to the Grand Commander of the Kingdom of Jerusalem.

124. All the secular knights who are in Jerusalem and are associated with the house should go and lodge near him and should ride under his banner. And all the brothers living in the town, and all those who come and go while he is there and the Marshal is absent, are under his command, and should do what they do with his permission.

Here Begin the Retrais of the Commanders of the Lands of Tripoli and Antioch

125. The Commanders of the lands of Tripoli and Antioch should each have four horses, and in place of a mule may have a palfrey; and a sergeant brother with two horses, one deacon with one horse, a turcopole with one horse, a Saracen scribe with one horse, and one foot soldier. And in all the places within their *baillies* they take the Master's place if he is absent. They should have a round tent and piebald banner, and one knight as companion, whom they may elevate in rank so that he may go from one land to another; and they should have the same rations of barley as the Master. And all the people who live in the houses in their *baillies* are under their command, either under arms or in peacetime; and they may hold chapter in the absence of the Master for as long as their authority lasts.

126. The Commanders should furnish the castles in their *baillies* with leather, wheat, wine, iron, steel and sergeants to guard the gates; and the castellans[1] should provide everything else; and if they lack anything, and they do not have the means with which to buy it, the Commanders should provide it for them or give them the money to buy it.

127. The marshalcies in their *baillies* are under their command, and they should provide food for the horses, mules of both sexes and other necessary equipment, and they should give to the brothers whatever they need. And if there is no marshal in the land, they should give the equipment to the brothers, and should issue the instructions of the house wherever the Marshal of the

by the Moslems at the battle of Hattin in 1187. Melville cites a story that a Templar escaped with it and buried it in the sand, but when he returned could not find it.

126.1 Officers commissioned to guard the castles of the Order. Their function is defined in more detail in §633.

convent is absent; and if they lack anything, the Commanders should provide the food for their stables; and they should also supply whatever is necessary for the drapery. And if there is a marshal in the land, the Commanders may appoint and dismiss him with the consent of the chapter of the land; and the Commanders may likewise appoint and dismiss the drapers and castellans who are in their *baillies*.

128. Nor may these Commanders offer an invitation or make large gifts to secular people or knights, wherever the Master happens to be, except to any friend or *confrère* of the house. And none may give permission to let blood, race horses or joust where he is without his permission. Nor do these Commanders have the power to increase or decrease the ration of barley; nor to put the brothers' horses to stud, except under instructions from the Master and chapter, if the Master is in the land; and if he is not there, they may do so with the advice of the brothers of the convent, except the fourth horse which it is at their discretion to put to stud or to keep on half rations.

129. And the Commanders, if they wish, may see the treasures of the castles and chief houses under their command, and the garrisons; and if they wish to take anything, they should take it with the consent of the commander of the house.

And these Commanders may give horses, robes and everything else that is said above for the Seneschal, for the benefit of the house. And every day that they spend in a house of the Temple in their *baillies*, three paupers should eat from the brothers' food, for love of God. And these Commanders may not give orders to any man without the Master's permission. And when the Commander of the land of Antioch goes to the land of Armenia he may take a chaplain and chapel.[1]

Here Begin the Retrais of the Draper
130. The Draper of the Order should have four horses, two squires and one man in charge of the pack animals; one pavilion like the Marshal; one tent for his squires and another for his tailors, and the pack animals should carry the tailoring equipment and his pavilion also.

The Draper should give the brothers whatever clothes and bed linen they require, except woollen blankets, for as long as his authority lasts.

When robes come from overseas, the Draper should share out the parcels, and he should take all the presents which come to brothers of the convent and distribute them accordingly. And he should ensure that the brothers are dressed decently;[1] and if any are not, he may order them and they must obey him; for after the Master and the Marshal, the Draper is superior to all the other brothers.

129.1 Because the Armenian rite differed from the Latin. The chapel comprises the vessels and vestments necessary for the celebration of mass. Bishops often used a portable altar when making their rounds.
130.1 *Cf.* §22.

131. The Draper should ensure that if any brother has an excess of anything or has anything he should not, he makes him remove it and put it back where it belongs, for all the brothers should be against him who does or says anything unreasonable.

When a man is made a brother, the Draper should take from him all his clothes except those of squirrel-fur or scarlet; and if he gives gold or silver to the house, ten besants should go to the drapery and the rest to the Commander of the Land.

And everything that is said about the Draper of the convent applies to the Drapers of the lands of Tripoli and Antioch, except the pavilion, which they should not have.

Here Begin the Retrais of the Knight Brothers, Commanders of the Houses

132. The Knight Commanders of the houses should have four horses and two squires each; and two of their horses should have the same rations as those of the Master and the other two horses the same as the convent. And when the brothers of the convent have three horses, they may have four; and when the brothers of the convent have two, they may have three. And these Commanders may give one hundred besants to the Marshal, fifty besants to the Draper, twenty besants to the Under-Marshal and ten besants to the Under-Draper; and to a brother of the convent he may give one besant, a *garnache*,[1] a shirt, a cope, a deerskin or a linen cloth.

133. The Knight Commanders of the houses may give to each other up to one hundred hogsheads from their kitchens and may give away some of their food; they may exchange or give one of their pack animals to a brother of the convent, and the brother involved should have the Marshal's permission, or place the animal in the caravan.

These Commanders may not make large gifts or offer an invitation to a secular person in a place where the Master or the Commander of the Land happens to be, except with their permission; unless it is a *confrère* or friend of the house, privately.

134. Nor may these Commanders or anyone else alone find guilty a brother in their charge for words which have passed between them: for that let them come to chapter; for the brother will be believed as much as the Commander; but the orders which the Commanders give to the brothers under their command will be believed, and they can find them guilty alone and take from them all that they can except the habit.

135. If the Commander wishes to give one of the horses from his string to a brother of the convent, he should have permission from his commander and the brother's horse should be placed in the caravan. But if the brother of the convent exchanges horses with the Commander with the permission of the Marshal, the

132.1 A sleeveless cloak.

brother's horse should remain with the Commander. And if the Commander has any fine foals he may give them to the brothers under his command, or other mounts if he has them, and they may give to their *caselier* brothers[1] a mule or the means with which to buy it and may buy from the villeins of their *casals* foals and pack animals for raising.

136. Nor may these Commanders build new houses of lime, mortar or stone without the permission of the Master or the Grand Commander of the Land. But they may rebuild and repair ruined houses.

Here Begin the Retrais of the Commander of the Knights

137. The Commander of the Knights should be under the command of the Commander of the Land, both under arms and in times of peace, in the absence of the Marshal, except for giving permission to the brothers to let blood, to bathe or to race horses at a gallop. And he may give a brother of the convent permission to sleep one night outside; and he may hold chapter in the absence of the Marshal and the Commander of the Land.

Here Begin the Retrais of the Knight Brothers and the Sergeant Brothers of the Convent

138. Each knight brother of the convent should have three horses and one squire; and a fourth horse and second squire, if he has them, are at the discretion of the Master; and they should have a communal ration of barley for their horses; a hauberk,[1] iron hose, a helmet[2] or *chapeau de fer*,[3] a sword, a shield,[4] a lance, a Turkish mace, a surcoat,[5] arming jacket,[6] mail shoes,[7] and three knives: a dagger, a bread-knife and a pocketknife. They may have caparisons, two shirts, two pairs of breeches and two pairs of hose; and a small belt which they should tie over the shirt. And all the brothers of the Temple should sleep thus, except when they are ill in the hospital, and then they should do so with permission. They should have a jerkin with tails back and front, and a covering fur jacket, two white mantles, one with fur and one without; but in summer they should give back the one with fur, and the Draper may put it aside for their use.

135.1 These are the officers commissioned to guard the *casals* or farms of the Order.
138.1 A coat of mail with coif enveloping the head and leaving just the face uncovered.
138.2 A heavy helmet, probably conical.
138.3 A wide-brimmed helmet.
138.4 The shield was triangular with the two long sides slightly curved, made of wood and covered in leather.
138.5 An overgarment of some kind.
138.6 A padded jerkin worn under armour.
138.7 Armoured protection for the feet.

139. And each should have a cope,[1] a tunic[2] and a leather belt to put round his waist; and three pieces of bed linen: that is to say a bag in which to put straw,[3] a sheet and a light blanket or whatever the Draper wishes to give him; also a rug, if he is given one, to cover his bed or his coat of mail when he rides out; moreover, the rug should be white or black or striped; and two small bags: one in which to put his nightshirt and one for his surcoat and arming jacket; and a leather or wire mesh bag in which to put his hauberk; but if he has one he may not have the other.

140. And each may have a cloth for eating[1] and another with which to wash his head;[2] and a rug on to which he can sift his barley; and a blanket to cover his horses; and if [he has] the rug for sifting he should not have the blanket. And he should have a cauldron for cooking and a bowl for measuring barley; and he may keep an axe and a grinder with permission, and if he goes from one land to another he may not always carry them, except with the Master's permission. And he may have three saddle bags: one for the brother and two for the squires; and two cups for drinking, and two flasks; a strap, and one girdle with a buckle and one without; a bowl made of horn and a spoon. And he may have one cloth cap and one felt hat; a tent and a tent peg; the surcoat should be completely white.

141. The surcoats of the sergeant brothers should be completely black, with a red cross on the front and back. And they may have either black or brown mantles; and they may have everything that the knight brothers have except the horses' equipment, the tent and the cauldron, which they will not have. And they may have a sleeveless coat of mail, hose without feet, and a *chapeau de fer*; and all these aforementioned things they may have according to the means of the house.

142. One brother of the convent may give to another a *garnache* that he has worn for a year, an old coat of mail, an old tunic, shirt, breeches and boots; and a lantern if he knows how to make it, a deerskin and a goatskin. And if any squire leaves his lord, and he has served his term in the house, his lord should not take from him any clothing that he has given him, except the year-old *garnache*, and he may give him a two-year-old one if he wishes.

143. There are five sergeant brothers who should have two horses each: these are the Under-Marshal, the Standard Bearer, the Cook brother of the convent, the Farrier of the convent and the Commander of the shipyard at Acre.[1] And each of these five may have two horses and one squire. None of the other

139.1 A heavy, hooded cloak enveloping the whole body and fastened by string or hook.
139.2 With short sleeves, worn over the shirt. Short at first, becoming longer in the twelfth and thirteenth centuries.
139.3 I.e. a mattress.
140.1 I.e. a napkin.
140.2 Presumably a flannel or face cloth.
143.1 This last acted as Admiral of the Fleet.

sergeant brothers may have more than one horse, and the other the Master may lend and take back when he wishes; and if it happens that any of the above-named five brothers is made the commander of a house, the Marshal should have the other horse.[2]

144. Nothing that a secular man gives to a brother of the convent for his own use should he take without permission, except any gift or any bequest which is given to the house as alms, and that he may take and give to the house.

No brother may shorten his stirrup leathers, nor his girth,[1] nor his sword belt, nor his breech-girdle without permission; but he may adjust his buckle without permission.

No brother may bathe, let blood, take medicine, go into town or ride a horse at a gallop without permission; and wherever he may not go without permission he should not send his squire or his horse without permission.

145. If the brothers are eating at table and any of them suffers a nosebleed, or the warcry is raised, or there is a fire or the horses are unsettled, to avoid harm to the house, they may get up from the table without permission, for all these things, and then return to eating at the table if they wish.

When the brothers are lodged in the dormitory, they should not leave without permission to sleep in another place; and when they are in camp and their tents are pitched, they should not move them from one place to another without permission; nor should they go to the lodging of a secular or religious person without permission, unless they are camped rope-to-rope with the [Knights of the] Hospital.[1]

146. When the bell sounds or the call given to say the hours or for the brothers to assemble, all the brothers should go to the chapel, if they are not ill, do not have their hands in feed, or the fire is not burning in the furnace to forge hot iron, or they are not preparing the horses' feet for shoeing, (or they are not washing their hair); and for these aforementioned things the brothers may absent themselves from nones and vespers. And when they have done what is listed above, they should go to the chapel to say the hours or to hear them, or go where the other brothers have gone. But they may not be absent from the other hours without permission unless they are ill.

147. And when the brothers hear together the mass or the hours, they should kneel down, sit and be on their feet together; for the Rule dictates it so. But the old and infirm should keep themselves to one part of the chapel, if they cannot behave like the other healthy brothers; and those who do not know when the brothers should kneel or be at the hours should ask those who know and learn how they do it, and should be behind the others.

143.2 Commanders of houses who were sergeant brothers were allowed only one horse (see §180).

144.1 Shortening the stirrup leathers implied fighting with the sword rather than the lance, i.e. in close combat, because the knight could rise in the stirrups to deliver a blow. Girth tightening similarly implied readiness for action.

145.1 I.e. the Hospitallers. Often in time of war the military orders installed themselves side by side.

How the Brothers Should Make Camp

148. When the Standard Bearer makes camp, the brothers should pitch their tents round the chapel and outside the ropes, each one coming in his troop. And those who are outside [the ropes] should pitch their tents outside and place their equipment inside; and each brother may select an area for all his following. But no brother should take a place until the cry has been raised: 'Make camp, lord brothers, on behalf of God,' and until the Marshal has taken his place, except the Master, the chapel, the mess tent and its commander and the Commander of the Land; and if any brother has taken his place the Marshal may give it to whomsoever he wishes, if he did it without permission. And each brother may take his place in the church or in the chapel; that is to say from the door up to the middle, for any farther in would annoy the priest, that is why it is forbidden. And when the hours are said, a brother should go in search of the one who should be next to him if he is not there.

149. No brother should send for forage or firewood without permission until the command has been given, unless he is near enough to camp to be able to hear the alarm. And they should cover their saddles with cloaks or rugs, etc.; and if they are going to carry rocks on them, they should have permission. And they should not send for the war-saddle without permission; nor should any brother with two squires send more than one, moreover only within the camp or nearby, so that he may have him with him if necessary. Nor should any brother go out for pleasure except as far as he can hear the alarm or the bell. And the brothers who are living in houses at time of war should not ride out except as is given above; neither in war nor in peace should any brother ride out a league without permission; nor may any brother of the convent ride out without permission without boots and in daytime between two meals. The crier [of orders] and the officer in charge of the grain store should camp with the Standard Bearer, and what he shouts should also be done for him as it is for him who has him give the alarm.

150. When the brothers are camped and the rations are called out, the brothers should fasten up their mantles and go quietly and in silence one after the other in their troops, and take what they are offered on behalf of God; and if secular people or brothers who are not in the camp send them gifts of food, they should send them to the Commander of the Victuals and they should not keep anything without permission. And if the Commander sends for them, they may eat the gifts and give them away as they wish; but it is better for the Commander to give them back than for the brothers to keep them. And if there is any brother who eats food from the infirmary because of his illness, the brothers who are camped with him may eat it in such a way that the brother does not suffer privation.

151. Each brother may invite in any worthy man who should be honoured who comes to his camp or passes before his lodgings; and the Commander of the Victuals should give to the brother so freely of the food he has that all those in the lodgings may have plenty, in honour of the worthy man; and this applies as much to the *baillis* as to the others. All searching for food is prohibited to the

brothers of the convent, the food of both the house and others, except for green vegetables from the fields, fish, birds and wild animals if they know how to take them without hunting; for hunting is forbidden in the Rule.[1] Nor should any brother have food in his lodgings, except what is handed over to the mess tent, if he has it without permission. And when the Commander of the Victuals arranges pieces of meat to give to the brothers communally, he should not put two pieces from the same place, neither two haunches nor two shoulders together; but he should share them out to the brothers as fairly as possible.

152. If the Commander of the Victuals wants the rations to be called, he should inform the Master's sergeant brother before he has it done; and when the Master's sergeant brother goes to the distribution, he should be given the best there is for the Master; and the Master's companions should take what the Commander of the Victuals gives them in the queue.

It is not at all a good thing for the Commander of the Victuals to give presents to any brother in the camp unless he is ill, rather he should distribute fairly to everyone alike; but to the sick he may give two or three pieces of the best meat he has, and when the healthy have only one dish the sick should have two; and so he should give alike to the sick and to the healthy in the queue. And when the healthy have two pieces of meat, the sick should have three or more; nor should they have fewer than two dishes when the healthy have only one dish.

153. The servings of meat for two brothers of the convent should be such that what is left by two brothers may sustain two paupers. And from two brothers' servings those of three turcopoles may be made up; and from two turcopoles' those of three sergeants.

Measures should be equal. When the brothers fast, two brothers should be given four measures of wine; and when they are not fasting, five measures between two brothers and three measures between two turcopoles; likewise with the measure of oil. This also applies to the lands of Tripoli and Antioch.

154. No brother should explicitly ask for a horse, a mule of either sex or anything else unless it is small; and if any brother has a restive or jibbing horse, or one that bucks or throws him, he should inform the Marshal or make sure that he is informed; and if it is true, the Marshal should not make him keep it, rather he should exchange it if he can. And if the Marshal does not wish to exchange it, the brother may go without his horse if he wishes, and not mount it, for as long as he keeps it; nor should the Marshal force him to ride it, by any command, if he does not do so willingly.

155. If the alarm is raised in the camp, those who are near the shout should leave that area with their shields and lances, and the other brothers should go to the chapel to hear the orders that are issued. And if the alarm is raised outside the camp, they should not leave without permission, not even for a lion or a wild beast.

151.1 §55.

How the Brothers Form the Line of March

156. When the convent wishes to ride, the brothers should not saddle up, nor load the baggage, nor mount, nor move from their places unless the Marshal has the order called or commands it; but tent pegs, empty flasks, the camping axe, the camping rope and fishing net may be put on the horses before the order to load the baggage is given. And if any brother wishes to speak to the Marshal he should go to him on foot, and when he has spoken to him he should return to his place; and he should not leave his place before the order to mount is given, for as long as his companions are in camp.

157. When the Marshal has the order to mount called, the brothers should look over their campsite so that nothing of their equipment is left behind, and then they should mount and go quietly with their troop, at a walk or amble, their squires behind them, and position themselves in the line of march if they find an empty place for themselves and their equipment; and if he does not find it empty, he may ask the brother who has taken it, who may give it to him if he wishes, but need not if he does not wish to. And when they have joined the line of march, each brother should give his squire and his equipment a place in front of him. And if it is night-time, he should keep silent except for any important task, and then he should go quietly and in silence within the line of march until the next day when they have heard or said prime, in the manner which is established in the house, and for as long as the camp lasts. The brother who has joined the line of march may give the place in front of him to another who has not joined it, but no-one should give up the place behind him; and then neither of these two brothers, neither the one who gave the place nor the one who took it in this way, may give it to another in front or behind.

158. And if two brothers wish to talk to one another, the one in front should go to the one behind in such a way that their equipment is in front of them; and when they have spoken, each should return to his troop. And if any brother rides beside the line of march for his own purposes, he should come and go downwind; for if he went upwind, the dust would harm and annoy the line of march. And if anything happens so that a brother cannot nor knows how to join his troop, one of the brothers should give him a place in front of him until daylight, and then he should return to his troop as best and as quickly as he can. And this also applies to the squires. And no brother should ride beside the line of march, nor two, nor three, nor four or more, either for pleasure or to speak, rather they should go behind their equipment and each one keep to his troop quietly and in silence.

159. No brother should leave his troop to water his horses or for anything else, without permission; and if they pass by running water in peaceful territory, they may water their horses if they wish; but they may not endanger the line of march. And if they pass by water whilst on reconnaissance, and the Standard Bearer passes by without watering his horses, they should not do so without permission; and if the Standard Bearer stops to water his horses, they may do likewise without permission. And if the alarm is raised in the line of march, the

brothers who are near the shout may mount their horses and take up their shields and lances, and keep calm and await the Marshal's order; and the others should go towards the Marshal to hear his command.

160. When there is war and the brothers are lodged in an inn or established in camp, and the alarm is raised, they should not leave without permission, until the banner is taken out; and when it is taken out they should all follow it as soon as possible, and they should not arm or disarm without permission; and if they are lying in ambush or guarding pasture, or somewhere they are reconnoitring, or they are going from one place to another, they should not remove bridle or saddle or feed their horses without permission.

How the Brothers should go in a Squadron
161. When they are established in squadrons, no brother should go from one squadron to another, nor mount his horse nor take up his shield or lance without permission; and when they are armed and they go in a squadron, they should place their squires with lances in front of them, and those with horses behind them, in such a way that the Marshal or the one who is in his place commands; no brother should turn his horse's head towards the back to fight or shout, or for anything else, while they are in a squadron.

162. If any brother wishes to try out his horse to learn what needs to be done for it or if there is anything to adjust to do with the saddle or saddle cloth, he may mount up to leave for a while without permission, and then return quietly and in silence to his squadron; and if he wishes to take his shield and lance, he should have permission; and whoever wishes to protect his head with his iron coif[1] may do so without permission; but he may not take it off. No brother may charge or leave the ranks without permission.

163. And if it happens by chance that any Christian acts foolishly, and any Turk attacks him in order to kill him, and he is in peril of death, and anyone who is in that area wishes to leave his squadron to help him, and his conscience tells him that he can assist him, he may do so without permission, and then return to his squadron quietly and in silence. And if he otherwise charges or leaves the squadron, justice will be done even as far as going on foot[1] to the camp and taking from him all that may be taken from him except his habit.

When the Marshal takes up the Banner to Charge
164. When the Marshal wishes to take the banner on God's behalf from the Under-Marshal, the Under-Marshal should go to the Turcopolier if the Marshal does not retain him. And then the Marshal should order five or six or up to ten

162.1 Formerly an integral part of the hauberk, in the thirteenth century the coif became a separate hood of mail.
163.1 This was a particular disgrace for a knight, who defined himself as a mounted warrior.

knight brothers to guard him and the banner; and these brothers should over-whelm their enemies all round the banner, to the best of their ability, and they should not leave or go away, rather they should stay as near to the banner as they can, so that, if necessary, they may assist it. And the other brothers may attack in front and behind, to left and right, and wherever they think they can torment their enemies in such a way that, if the banner needs them they may help it, and the banner help them, if necessary.

165. And the Marshal should order the Commander of the Knights to carry a banner furled round his lance, and he should be one of the ten. And this brother should not leave the Marshal, rather he should keep as near to him as possible, so that if the Marshal's banner falls or is torn or any misadventure befalls it, which God forbid, he can unfurl his banner; or if not, he should act in such a way that the brothers may rally round his banner if necessary. And if the Marshal is so badly wounded or afflicted that he cannot lead the attack, the one who carries the furled banner should lead the attack. And those who are ordered to guard the banner should go to him; neither the Marshal nor the one who carries the furled banner into battle should charge with it or lower it to charge for any reason.

166. And those especially who lead a squadron of knights should not charge or leave the squadron unless they do so with the permission or consent of the Master, if he is there, or of the one who is in his place. If he does not agree to do it through difficulty, or because he is surrounded, he cannot lightly have per-mission; and if it happens any other way, severe punishment will be given, and he cannot keep the habit. And each squadron commander may have a furled banner and may command up to ten knights to guard him and the banner. And everything that is said about the Marshal is true for all the commanders who lead squadrons.

167. And if it happens that any brother cannot go towards his banner be-cause he has gone too far ahead for fear of Saracens who are between him and the banner, or he does not know what has become of it, he should go to the first Christian banner that he finds. And if he finds that of the Hospital, he should stay by it and should inform the leader of the squadron or someone else that he cannot go to his banner and he should remain quiet and silent until he is able to go to his banner. Nor should he leave the squadron because of cuts or wounds without permission; and if he is so badly hurt that he cannot obtain permission, he should send another brother to get it for him.

168. And if it happens that the Christians are defeated, from which God save them, no brother should leave the field to return to the garrison, while there is a piebald banner raised aloft; for if he leaves he will be expelled from the house for ever. And if he sees that there is no longer any recourse, he should go to the nearest Hospital or Christian banner if there is one, and when this or the other banners are defeated, henceforth the brother may go to the garrison, to which God will direct him.

Here Begin the Retrais of the Turcopolier

169. The Turcopolier brother should have four horses, and in place of a mule he may have a turcoman; and he should have a small tent and the same rations as the convent; and the pack animals should carry the rations, the tent and the cauldron. And if he is in lodgings or in camp and the alarm is raised, he should not leave without permission; but the Marshal should indicate to him once what he should do. And if he has to go anywhere he should send one or two turcopoles to that area where the alarm is, to see what it is; and then he should inform the Marshal or the one who is in his place, so that he may order and issue his command.

170. And when the Turcopolier goes with the scouts and is given five or six or eight knights, or up to ten, they are under the command of the Turcopolier; and if there are ten, and there is a Commander of Knights with a piebald banner, the Turcopolier will be under his command. And when the squadrons of the convent are lined up, the Turcopolier should keep his men in the squadron and be like the others, and behave in such a way as to carry the banner, as is given above for the Marshal. Nor should he charge or attack unless the Master or Marshal orders him to.

171. All the sergeant brothers, when they are under arms, are under the command of the Turcopolier, but in peacetime they are not; and the turcopoles are [under his command] in time of war and in time of peace.

The Under-Marshal, the Standard Bearer, the Master's sergeant brother, and those of the Marshal and the Commander of the Land, if they are not in the Turcopolier's squadron are not under his command.

172. The sergeant brothers who are armed in mail should conduct themselves under arms as is given for the knight brothers; and the other sergeant brothers who are not armed, if they act well, will receive thanks from God and the brothers. And if they see that they cannot resist or that they are wounded, they may go to the back, if they wish, without permission, and without harm coming to the house.

If brothers are placed to command the sergeants at arms, they should not leave in order to charge or for any other reason, without permission; but if the Marshal or the brothers charge, they should lead the sergeants lined up in close ranks behind them, to the best of their ability, so that if the brothers need them, the sergeants may come to their aid.

Here Begin the Retrais of the Under-Marshal

173. The Under-Marshal should have two horses and a tent and the same rations as the convent; and the pack animals should carry the tent. And he should give to the brothers the small items of equipment, and have them loaded and repaired if he can and if he has them, and may distribute old saddles, rugs, barrels, fishing nets, lances, swords, *chapeaux de fer*, old Turkish arms and crossbows, which belong to the marshalcy, and saddle pads; and henceforth he may

give and distribute all small items of equipment, wherever the Marshal is or is not, unless it is something that the Marshal has forbidden. And the Under-Marshal may not give out any of the large items of equipment unless the Marshal orders him to.

174. And if a brother goes overseas or passes from this world, and the Marshal wishes to give away the entire equipment, or keep it for as long as he wishes, he should order and command the Under-Marshal, who should do it; the Under-Marshal may not give any of it away until the Marshal has seen it. And if the Marshal does not order him, until he has seen it or forbids it, he may give away what suits him.

175. All the craftsman brothers of the marshalcy are under his command, and should answer to him or the one who is in his place for their work, and he should provide them with and ensure that they have everything appertaining to their work. And he may send them out in the service of the house and give them permission to go from one house to another to enjoy themselves on feast days. And where the Marshal is absent, the Standard Bearer is under his command as is given above. And if there is a squire without a master, and the Under-Marshal asks for him to put him in the horse caravan, and if he asks him for any squire from the caravan to give to a brother, he should do it; and he should give the Standard Bearer as many squires as he asks for, if he has them, to put in the caravan, and he should obey him. And the Under-Marshal, if he has too many squires in the caravan, and the Standard Bearer has need of them, should give them to him, except for the garrison of the caravan.

176. And wherever the Standard Bearer is absent, the Under-Marshal may punish the squires if he wishes and if they have committed some crime against him; he may take squires from the caravan and give them to the brothers who he sees are in need of them, and place caravan squires in the horse caravan. And if the Standard Bearer assembles a chapter of squires, and the Under-Marshal wishes to go to it, he may hold the chapter and may punish the squires if he wishes. And all the squires who have been lent to craftsman brothers or to brothers who have only one horse, should go to the Standard Bearer when the order is called for the caravan squires to go there.

Here Begin the Retrais of the Standard Bearer
177. The Standard Bearer should have two horses and a tent and the same rations as the convent; and the pack animals should carry the tent; and all the squires of the house are under his command wherever he happens to be; he should engage them and hear their vows, and should tell them all the laws of the house, and the things for which they may be expelled from the house, put in irons and flogged; and ensure that they are paid when they have served their term. And he may hold chapter and assemble them whenever he pleases and there is need, and he may punish those who have committed a crime against him, in the manner which is established in the house; and he should ensure that

they are given barley, straw and lodging. The officers in charge of the grain store and the sentries are under his command and should each have one horse.

178. And if the brothers are together and they send their horses and squires to the house's baggage train or pasture, or to another communal area, the Standard Bearer should lead them out and back in a troop, a piebald banner at the head of the troop. And wherever the squires and brothers eat in the convent, the Standard Bearer should keep table; and wherever the brothers are camped and the squires take rations, they should not mix with them if they do not wish.

179. When the convent is on the march, the Standard Bearer should go in front of the banner and should have a squire or sentry carry it, and should lead the line of march in such a way as the Marshal commands. And in time of war, when the brothers go in squadrons, a turcopole should carry the banner, and the Standard Bearer should form the squires into a squadron. And if the Marshal and the brothers charge, the squires who lead the destriers[1] should charge behind their lords, and the others should take the mules which their lords ride and should remain with the Standard Bearer. And he should have a banner furled round his lance; and when the Marshal charges he should have the squires formed into squadrons and should unfurl his banner; and he should go after those who are attacking as best, as soon and in as orderly a fashion as he can, at a walk or amble, or whatever seems best to him.

Of the Sergeant Brothers, Commanders of the Houses

180. The sergeant brothers commanders of the houses should have one horse and the same rations as the convent; he may give four deniers to a brother, and may have one of their sergeants as a squire. And if it pleases the Standard Bearer to give him a squire, he may take him.

Of the Casalier Brothers

181. The casalier brothers should have two horses and one squire and the same ration of barley as the Master; and they may give four deniers to a brother; and may keep one girth for the horses that they ride.

How the Master and the Brothers should Eat in the Convent

182. The Master and all the other strong and healthy brothers should eat at the convent's table and hear the blessing; and each brother should say one paternoster before he cuts his bread and not while he is eating. And when he has eaten he should give thanks to God for what He has given; and he should not speak until he has given thanks in the chapel if it is nearby, and in the same place if it is not nearby.

179.1 War horses which were led by squires and mounted by knights only when battle was joined.

183. Neither the Master nor any other brother should have flasks of wine or water at the convent's table, nor allow any brother to bring them there. And if a secular man sends a gift of wine or meat, only the Master may send the present to the infirmary or wherever he pleases, except to the convent's table. And all the other brothers, if anything is presented to them, should send it to the Master if he is at the convent's table, and if he is not, to the brothers in the infirmary. And if the Master eats at another table or at the infirmary table, when he does not eat in the convent, the gift should be sent to him.

184. If it happens that anyone gives beef and mutton to the convent's table, the commander of the house should place those who do not eat beef in one area of the table, except the Master and the chaplain. Each brother may ask for some of the sergeants' meat.

If anyone brings to the brothers raw or rotten meat, or meat which smells, they may take it back and it should be exchanged if there is sufficient.

185. Often, two kinds of meat are given to all the brothers in the convent, because he who does not eat one eats the other, as at Christmas and Easter, and at the two Shrovetides;[1] and three kinds of meat when the houses have sufficient, and the commanders wish it. And the servings should be communal as is written for the Commander of the Victuals.[2]

186. On the days when they do not eat meat they should have two cooked dishes; but if they are given either cheese or fish they should have only one cooked dish, if the commanders do not wish to give them two. But at the two Shrovetides they should be given two or three dishes, so that he who does not want one may have the other. And when it comes to Sundays, Tuesdays or Thursdays, it is usual to give them fresh or salted fish, or something else to be eaten with bread. But if they have fish on Monday, Wednesday, Friday or Saturday, the commander of the house may take away from them one of the cooked dishes if he wishes, if he pays for the fish he gives them.

187. It is usual on Fridays to give them one cooked dish and then green vegetables or something else to be eaten with bread; and each brother may ask for what is eaten at the convent's table and what is given to the other brothers. But each brother should speak quietly and keep silence, and listen to the clerk who reads the lesson. And each may give some of his food to those around him, but only as far as he can stretch out his arm.

188. The Master may give some of his food to the brothers who eat on the floor and do their penance. And for this reason enough food for four brothers should be put in the Master's bowl, either meat, fish or anything else to be eaten with bread; neither the Master nor anyone else should have any other food, to

185.1 The Templars observed two fasts per year (cf. §76 and 351), before Easter and before Christmas. The two Shrovetides were Shrove Tuesday and the Sunday before St Martin's Day (11 November).

185.2 Cf. §151.

eat or drink, except what is given communally to the brothers of the convent. Nor should any brother have his own place at the convent's table, except the Master and the chaplain brother who eats next to him. Wherever the Master is, three paupers should eat of the brothers' food, four in each major house and castle, for love of God and the brothers. When the bell sounds, the chaplain brother, the paupers and all the knight brothers may sit, and the sergeant brothers should wait until the small bell is rung, and then they should sit. They should fill the table on the inside and then on the outside. Cups, bowls and napkins should be communal, except for the Master and the chaplain brother who have been permitted cups.

189. When the convent has three dishes of meat or other food, the household should have two. But the turcopoles and all those who eat at their table should have what is eaten by the convent. And the paupers who are fed at the house where they are established should have as much meat and other food as the brothers of the convent.

The Retrais of the Infirmarer Brother

190. The Infirmarer brother should have so much good sense as to ask the sick brothers who cannot eat, and dare not, from the communal food of the infirmary, which food they are able to eat, and they should tell him when he asks them; and he should prepare and give to them as much of the communal food of the infirmary as they can eat. And especially for those brothers who are feeble, suffering and recuperating from illness he should do as is said above. And to those who have quartan fever[1] he may give meat every weekday except Friday, likewise from the fast of St Martin until Advent, and during Advent on three days a week.

191. All the sick and ageing brothers who cannot tolerate the food of the convent should eat at the infirmary table; and the healthy brothers, when they are bled, should eat only three times. And if a brother who has been bled, or an elderly one, or one who has quartan fever asks for the food of the convent, he should be given it. But to those other brothers who eat according to their illness, none of it should given, except to see if they can endure the [food of the] convent; and for this reason they may be given it once or twice. And if they can tolerate it, they should go and eat in the convent.

192. Not lentils, nor shelled broad beans, nor cabbage that has not flowered, nor beef, nor trout, nor nanny-goat, nor billy-goat, nor mutton or veal, nor eels should be given to the infirmary table, except when the convent eats it, or those whom we have mentioned above, or when any brother eats at the invitation of anyone who may invite him to do so. Cheese may not be given as a dish in the infirmary.

190.1 A fever characterised by a paroxysm every third (or, by inclusive reckoning, every fourth) day.

193. When the Master wishes to eat at the infirmary table he should ask the Infirmarer to prepare the food. And on the table nearest the infirmary should be placed a napkin, wine and water in flasks, and a glass goblet; and then the Infirmarer brother should prepare so much food that all the other brothers may be nourished by him.

No brother who eats at the infirmary table may have glass flasks or goblets, unless it is for a worthy man or great friend of the house.

194. All the brothers who cannot hear the hours or go to the chapel because of their illness should go and sleep in the infirmary. But it is a good thing if they confess and take communion beforehand, and that they ask the chaplain for extreme unction if necessary. Moreover, only the Master may sleep in his room when he is ill. And each brother, when he is ill, may eat three times in his own bed, if he wishes: that is to say, the day he cannot go to the chapel because of his illness, the next day until vespers, and then he should go to the infirmary if he has not recovered. But those brothers who suffer from dysentery, or a serious wound, or vomiting, or delirium, or any other grave illness which the other brothers cannot tolerate, should be given a room as near as possible to the infirmary until they are fully recovered and the other brothers can tolerate their presence.

195. The Infirmarer brother should have as much food prepared for the brothers who lie in the infirmary as each asks for, if he can find it in the house or for sale in the town, and syrup if they ask for it. And the Infirmarer may give them permission to let blood and shave their heads. But to shave their beards, or cut into mortal wounds, or to take medicine, permission must be obtained from the Master or from the one who takes his place.

196. The commander of the house should provide the Infirmarer brother with whatever is necessary for the infirmary table, and for the infirmary where the brothers lie sick; and he should place under his command the cellar, the large kitchen, the oven, the pigsty, the henhouse and the garden. And if the commander does not wish to do this, he should give to the Infirmarer brother as much money as is necessary for the needs of the infirmary.

The Commander of the Land should ensure that the brothers have what they require, and the means with which to buy the medicines they need.

197. When brothers leave the infirmary, they should firstly go to the chapel to hear mass and the divine office of Jesus Christ, and afterwards they may eat three times in the infirmary, and then they may leave, if they are recovered to such an extent that they can go to the chapel to hear all the hours. And then they should eat at the infirmary table until they can safely eat the food of the convent.

The Commander of the Land, or the Master, should find a doctor for the sick brothers so that he may visit them and advise them on their illnesses.

Election of the Grand Master

On the Election of the Master of the Temple

198. When the Master of the Temple dies and God summons him, if he dies in the Kingdom of Jerusalem, and the Marshal is present, he remains in place of the Master, and should hold chapter because of the office of the Marshalcy that he holds until he and the convent and all the *baillis* from this side of the sea[1] have determined and elected a Grand Commander who will hold the office of Master. And so he should assemble all the worthy men of the *baillie*, and should ask all the prelates of the land and the good people of religion to be at his funeral and interment. And with a great lighting of candles his service should be celebrated, and he should be buried with great honour. And this lighting of candles is granted to him only, in honour of his Mastership.

199. And all the brothers who are present should say two hundred paternosters during the next seven days, and all the brothers in the same *baillie* as that house should do likewise; and so they should be there unless it is not suitable for them to remain for any reason. And one hundred paupers should be fed for the sake of his soul at dinner and at supper. Afterwards, his equipment should be distributed as if for any other brother of the convent, except his clothes and night clothes, which should go to the Almoner, and should be given entirely to the lepers, for love of God, as he did with his old clothes when he took new ones.

200. As soon as possible afterwards, the Marshal should inform all the commanders of the provinces this side of the sea of the Master's death, so that they may come to advise the house on a given day and elect a Grand Commander who will take the place of the Master. And if it can be done without great harm to the house, the election of the Master should be celebrated in Jerusalem[1] or within the Kingdom. For he is the head of the house and the chief province of all the Temple.

201. But if it happens that the Marshal or all the convent is in the land of Tripoli or Antioch, and the Master dies there, what is said above for the Marshal of the Temple in the Kingdom of Jerusalem should be understood for each and both of these two commanders of these two provinces. Just as the Marshal should hold chapter to elect the Grand Commander if it happens in the Kingdom of Jerusalem, the Commander of the land of Tripoli or Antioch should act in the same way. And if he dies in the Kingdom of Jerusalem and the Marshal is not in the Kingdom, the Commander of the Kingdom of Jerusalem should arrange his funeral like one of the other commanders of the provinces, and should inform the Marshal, the convent and the other commanders of the Master's death as soon as possible, in the name of the Holy Trinity.

198.1 I.e. in the East.
200.1 This section must have been written before 1187, prior to the fall of Jerusalem.

202. And if the Grand Commander who is to take the place of the Master is within the Kingdom of Jerusalem, the Marshal should hold chapter as is said above, and he[1] should be elected by the common consent and will of all the brothers or of the majority, on behalf of and in the name of God.

203. The Grand Commander should retire apart with the Marshal and the commanders of the three provinces, if they can be present, and are not prevented by canonical impediment with the other worthy *baillis*, and those others who to him and to the other worthies it seems that they should be called to give advice, and by no means all. And together with them he should decide the time and day on which they may suitably assemble to make the election. And each of the commanders of the provinces should come on the appointed day, without being sent for, with a party of worthy men from his *baillie* whom he may bring without harm.

204. And from that day on, the Grand Commander should carry the Master's seal and issue all the commands of the house in place of the Master until such time as God has provided the house with a Master and governor. And so he should be obeyed like the Master if he were alive.

205. And all the brothers of the Temple overseas[1] should fast for three Fridays on bread and water, from that moment until the day appointed for the election. And from that day on each commander should go to his *baillie* and take care of the work of the house in the finest and best way that God will show him, and should ask and command his brothers to pray that God advise the house in the matter of a Father and Master. And this same request should be made to all good people of religion.

206. When the day for the election of the Master arrives, the convent and all the *baillis*, as is given above, should assemble in the appointed place, according to what seems good to them. And after matins on the day the election is to take place, the Grand Commander should summon the majority of the worthy men of the house, but not all the brothers, and they should with advice select two or three worthy men of the house, and more if necessary, who are brothers and the best-known; and they should be ordered to leave the council, and they should obey.

207. And afterwards, the Grand Commander should ask them, and the one on whom all the council, or the majority agrees, will be the Commander of the election. Then, he should recall them and make known to the one who is elected that he is made the Commander of the election of the Master on behalf of God. And the one who is elected should be such that he loves God and justice, and should be able to speak all languages and to all the brothers; he should love peace and concord within the house, and should not encourage differences. And all the thirteen electors of the Master should be such, from

202.1 I.e. the Grand Commander.
205.1 I.e. in the West.

divers provinces and divers nations. And before they leave the council, the Grand Commander should give himself and all the other brothers of the council, a knight brother as a companion, as is given above. And this council and this assembly should always be held without change.

208. After matins on the day of the election, so that they may stay awake to pray to God until daybreak, henceforth the two brothers should go to the chapel to pray that God guide and counsel them, so that they may perfectly and according to His will accomplish the office and command with which they are charged. And each one should pray to himself and they should not speak to any other brother, nor any other brother speak to them; nor should they assemble together unless it is to speak of that thing which they have to decide. And they should stay all night in prayer and discuss the business of the election, and none of the other brothers of the council should leave, and those who are ill should rest in their beds and pray that God advise the house, and the other healthy brothers according to the strength of their bodies should be at their prayers until daybreak.

209. When the bell has rung for prime and the brothers have gone to the chapel to hear prime, and the mass of the Holy Spirit has been sung with great devotion, and terce and sext heard, they should enter the chapter silently and humbly and hear the sermon and prayer said according to the custom of the Order of Knighthood. And afterwards, the Grand Commander should ask and command the brothers to call upon them the grace of the Holy Spirit, through which they may have such a Master and shepherd by whom the house and all the Holy Land may be advised, and in whose service the house is established and ordained. And all the brothers should kneel on the ground and say those prayers which God has taught them.

210. And afterwards, the Grand Commander should have the Commander of the election and his companion come before him and all the chapter, and should charge them in virtue of obedience with this office which is given above, in peril of their souls and with the reward of Paradise, that they may have all wisdom and all understanding to elect their companions who will be with them in that office. And so he should order them also not through mercy, nor hatred, nor love, but seeing only God before their eyes, to choose such companions by their wisdom, who strive for the peace of the house as is said of them above, and they should leave the chapter.

211. And these two brothers should choose another two brothers so that they are four. And these four should choose another two brothers so that they are six. And these six brothers should choose another two brothers so that they are eight. And these eight brothers should choose another two brothers so that they are ten. And these ten brothers should choose another two so that they are twelve, in honour of the twelve apostles. And the twelve brothers should elect together the chaplain brother to take the place of Jesus Christ; he should endeavour to keep the brothers in peace and love and in harmony: and they will be

thirteen brothers. And of these thirteen, eight should be knight brothers, four sergeant brothers and the chaplain brother. And these thirteen brother electors should be as is given above for the Commander of the election, from divers nations and countries, in order to keep the peace of the house.

212. Afterwards, all the thirteen electors should go before the Commander and the brothers, and the Commander of the election should ask all the brothers together and the Grand Commander to pray to God for them, for they are charged with a heavy task. And straightaway all the assembled brothers should throw themselves on the ground in prayer and pray to God and all the saints, through whom the house had its beginning, that He advise them and indicate such a Master as He knows the house and the Holy Land require.

213. Afterwards, all thirteen should stand up in front of the Grand Commander, and he should command each and all of the thirteen electors in that office with which they are enjoined, to have God before their eyes and strive for nothing but the honour and benefit of the house and the Holy Land. And that person who seems most beneficial to all or to the majority they will not fail to put in that office which is the Master's, out of hatred or any ill will. And he who does not seem beneficial to all or to the majority, neither out of any favour or love should they call or elect him to hold such a high office as that of Master.

214. And this order should be given to all the thirteen electors in front of the whole chapter by the Grand Commander in this way: 'We implore – on behalf of God and My Lady St Mary, and My Lord St Peter, and all the saints of God, and on behalf of all the chapter, in virtue of obedience, under pain of the grace of God that on the Day of Judgement, if you act in this election in a manner in which you should not, you will be held to give account and reasons before the face of God and all these saints – that you elect that brother of the Temple who seems to you most worthy and beneficial and most acceptable to all the brothers and to the house and the Holy Land and who is of the best reputation.'

215. And the Commander of the election should ask the Grand Commander and all the brothers to pray to God for them, that He advise them. And all the thirteen electors will leave the chapter together and will go to such a place as is suitable for the election.

216. In the name of the Holy Trinity, that is of the Father and of the Son and of the Holy Spirit. Amen. – There they will begin to treat of the election and to name the persons who it seems to them beneficial to elect as Master. Firstly, the persons of the brothers who are this side of the sea, either in the convent or in the *baillies*. And if it happens that God wishes that he is found beneficial to hold that office, and he has the common accord of all thirteen or of the majority, that one will be elected Master of the Temple. But if it happens that the most beneficial person is found in a land across the sea,[1] with the agreement of all thirteen or of the majority, that one will be elected Master of the Temple.

216.1 I.e. in the West.

217. And if it happens, from which God protect them, that the thirteen brothers are divided into two or three groups and are not in agreement, the Commander of the election, with any of the other worthy men, should go to the chapter in front of the Commander and all the brothers, and should request them to pray that God direct them; without withholding any word of the discord which is among them, from which God protect them. And these prayers should be offered several times, at the request of the electors. And all the brothers should kneel and bow down on the ground, and pray that the grace of the Holy Spirit advise and direct the electors to appoint a Master. – Afterwards, they should return to their companions in the place chosen for the election.

218. And if it happens that they are able to agree on the person to elect, he is Master who by common agreement of the majority is named and elected.

And he who is thus communally elected, if he is this side of the sea, as we have said above, and is in the chapter with the other brothers, all the thirteen electors should go before the Commander and all the other brothers of the chapter.

219. And the Commander of the election should say, for himself and all the companions together, to all the brothers: 'Good sirs, give thanks to Our Lord Jesus Christ and to My Lady St Mary and all the saints, that we are all together in agreement. And so we have, on behalf of God, elected according to your orders the Master of the Temple; do you give your assent to what we have done?' And they should say all together and each one for himself: 'Yes, on behalf of God.' – 'And do you promise to obey him all the days of his life?' – And they should reply: 'Yes, on behalf of God.'

220. Afterwards, the Grand Commander should be questioned using this formula: 'Commander, as God and we have elected you as Master of the Temple, do you promise to be obedient to the convent all the days of your life and to keep the good customs and practices of the house?' and he should reply: 'Yes, if it please God.' And this question should be put by three or four of the most worthy men of the house.

221. And if the elected person is present, he should go to speak to him in this manner and name him by his name, and say: 'And we, in the name of the Father and of the Son and of the Holy Spirit, have elected and elect you Master, brother N...' – And then the Commander of the election should say to the brothers: 'Good lord brothers, give thanks to God; here is our Master.' And immediately the chaplain brothers should begin the *Te Deum laudamus*. And the brothers should immediately rise and take the Master with great devotion and great joy, and carry him in their arms to the chapel, and offer him to God before the altar, whom He has provided for the governance of the house; and he should be kneeling in front of the altar while prayers are said to God for him. And the chaplain brothers should say:

222. Lord have mercy upon us. Christ have mercy upon us. Lord have mercy upon us.

Our Father . . . And lead us not into temptation. R. But deliver us from evil.
Make safe your servant. R. My Lord, who puts his trust in you.

Send to him, Lord, help from the sanctuary. R. And watch over them out of
Zion.

Be to him, Lord, a tower of strength. R. In the face of the enemy.

Lord, hear my prayer. R. And let my cry come to you. The Lord be with you.
R. And with your spirit.

Prayer

Let us pray. Almighty and everlasting God, have mercy upon your servant and
lead him according to your mercy in the way of eternal salvation, that, you being
willing, he may desire those things pleasing to you and perfect them in all virtue,
through Our Lord . . .

223. All the things which have been said and recounted between the brother
electors should be kept secret and concealed like the chapter; for great scandal
and great hatred may spring from it, for whoever would allow to be repeated the
words which have been said and recounted among the brothers.

Penances

These are the Things for which a Brother of the House of the Temple may be Expelled from the House

On Simony
224. The first thing for which a brother of the Temple may be expelled from the house is simony, for a brother who enters the house through simony should be expelled because of it; for he cannot save his soul. And simony is committed by gift or promise to a brother of the Temple or to another who may help him to enter into the Order of the Temple.

On Disclosing the Affairs of the Chapter
225. The second thing is if a brother discloses the affairs of his chapter to any brother of the Temple who was not there, or to any other man.[1]

On He who Kills or Causes to be Killed a Christian Man or Woman
226. The third thing is he who kills or causes to be killed a Christian man or woman.

On Theft
227. The fourth thing is theft, which is understood in several ways.

Whoever Leaves a Castle or Fortified House except by the Gate
228. The fifth thing is whoever leaves a castle or fortified house by any other way except by the prescribed gate.

On Conspiracy
229. The sixth thing is to conspire; for conspiracy is committed by two or more brothers.

On the One who Flees to the Saracens
230. The seventh thing is he who leaves the house and goes to the Saracens; (he will be expelled from the house).

On Heresy
231. The eighth thing is heresy, or whoever goes against the law of Our Lord.

225.1 Keeping the secrecy of the chapter was not unique to the Templars, although it formed the basis for one of the accusations laid against them which led to their dissolution.

On the One who Leaves his Banner for Fear of the Saracens
232. The ninth thing is if a brother leaves his banner and flees for fear of the Saracens; (he will be expelled from the house).

These are the Things for which a Brother of the Temple Loses his Habit

Whoever Disobeys the Commandment of the House
233. The first thing is, if a brother disobeys the commandment of the house and persists in his folly, and does not wish to carry out the order he has been given, his habit should be taken from him, and he may be put in irons; and if he repents before his habit has been removed, and no harm has come to the house, the habit is at the discretion of the brothers, whether to take it from him or let him keep it. For it is said in our house that when a brother is commanded to do the work of the house, he should say, 'On behalf of God.' And if he says, 'I will not do it,' immediately that commander should assemble the brothers and hold chapter, telling the elders of the house that the habit may be removed from him because he has disobeyed the order; for the first promise that we make is obedience.

On a Brother who Strikes another Brother
234. The second thing is, if a brother lays his hand on another brother out of anger or wrath, he should not keep his habit; and if the blow is serious, he may be put in irons. And so he should not carry the piebald banner, nor the silver seal, nor take part in the election of a Master; and this has been done many times. And before the fault is examined, he should be absolved, for he is excommunicated; and if he is not absolved of it, he should neither eat with the brothers nor go to the chapel. And if he strikes a man of religion or a clerk, he should be absolved before the fault is examined.

On a Brother who Strikes a Christian Man or Woman
235. The third thing is, if a brother strikes a Christian man or woman with a sharp instrument or a stone, or stick, or with anything with which he may kill or wound with one blow, the habit is at the discretion of the brothers, whether to take it from him or let him keep it.

On a Brother who has Contact with a Woman
236. The fourth thing is if a brother has contact with a woman, for we consider guilty a brother who enters an evil place, or a house of iniquity, with a sinful woman, alone or in bad company; he may not keep his habit, and he may be put in irons. And he should not carry the piebald banner, or the silver seal, nor take part in the election of a Master; and this has been done several times.

On a Brother who Falsely Accuses another Brother of something for which he should be Expelled from the House
237. The fifth thing is, if a brother accuses another brother of something for

which he may be expelled from the house if he is guilty, if the brother who accuses him cannot prove it, he may not keep his habit, after he makes him plead for mercy in chapter; and if he repents in chapter, the habit is at the discretion of the brothers, whether to take it from him or let him keep it; and unless he makes him go to chapter, he may not have back his habit whatever he may say, even if he repents and does not wish to persist in his folly.

On a Brother who Puts Blame on Himself

238. The sixth thing is, if a brother falsely accuses himself in order to have permission to leave the house, and is found guilty, he may not keep his habit.

On a Brother who Asks Permission

239. The seventh thing is, if a brother asks permission in chapter to go and save his soul in another order, and they do not wish to give it to him, and he says he will leave the house, the habit is at the discretion of the brothers, whether to take it from him or let him keep it.

On a Brother who Says He Will Go to the Saracens

240. The eighth thing is, if a brother says he will go to the Saracens, even if he says it out of anger or wrath, the habit will be at the discretion of the brothers, whether to take it from him or let him keep it.

On a Brother who Lowers the Banner in Battle

241. The ninth thing is, if a brother of the Temple who carries the banner in battle lowers it in order to strike, and no harm comes of it, the habit is at the discretion of the brothers, whether to take it from him or let him keep it. And if he strikes with it and harm comes of it, he may not keep his habit, and so it may be decided to put him in irons; he may never carry the banner or be a commander in battle.

On a Brother who Carries the Banner and Charges Without Permission

242. The tenth thing is, if a brother who carries the banner charges without the permission of the one who may give it, if he is not at that time surrounded or in a place where he cannot obtain permission as is given in the *retrais*, the habit is at the discretion of the brothers, whether to take it from him or let him keep it. And if great harm comes of it, it may be decided to put him in irons; he may never carry the banner or be a commander in battle.

On a Brother who Charges without Permission

243. The eleventh thing is, if a brother who is in battle charges without permission, and harm comes of it, the habit is at the discretion of the brothers, whether to take it from him or let him keep it. But if he sees a Christian in peril of death, and his conscience tells him that he can help him, as it is given in the *retrais*,[1] he may do so. But in no other circumstances should a brother of the Temple charge without permission.

243.1 See §163.

On a Brother who Refuses the Food of the Temple to Another

244. The twelfth thing is, if a brother refuses the bread and water of the house to another brother, coming or going, so that he does not let him eat with the other brothers, he should not keep his habit: for when a man is made a brother, he is promised the bread and water of the house, and no-one may take them from him for anything that he does, except as is established in the house. Or whoever refuses to open the gate to a brother so that he may not enter within the gate.

On a Brother who Gives the Habit to a Man to whom he Should Not

245. The thirteenth thing is, if a brother gives the habit of the house to a man to whom he should not give it, or to anyone to whom he has not the authority to give it, or without the consent of the chapter, he may not keep his habit. And he who has the authority to give it may not take it away from him without the consent of the chapter, and if he does so he may not keep his habit.

On a Brother who Takes Something from Another, for which he Helps him to Become a Brother

246. The fourteenth thing is, if a brother takes something from a secular man, for which he should help him to become a brother of the Temple, he may not keep his habit because of it: for he commits simony.

On a Brother who Breaks the Seal of the Master or of Another

247. The fifteenth thing is, if a brother breaks the seal of the Master or of the one who takes his place, without the permission of the one who may give it, the habit is at the discretion of the brothers, whether to take it from him or let him keep it.

On a Brother who Breaks a Lock

248. The sixteenth thing is, if a brother breaks a lock without the permission of the one who may give it, and no other harm comes of it, the habit is at the discretion of the brothers, whether to take it from him or let him keep it.

On a Brother who Gives the Alms of the House to a Secular Man

249. The seventeenth thing is, if a brother of the Temple gives the alms of the house to a secular man, or to anyone except a brother of the Temple, without the permission of the one who may give it, his habit is at the discretion of the brothers, whether to take it from him or let him keep it. And if the thing is great, or if he alienates land, he may not keep that habit; and because of the great harm to the house, it may be decided to put him in irons.

On a Brother who Lends Anything Belonging to the House without Permission

250. The eighteenth thing is, if a brother lends anything belonging to the house without the permission of the one who may give it, in a place where the house may lose it, he may not keep the habit; and the loan may be so great, and in such a place, that he will be put in irons.

On a Brother who Lends his Horse to Another Brother without Permission

251. The nineteenth thing is, if a brother lends his horse to another brother in any place where he cannot go without permission, and the horse is lost, or dies, or is wounded, the habit is at the discretion of the brothers, whether to take it from him or let him keep it. But he may lend it for pleasure in the town where he is.

On a Brother who Places Things Belonging to Another with those of the House

252. The twentieth thing is, if a brother places the things of another with those of the house, by which the lords of the lands will lose their rights over them, the habit is at the discretion of the brothers, whether to take it from him or let him keep it.

On a Brother who Knowingly says that the Things of Another Belong to the House

253. The twenty-first thing is, if a brother knowingly says that the lands or goods of another belong to the house and they do not, and it is proven that he did it out of malice or covetousness, the habit is at the discretion of the brothers, whether to take it from him or let him keep it. But if his conscience tells him to, he may say so or give a guarantee without coming to harm.

On a Brother who Kills, or Wounds, or Loses a Slave

254. The twenty-second thing is, if a brother kills, or wounds, or loses a slave through his own fault, the habit is in the hands of the brothers, whether to take it from him or let him keep it.

On a Brother who Kills, or Wounds, or Loses a Horse

255. The twenty-third thing is, if a brother kills or wounds a horse, or loses it through his own fault, the habit is in the hands of the brothers, whether to take it from him or let him keep it.

On a Brother who Hunts, and Harm Comes of It

256. The twenty-fourth thing is, if a brother hunts, and harm comes of it, the habit is at the discretion of the brothers, whether to take it from him or let him keep it.[1]

On a Brother who Tries Out his Arms

257. The twenty-fifth thing is, if a brother tries out his arms and equipment and harm comes of it, the habit is at the discretion of the brothers, whether to take it from him or let him keep it.

On a Brother who Gives Away any Animal except a Dog or Cat

258. The twenty-sixth thing is, if a brother from the sheepfold or the stable gives away any animal except a dog or cat, without the permission of his commander, the habit is at the discretion of the brothers, whether to take it from him or let him keep it.

256.1 *Cf.* §55, where all forms of hunting are forbidden.

On a Brother who Builds a New House without Permission

259. The twenty-seventh thing is, if a brother builds a new house of stone or lime without the permission of the Master or of the Commander of the Land, the habit is at the discretion of the brothers, whether to take it from him or let him keep it. But other ruined houses he may repair without permission.

On a Brother who Knowingly Causes Loss to the House

260. The twenty-eighth thing is, if a brother knowingly or through his own fault causes loss to the house, of four deniers or more, the habit is at the discretion of the brothers, whether to take it from him or let him keep it: for all loss is forbidden to us. And the loss may be so great that he may be put in irons.

On a Brother who Passes Through the Gate with the Intention of Leaving the House

261. The twenty-ninth thing is, if a brother passes through the gate with the intention of leaving the house, and then repents, he could forfeit the habit; and if he goes to the Hospital, or anywhere else outside the house, the habit is at the discretion of the brothers, whether to take it from him or let him keep it. But if he spends one night there he may not keep the habit.

On a Brother who Leaves the House and Sleeps Two Nights Outside

262. The thirtieth thing is if a brother leaves the house and goes away, and sleeps two nights outside the house, he will lose his habit because of it, and should not recover it for a year and a day. And if he keeps the things which are forbidden for more than two nights, he will be expelled from the house.

On a Brother who Wilfully Gives Back his Habit, or Throws it out of Anger

263. The thirty-first thing is, if any brother wilfully gives back his habit or throws it to the ground out of anger, and does not wish to pick it up despite the pleas and requests made to him, and other brothers pick it up before him, he will lose his habit, and should not recover it for a year and a day. But if he willingly picks it up before them, it will be at the discretion of the brothers, whether to take it from him or let him keep it.

264. And if by any chance he does not wish to pick it up, and any brother takes the habit and places it round the neck of the brother who has given it back, that brother will lose his own: for no brother should give back the habit nor make a brother outside the chapter. And the one to whom the habit is returned in this way will be at the mercy of the brothers, whether to take it from him or let him keep it.[1]

265. And in all the other things – except the last two, the one who sleeps two nights outside the house, and the one who wilfully gives back his habit, which are a year and a day as we have said above – the other faults of the habit are at the discretion of the brothers, according to the fault and the conduct of the brother, whether to take it from him or let him keep it.

264.1 Cf. §224 where a brother who enters the Order through simony is punished by expulsion from the Order.

266. And when a brother's habit is considered, it is taken from him as is said in the house; and if a brother has his habit taken from him, then he is quit of all the penances that he had to do.

And when the habit is taken from a brother and he is put in irons, he should lodge and eat in the Almoner's house and does not have to go to the chapel; but he should say his hours, and should work with the slaves. And if he dies whilst doing his penance, he should be given the service of a brother.

And no brother who does not have the authority to make a brother has the authority to remove the habit without the permission of the one who may give it.

These are the Faults which may be Examined by the House of the Temple

267. The first thing is being expelled from the house; and so there are things for which he may be put in irons and in perpetual imprisonment.

The second thing concerns the habit; and so there are things for which he may be put in irons.

The third thing is, when any brother is allowed to keep his habit for love of God, he is on three days until God and the brothers release him; and he should be made to do his penance at once without delay.

The fourth thing is two days, or three days the first week.

The fifth thing is two days only.

The sixth thing is one day only.

The seventh thing is on Fridays and corporal punishment.

The eighth thing is when a brother's sentence is deferred before the Master or any worthy men of the house, in order to be guided in things of which the brothers may not be certain.

The ninth is when a brother is sent to the chaplain brother.

The tenth is when a brother is acquitted.

These are the Retrais of the Chaplain Brothers

268. The chaplain brothers should make the same promises as the other brothers; and should conduct themselves like the other brothers; except for the right of the paternoster, they should say the hours. And they should wear a closed robe, and shave their beards, and may wear gloves. And when they are in the presence of a dead brother, they should sing the mass and say the office,[1] instead of the hundred paternosters.

And the chaplain brothers should be honoured, and given the best robes of the house, and should sit next to the Master at table, and should be served first.

269. The chaplain brothers should hear the confessions of the brothers; no brother should make confession to anyone else but him, because he may see the chaplain brother without permission. For they have greater power to absolve them on behalf of the pope than an archbishop.

268.1 I.e. the office for the dead.

270. If a chaplain brother sins, he should plead for mercy in his chapter like any other brother, without kneeling, and should do what the brothers decide. If a chaplain brother leaves the house and then returns, pleading for mercy at the gate, he should undress himself at the door of the chapter, and go before the brothers in chapter, and plead for mercy without kneeling. And if he does not do something for which he should be expelled from the house, he should be made to do his penance, and should be without his habit for a year and a day; and he should eat at the household's table without a napkin, and should observe all the fasts observed by the other brothers who are doing penance, until the brothers release him; and on Sundays he should go for corporal punishment, to the chaplain brother privately, and he should also receive all the punishment that he should; and he may sing privately during the week without music. And when the other brothers who are doing penance work with the slaves, the chaplain brother should say his psalter instead of working.

271. And if there is a chaplain brother who leads a wicked life, or who engenders discord between the brothers, or causes scandal, he may be more readily got rid of than another brother; for thus the pope commanded us when he gave us chaplain brothers.[1] And if he does penance with his habit, he should eat at the turcopoles' table without a napkin. And he may do something for which he will be put in irons or in perpetual imprisonment.

These are the Things which a Chaplain Brother may not Absolve

272. These are the things for which a chaplain brother may not absolve a brother of the Temple. That is to say, if he kills a Christian man or woman.

The other is if a brother lays his hand upon another brother in such a way that he causes blood to flow from a wound.

The other is if a brother of the Temple lays his hand on any man of another order, either a clerk or a priest who is ordained in the Holy Church.

The other is if a brother is in orders and he renounces them when he enters the house, and afterwards confesses; and when he enters the house through simony.

273. The chaplain brother may not absolve them, for the pope has kept them in the Church of Rome; and for this reason it is proper that they be absolved by the patriarch or the archbishop or bishop of the country where they are.

Formulae of Profession

274. 'Are you willing to renounce the world?' R. 'I am willing.' – 'Are you willing to profess obedience according to canonical institution and according to

---

271.1 Innocent II's bull *Omne datum optimum* of 1139 gave the Templars permission to have their own chaplain brothers (see Introduction).

the precept of the lord pope?' R. 'I am willing.' – 'Are you willing to take upon yourself the way of life of our brothers?' R. 'I am willing.'

Then he who addresses him shall say: 'May God help and bless us'; the entire psalm is to be said.

275. Then he shall say his profession to him: 'I N... am willing and I promise to serve the Rule of the Knights of Christ and of His knighthood with the help of God for the reward of eternal life, so that from this day I shall not be allowed to shake my neck free of the yoke of the Rule; and so that this petition of my profession may be firmly kept, I hand over this written document in the presence of the brothers for ever, and with my hand I place it at the foot of the altar which is consecrated in honour of almighty God and of the blessed Mary and all the saints. And henceforth I promise obedience to God and this house, and to live without property, and to maintain chastity according to the precept of the lord pope, and firmly to keep the way of life of the brothers of the house of the Knights of Christ.'

276. Then he shall lay across the altar, and prostrate shall say: 'Receive me Lord in accordance with your word and let me live.' Then the others: R. 'And may you not confound me in my hope.' Then he shall say: 'The Lord is my light.' R. 'The Lord is the protector of my life.' Then: 'Lord have mercy upon us. – Christ have mercy upon us. – Lord have mercy upon us. – Our Father.' – Then the priest shall say: 'And [lead] us not . . .'

The psalms: I have lifted up my eyes. – Reveal to us Lord. – Keep safe your servant. – May my supplication enter into your consideration, Lord. – I have gone astray like a lost sheep. – Behold how good. – Blessed be the name of the Lord. – Lord hear the prayer.

Prayer
277. Let us pray. – Receive, we beseech you, O Lord, this your servant fleeing to you from the tempests of this world and the snares of the devil, so that having been received by you he may happily enjoy both protection in the present world and reward in the world to come: through Christ . . .

Prayer
278. Lord, who through yourself and our holy fathers have sanctioned es-pecially the authority of the Rule, we ask your mercy that, calmed by the intercession of all your saints, you may look mercifully upon this your servant who has renounced the world, and you may turn his heart from worldly vanity and inspire him towards love of his eternal vocation, and pour out on him the grace which abides in you, so that, fortified by the aid of your protection, he may fulfil this which, you being willing, he promises, and, having completed the execution of his profession, he may deserve to attain those things you have deigned to promise to those who persevere in you.

285.1 I.e. Satan.

Conventual Life

Rules for the Day-to-Day Life of the Brothers

279. Each brother of the Temple should know that he is not committed to anything so much as to serve God, and each one should apply all his study and understanding to this, and especially to hearing His holy office; for none should fail or be lacking in this, as long as he is content in it. For as our Rule says, if we love God, we should willingly hear and listen to His holy words.

280. And no brother should be without his habit when the hours are sung. And if any brother is drinking or eating, he should not be without his habit; and he should wear his habit in such a way as to have the laces of his cloak round his neck. And if he has his cope when he hears the hours, he should be dressed in his tunic, if he does not have a mantle; and a brother may eat in the same way if he does not have a mantle.

281. When the bell rings for matins, each brother should get up immediately, put on his hose, and fasten his cloak, and go to the chapel and hear the office; for none should stay [in bed] during the day unless he has been working or is ill, and for these things he may remain in his bed. But he should obtain permission from the Master or from the one who is in his place. And each brother should come to matins in breeches and shirt, without any belt except the small one, and with his hood up. Moreover, he should be dressed in hose and shoes, and should have his habit as is said above. And all the other hours the brothers should hear completely dressed and in hose, according to the requirements of the weather and the season.

282. When the brothers are in the chapel and matins are sung, each one should keep silent and hear the office quietly and in silence; and he should say the paternoster thirteen times for the matins of Our Lady, and thirteen times for those of the day if he wishes. But if he wishes, he may refrain from saying them, since he hears them, but it is better that he says them than that he does not.

283. When the brothers leave matins, each one should go and look at his horses and equipment, if they are in a place where he may and should go, and if there is anything to be repaired, he should repair it or have it repaired. And if he needs to speak to his squire, he should speak to him quietly, and afterwards he may go to sleep again. But he should say one paternoster when he lies down so that, if he has sinned in any way, either in breaking the silence or in anything else, Our Lord may pardon him.

284. When the bell rings for prime, each brother should get up immediately and dress himself completely in his hose, as is said above, and should go to the chapel and hear the entire office. Firstly he should hear or say prime; and

afterwards he should hear mass if he can; and after mass he should hear or say terce and sext: for this is the custom of the house. And if any brother hears or says terce or sext before mass, he may do so. And when the first mass has been sung, if more masses are sung in the chapel, each brother may hear them: he should rather hear them than not if he has nothing else to do; and always if the brother wishes to go when the first mass has been said and he has heard terce and sext, he may do so. But before he goes anywhere else, each brother should go and look at his equipment, as is said above.

285. When the brothers have left the chapel, if they are not waging war or they have not been given any other order, each one should go to his place and repair his armour and his equipment, if there is anything to repair, or he should have it repaired, or should make tent-posts or pegs or anything else that befits their office. And each brother should ensure that the Enemy does not find him lazy, for the Enemy[1] assails more boldly and more willingly with evil desires and vain thoughts and mean words, a lazy man than he does one whom he finds busy in good work.

286. When the bell rings for meals, each brother should eat at the first sitting,[1] so that none remain behind without permission except for the things which will be named hereafter. But each brother should studiously take care that, before he eats anything, he has said or heard matins, prime, terce and sext, and above all the sixty paternosters which each brother of the Temple is required to say every day, for the brothers and other benefactors dead and alive; that is to say thirty for the dead, that God may deliver them from the pains of Purgatory and place them in Paradise, and the other thirty for the living, that God may deliver them from sin and pardon them the sins they have committed, and lead them to a fine end. And these sixty paternosters no brother should omit to say in their entirety every day, unless he is so ill that he cannot say them without harm to his body.

287. When the brothers have come to the table to eat, if they have a priest, they should send for him and wait until he arrives, if he is in such a place that he can come quickly; and afterwards they should ensure that he has at table bread and wine and water, if they should not eat anything else,[1] and if there is what ought to be there. The priest, if he is there, should give the blessing, and each brother should say one paternoster standing, and then he should sit and may cut his bread; and before he has given the blessing in such a manner, he should not cut his bread nor eat nor drink. And in this same way, if they do not have a priest, each brother should say the paternoster and the other things; and afterwards he may eat, for love of God.

288. And wherever there is a convent, when the convent eats, a clerk should read the holy lesson; and this was established so that the brothers may better

285.1 I.e. Satan.
286.1 The first sitting was for the knights, the second for sergeants.
287.1 Because it is a fast day.

keep silence, and listen to the holy words of Our Lord; and thus the Rule commands it. For let it be known that, in all the places where the convent eats, silence should be kept, both by the brothers and by all other people. And also where the brothers eat at the infirmary table, each one should eat quietly and keep silence.

289. When the brothers eat in the convent, none should eat or drink any food except what the convent eats and drinks communally, not the Master nor any other, unless it is changed, that is to say if a brother is given different food because he did not eat what the convent had been communally served with beforehand. When the convent is served, the alternative should always be brought, after the dish, because if there is anyone who does not eat the dish, he may eat the other if he wishes. And the alternative for the convent should always be worse than the dish which is given before; and each brother who does not eat the communal dish may take the other if he wishes.

290. Each brother who eats in the convent may ask for the household's food if he does not like the convent's food, and he should be given it. But if he eats the household's food, he should not eat the convent's food; or if he eats that of the convent, he may not eat that of the household. And so each brother who eats in the convent may ask for what the other brothers eat, but he should ensure that he does not eat the alternative.

291. When the brothers eat in the convent, none should give the food in front of him, not bread nor anything else, to any man, nor to any bird, nor to any other animal. He should not invite any man to drink from his cup, unless it is such a man who is worthy of eating in the convent. But if any other man comes to talk to a brother who eats in the convent, the brother may invite him to drink; but he should bring the wine from the cellar or anywhere else but from the convent's table.

292. And any worthy man who comes to the palace when the brothers are eating may be invited to eat; and he may be seated at one of the tables in the palace that befit such a man. But always the brother should speak or send word to the commander of the house, or that of the palace; and they should not refuse him. – And also when they eat at the infirmary table, none should give the food in front of him to any man, nor to a bird, nor to an animal; nor should he invite a man to drink or to eat, unless it is as is said above for the brothers who eat in the convent. But always it is worse if it is done in the convent than if it is done in the infirmary; and everything is forbidden.

293. No brother who remains in the convent should wear breeches, nor two pairs of hose; nor should he lie on a mattress without permission, nor should he keep a cloak or rug, nor anything else for the comfort of his body, on his palliasse without permission, except only a sheet.

294. When the brothers are sitting down to eat in the convent, when they have broken their bread, none who has broken it or who has eaten and drunk anything, either at dinner or at supper, should get up at all or sit down until he

has eaten everything. And if they are at the first sitting, none should get up until they all get up together, unless any brother has a nose bleed; for this he may get up without permission, and then return to the meal when the flow of blood has been stanched. And for the cry to arms, if they are sure that the cry is raised by a brother or by any worthy man, and for a disturbance among the horses, and for a fire, if it takes hold in their house, they may also get up without permission, and then return to the meal.

295. When the brothers have eaten at the first sitting they should get up all together, when the clerk who is reading says *Tu autem Domine*, etc., and none should remain at the table, and they should all together go to the chapel if it is nearby, and should give thanks to Our Lord for what He has given them; and each one should say a paternoster, and the priest and the clerk, if there are any, should go to the chapel before the brothers, and should give thanks to God, and have those prayers said as is the custom of the house. And if the chapel is not nearby, they should say their prayers and give thanks in the same place, as is said above as if they were in the chapel. And when the brothers have got up from the table they should say neither good word nor bad, until they have given thanks to God, as is said above.

296. When the brothers go to the table to eat at the last sitting, they should say the blessing as it is said of those who eat at the first sitting; and they should be served the same food and the same quantity as the first, and in the same manner; and no other food should be given to the last, except what the first have had, if there is any of the same. But if the last sitting lacks that food, it is fitting that the brothers be served other food. But that food should under no circum-stances be better than that which was served to the other sitting; and let it be known that the brothers should take it with patience and remain silent. More-over, let it be known that the one who serves the brothers and the one who distributes the food should share it out so that the last has the same as the first.

297. When the brothers eat at the last sitting, the holy lesson is not read; but always the brothers should keep silence and do the other things as is said above for those who eat at the first sitting, except that each brother who eats at the last sitting may get up from the table when he has eaten; but he should give thanks and do the other things as is said above of those who eat at the first sitting.

298. And each brother who eats in the infirmary may act in the same way, be it at the first sitting or the last, in getting up and giving thanks. But let it be known that the brothers who eat at the last sitting in the infirmary should not be served any other food except what the first sitting was served, unless the food is wanting, for then it would be suitable to give them some other. And whoever does so will be charged with gluttony and a great penance should be given to the one who has done it; and this includes those brothers who can tolerate the communal food of the infirmary; for it is fitting to favour those who are more sick and the old and feeble; for thus the Rule commands.[1]

298.1 See §60 and 61.

299. When the commander of the palace sees that there is a great abundance of food in the infirmary and little in the convent, he may tell the brothers who should eat at the last sitting of the convent's table to go and eat with him at the infirmary table; they should obey him, and the commander of the palace may have those brothers served from the food of the infirmary, just as the first sitting was served.

When the brothers have given thanks to God as is said above, they may go to their places and should do the best that Our Lord instructs them.

300. When it is nearly time for nones or vespers or whatever hour it may be, each brother should be in such a place where he can hear the bell, or where he may be found if anyone searches for him in order to hear the hours. Afterwards, when the bell sounds for nones, each should go to the chapel to hear nones. And afterwards, when the bell sounds for vespers, each brother should go to hear vespers, and none should remain behind without permission, except the brother in charge of the oven, if he has his hands in pastry, and the brother of the large forge if he has iron burning in the fire, who may stay until he has forged the hot iron; and the blacksmith brother, if he is preparing the shoe of a horse or any other saddled animal, or if he has prepared it, he may stay until he has shoed it. But as soon as they have done this work, they should go to the chapel where the hours are sung, and they should hear them, or say them if they cannot hear them.

301. And you should know that no brother, unless he is ill, should drink wine between dinner and vespers; and those who eat in the convent should not drink it at all except once nones have been sung.

302. When the brothers have heard or said vespers, all those who eat twice a day should go to the first sitting of supper, and none may remain behind without permission, except as is said above of those three, who may absent themselves from dinner and supper, and from nones and vespers, for those things which are named above; and at supper they should say the blessing, the lesson and grace and do the other things that it is said above they should do at dinner.

303. When the brothers fast, they should hear or say nones before they eat,[1] and then they may eat, unless it is Lent; for during this fast, after the first Sunday has passed, each brother should hear and say vespers before he eats,[2] on the day that he fasts.

304. When the bell sounds for compline, all the brothers should assemble in the chapel or where they are accustomed to assemble,[1] and may all drink communally, those who wish to drink, water or diluted wine, if it please the Master, or according to what is the custom in that house; but they should do it in such a

303.1 This meant that during periods of fasting the brothers ate only one meal a day, at about 3 p.m.
303.2 The one meal of the day would therefore be at about 4 p.m.
304.1 In the small houses which did not have a chapel, the hall acted as place of worship, chapter room and refectory.

manner as there is no excess; for in such a way the Rule commands.[2] Then, if it is commanded, they should obey quietly and in silence. Afterwards, each brother should hear compline, or say it if he is not in a place where they can hear it.

305. And when compline has been sung, each brother should go and look at his horses and equipment, if they are in place, as is said above; and if he wishes to say anything to his squire, he should say it quietly and calmly, and then may go to sleep. And when he is lying down he should say one paternoster so that if he has sinned in anything since compline was said, God may pardon him. And each brother should keep silence from when compline is begun until after prime, except in an emergency.

306. And each brother should know that, if he is not in a place where he may hear the hours, each one should say for each of those hours named below the paternoster as many times as is given below, that is to say for prime, terce, sext, nones and compline. For each hour fourteen paternosters: seven times for the hours of Our Lady, and seven times for the hours of the day. And the hours of Our Lady should always be said and heard standing; and those of the day may always be said and heard seated.

And for vespers each one should say the paternoster eighteen times: nine times for those of Our Lady, and nine times for those of the day. And the hours of Our Lady should always be said first in the house, except the compline of Our Lady, which should always be said last in the house, because Our Lady was the beginning of our Order, and in her and in her honour, if it please God, will be the end of our lives and the end of our Order, whenever God wishes it to be.[1]

307. And each brother who hears the hours may refrain from saying them if he wishes; but it is better that he says them, than that he does not, and it is more healthy. And let it be known that, when the brothers are in the chapel, all should kneel or be standing or seated together, while the office is sung; except for any who cannot do so in this manner because of his illness, and he should be apart behind all the other brothers.

308. Each brother is required to hear the hours in their entirety, and no brother should leave the chapel until these hours are finished, except for a task which he cannot avoid, or if he goes in search of the one who has the place next to him in the chapel, whom he should seek if he has not come when the office is begun, and so he should look for him at least in his bed or with his horses.

309. Each brother should ensure that he is present at the end of the hours, because it is customary in the Order that appeals and commands are issued at the end of the hours, except compline: for then they should be issued with collation,

304.2 See §30.

306.1 This reflects the medieval cult of the Virgin Mary by which it was fashionable for churches and orders to be dedicated to Christ's mother. St Bernard influenced the devotion to the Virgin for the Cistercian order, which was dedicated to her and which began the custom of building a special Lady chapel in their churches. M. Warner, *Alone of All her Sex* (London 1976), p. 131.

before compline begins. And they are given beforehand because if it were done afterwards, silence would be broken; nevertheless it may be done out of necessity, but it is better if it is done before, without sin, than afterwards. – And no brother should depart from the place of collation until the small bell rings, except by order; even if a brother does not wish to drink, he should go there with the others to see if any orders will be given.

310. Each brother is required to hear the orders willingly. Each brother who has not been present at the end of the hours should ask the others who were there if any commands were given, and they should tell him, unless it is anything which is forbidden to them. But if an order was issued such as placing brothers on duty, or many other things, he should go immediately to him who gave the command and should say to him, 'Good sir, I was not at the issuing of the order.' And then he should do what he commands him.

311. When the bell rings to assemble the brothers, no brother should remain behind without permission. No brother should obtain leave for another brother, not from the hours, nor from the appeal, nor from chapter, nor from anything else, unless the brother for whom he obtains permission has asked or commanded him.

When a brother tells another to obtain leave for him from anything to which leave is appropriate, that brother should obtain permission for him; and if he does not obtain it, he is guilty and the other is acquitted.

312. When a brother wishes to obtain leave from the hours for another brother, he should speak in this way, 'Sire, give permission to such-and-such a brother,' and he should name him, and should give the reason why the brother wishes to absent himself from the hours, be it either through illness or anything else; and it was established in this manner because the commander knows the brother. And if he sees that a brother is accustomed to miss the hours too often, the commander should admonish him, and ask him to behave as the Rule commands; and if the brother does not wish to reform, the commander should pass him over to the justice of the house and may refuse him permission.

313. When the Master gives a brother an order, the brother should say, 'On behalf of God' and should carry it out if he can and knows how to. And if he cannot or does not know how to, he should ask someone to ask the Master to release him from the command, because he cannot do it or does not know how to, or because the order is unreasonable;[1] and the Master is obliged to release the

313.1 This seems a strange phrase to find here, bearing in mind discipline was so important to the Order. However, it does echo the rule of St Benedict. Cf. 'If it happen that something hard or impossible be laid upon any brother, let him receive the command of his superior with all docility and obedience. But if he see that the weight of the burden altogether exceeds the measure of his strength, let him explain the reasons of his incapacity to his superior calmly and in due season, without pride, obstinacy, or contentiousness. If after his representations the superior still persist in his decision and command, let the subject know that it is expedient for him, and let him obey out of love,

brother if he sees that it is so. And in such a way should each commander behave to every brother who is under his command; and also each brother should say, 'On behalf of God' to every order that his commander gives him, and then do as is said above. Each brother should guard against doing what is forbidden in the house.

314. When a brother goes to prime, he should be fully dressed in his hose; for he should not go in his shirt, nor in his *garnache* if he does not have a coat of mail or tunic, nor with his hood up. No brother should comb his hair after compline; no brother should wear a mantle over his head except when he is in the infirmary and when he goes to matins, for then he may wear it; but he should not keep it on when the office is being sung.

315. Each brother should zealously take care of his equipment and horses. No brother should run his horse if it is not rested, nor gallop without permission, and especially the one he is not using; he may go out for pleasure at a pace or amble. No brother should run his horse over a complete course without permission. If he does not carry a crossbow and wishes to ride a horse on the course, he may run his horse over one course or two or three without permission if he wishes. No brother may impetuously race his horse against another person over half a course without permission. No brother should run his horse over a complete course, nor carry arms in hose without permission; but he may over half a course. When brothers go with the intention of running a course, they should pull on their boots. When brothers joust, they should not throw lances, for it is forbidden because of the injury which could arise. No brother should groom his horse, nor do anything for which it would be necessary to remain there, without permission.

316. None should take anything from another's campsite without the permission of the brother whose site it is. If any brother finds another brother's horse in his space, he should not take it away or move it, but he should tell the brother whose horse it is to return it to its proper place, and the brother should return it; the Marshal or the one who is in his place should make him take it back.

Each brother who rides out for pleasure should leave his place and his equipment under the command of another brother.

317. None should place a wager, not on a horse nor on anything else, except an arrow without iron, or anything else which does not cost him or anyone else money, like an open lantern, or wooden mallet, or camping or tent pegs. And these same things, which do not cost money as is said above, one brother may give to another without permission. And each brother of the Temple may wager against another brother, with his crossbow, ten pieces of candle without permission, but no more; and he may lose as much in a day; and he may wager the worn (*fausse*) string of his crossbow for the pieces; but he may under no circum-

trusting in the assistance of God.' *The Rule of St Benedict*, ed. & tr. Justin McCann (London 1952), p. 115.

stances leave the string overnight without permission. And the brother may not and should not place another wager on the draw of a crossbow. No brother should belt his sword over his *garnache* or his waist at daybreak.

Each brother may play with wooden tent pegs without iron, or *forbot*[1] if the wood is his. And let it be known that a brother of the Temple should play no other game except *marelles*,[1] which each may play if he wishes, for pleasure without placing wagers. No brother should play chess, backgammon or *eschaçons*.[1]

318. And if a brother finds another's equipment he should not keep it; but if he does not know whose it is, he should carry it or have it carried to the chapel; or if he knows whose it is he should return it. If equipment which has been found is brought to the chapel, and the equipment belongs to the house, but otherwise it is not known to which brother it belongs, if the equipment is suitable for the marshalcy it should be returned to the marshalcy, or the tailor if it belongs to the tailor, or to any of the other craftsmen in the same way.

319. No brother should give greater rations to any of his horses in such a way that the other horses suffer. No brother should seek to obtain barley for his horses without permission, except the ration which he is given communally at the grain store. No brother should keep one ration of barley in his place when he takes another ration, and if he does he should say so. When the brothers knowingly give half-rations to their horses, the half-rations should be ten [measures]; and let it be known that horses in the caravan should always be given half-rations and they should be ten [measures]; and the horses which the craftsman brothers keep should also have half-rations of ten [measures]. And it should always be thus, unless the house has other customs, namely that the half-rations are larger or smaller.

320. No brother of the convent should enter a town, *casal*, castle, garden, farm or dwelling, within a league of the house, without permission; unless he goes with any *bailli* brother who has the authority to take him to that place.

And let it be known that each brother of the convent or craftsman brother should ensure that he does not enter a town, garden or farm unless it is under his command. No brother, either of the convent or a craftsman brother, should eat or drink wine without permission in a place which is a league or less from a house where there are brothers living, except in an emergency; but he may drink water if necessary. And he may drink wine if he is with a bishop or archbishop, or with any other person of the Church of greater dignity than a bishop. And he may drink at the Hospital of St John if he wishes, and if it is necessary; but he should do so in the same way he would if he were in the house.

321. When any brother goes to any of the workshops in the course of his duty, he should not enter the cupboard without permission from the brother who is in that office or from a superior. When the brothers of the convent ask the

317.1 These appear to be board games played using counters, although their exact nature is not known.

craftsman brothers for something they need, they should ask for it quietly and calmly; and the craftsman brothers should give it to them quietly and without argument or disturbance, if they have it; and if they do not have it, they should refuse them quietly and calmly.[1] And if they do so in any other way, justice should be done, for discord could arise between the brothers because of it; and let it be known that each brother should take care not to move his brother to anger or to wrath, and this is a strict commandment of the Rule.[2]

322. No brother should carry his hauberk or his iron hose in a bag, neither in a *guarelle*[1] nor in a *profinel*, but he should carry it in a leather or wire mesh bag; moreover, he should not hang the wire mesh bag by the straps in order to carry his hauberk, but he should carry it in his hand for as long as he or a sergeant can each hold it; and with permission he may hold it or hang it by the straps.

323. No brother should eat in the palace dressed in his cope, neither in the convent, nor in the infirmary, and no brothers who have eaten in the morning in the convent may take supper in the evening anywhere except in the convent, neither the Master nor any other. But if it happens that the Master has eaten in the morning in the infirmary and rides out during the same day for pleasure or anything else, and takes with him brothers who have eaten in the morning in the convent, the Master may invite them to take supper with him in the same palace where they ate in the morning. But if the Master has eaten in the morning in the convent, if he takes supper in the evening he should have it in the convent and nowhere else. And when the Master eats at any table but the convent's, the Almoner should take the food which is served at that table to give to the sick sergeants and squires who are in the infirmary, and he should take from the infirmary table the meat juices, and roast and white foods,[1] if there are any.

324. No brother may wear a hood on his head. No brother may wear a coif without a cloth cap. No brother should hang his mantle round his bed on hooks, for each brother is obliged to honour his habit. No brother may throw his lance without permission, nor may he repair his sword without permission, nor his *chapeau de fer*, nor his coat of mail, nor throw his *chapeau de fer*.

325. No brother should ever swear when angry or calm, nor should he ever say an ugly or vile word, even less do such a thing. Each brother is required to do all noble actions and say all good words. No brother should wear leather gloves, except the chaplain brothers who are permitted to wear them in honour of Our Lord's body, which they often hold in their hands; and the mason brothers may wear them sometimes, and it is permitted them because of the great suffering they endure and so that they do not easily injure their hands; but they should not wear them when they are not working.

321.1 An example of this is given in §604.
321.2 Cf. for example §234.
322.1 I have not been able to ascertain exactly what kind of bag this is.
323.1 I.e. milk, butter, cheese, eggs.

Each brother should wear arming gauntlets when he has put on his arming jacket in order to arm himself, but otherwise he should not wear them without permission.[1]

326. No brother should have the *retrais*[1] or the Rule, unless he has them with the permission of the convent, for by the convent they have been and were forbidden to be kept by the brothers, because the squires found them once and read them, and disclosed them to secular men, which could have been harmful to our Order. And so that no such thing may happen, the convent established that no brother may keep them, no brother unless he is a *bailli*, who may keep it for the office of the *baillie*.

327. None may carry or keep money without permission.

When a brother asks any brother of our *baillie* for money to buy something, he should buy as soon as possible that for which he asks it, and he may not buy anything else without permission; but he may do so with permission, and each *bailli* brother of the Temple may do so and give such permission; and each *bailli* brother may give permission to another brother to give a dagger from Antioch or England. And if brothers are in a place where there is no commander of knights over them, and there is any knight *bailli* brother among them, they should obtain permission from him when necessary.

328. And if they have neither a commander of knights nor any other knight *bailli* brother, the brothers themselves by agreement may make one of the brothers in their number a commander of knights, he who seems to them most reasonable, and from whom henceforth they should obtain permission. And if the brothers are sergeant brothers, they may obtain permission from any sergeant *bailli* brother, if there is one and if there are no other commanders of knights. But let it be known that no sergeant brother should be a commander of knights, nor hold chapter in a place where there are knights.[1]

329. Each brother of the Temple, both the Master and others, should assiduously take care that he does not keep money for himself, neither gold nor silver; for a person of religion should not have anything of his own, as the saint said, 'A man of religion who has coppers is not worth a halfpenny.'[1] No brother should have anything of his own, neither a little nor a lot, whether given in trust or not, and money is especially forbidden above all else. The *bailli* brothers may have the things which they require for their office, but they should keep them in such a way as to show them to him under whose command they are, if he asks them, for

325.1 The arming gauntlets and arming jacket were only put on prior to arming for battle.

326.1 Much emphasis was placed on the existence of a 'secret rule' during the trials. It is difficult to know why harm should come to the Order if the Rule were revealed to seculars, unless it was regarded as of military value to an enemy.

328.1 Sergeants were commanders, but only in houses consisting only of sergeants. In such houses, reception into the Order was conducted by a knight who came for that specific purpose.

329.1 The French text has *maille*, the smallest coin, worth half a denier.

if they refuse and are guilty of [having] it, it will be counted stolen by them and they will be expelled from the house, from which God keep every brother of the Temple.

330. All the things of the house are common, and let it be known that neither the Master nor anyone else has the authority to give a brother permission to have anything of his own, neither a denier nor more, nor to do anything except what he has promised to God and vowed especially and particularly, that is to say obedience and chastity, and to live without possessions. But the Master may give a brother permission, when he goes from one land to another, or when he moves from one place to another, to carry money in order to perform his duties and to buy what he requires, and this same permission another commander may give him if there is one; but as soon as the brother is where he is to stay, he should give back what remains of the money to the treasury or to the one who gave it to him, if he can return it, and he should, for he should not keep it whether it be a little or a lot.

331. For if it happens that a brother dies, and money is found on him, in his habit or night clothes or in his pouch, it will be considered his and stolen. And these wicked brothers should not be buried with the other good brothers who have gone from this world, nor should they be placed in hallowed ground, and the brothers are not obliged to say the paternosters for them, nor to perform the office that they should perform for a dead brother; but they should have him buried like a slave, from which God keep all the brothers of the Temple.

332. But if it happens that a brother dies and it is found afterwards that he had money in the treasury in trust, or by order of any other *bailli* brother, that brother should not be treated as it is said above for the wicked brother, because he did not have it on him nor in a place where the house might or should reasonably lose it. Although he had failed badly and sinned against his vow and his promise, he should be forgiven and treated, out of pity and mercy, like any other brother, and his soul should be prayed for, that God may pardon him. But if the fund entrusted is found outside our house, and the brother to whom the fund was given is dead, and he had not confessed it to such a man from whom the house may or should recover it, such a brother should be treated as it is said above of that wicked brother on whom money was found.

333. And let it be known that if the Master himself places the fund outside the house in such a manner, and dies, and has not confessed in such a way that the house may or should recover it, he should be treated the same and worse as is said above for the false and wicked brother; for let it be known that the more a person has, the more he owes to our house, if he knowingly commits such a hideous crime.

334. And let it be known that no brother, neither the Treasurer nor any other, should thus keep another brother's fund for a long time, and especially money, neither gold nor silver; and he who does so fails badly and partakes in vile sin; rather the brother who looks after the sum should admonish the brother

to whom it belongs to buy that for which the money was given, or to return it to the treasury or to the one who gave it to him, and he should obey.

335. And let it be known that no brother may place a fund of money anywhere except in the treasury, and if there is no Treasurer, he should give it to the commander of the palace or to the commander of the house where he lives. And deposits of cloth, made-up and otherwise, should be placed in the tailor's workshop, except made-up squires' tunics, and shirts, breeches, and camping *garnaches*, which should be placed in the saddlery; and all the equipment which is sold to the tailor's workshop should be deposited in the tailor's workshop, and that which is sold to the Under-Marshalcy, and each brother when he puts his equipment on deposit. And no brother should take another brother's property without his permission.

336. No craftsman brother, neither one from the prison, nor any other, should strike a slave in such a way that he places irons round his neck without permission, if he has deserved it; none should put him in a pillory nor pierce him with a sword without permission; but he should beat him and may without permission with a leather strap if he has deserved it, but he should take care not to maim him.

337. No brother, unless he is the son of a knight or descended from the son of a knight, should wear a white mantle,[1] nor should the other brothers permit him to do so. But if the father of any worthy man died before he could be received into the knighthood, and was such a man as should and could be a knight, his son should not lose his nobility because of it; rather, he may be a knight and brother of the Temple and wear a white mantle. No brother who is not born of a legal marriage should wear a white mantle, even if he is a knight or the son of a knight.

338. When any brother of the Temple is so old that he cannot use arms, he should speak to the Marshal in this way, 'Good sire, I pray you for love of God to take your equipment and give it to such a brother who may use it in the service of the house, for I can no longer do what is required of me and of the house.' And the Marshal should and may do so, but he should give to the worthy man any gentle, ambling horse for his pleasure, if the brother wishes to have it; but always he should speak to the Master about it before taking the brother's equipment. For neither the Marshal nor any other may take the equipment from a brother, either voluntarily or against his will, without talking to the Master or to him who takes the Master's place, in such a way that all his equipment is taken from him.

339. But if a brother has a horse with which he cannot carry out the duties customary in the house, he may return it to the Marshal, and the Marshal should

---

337.1 This reflects the development of the knightly class in the thirteenth century; also the fact that the Order did not train men for knighthood, but normally accepted as knight brothers only those men who were already knights.

and may take it, without speaking to the Master or anyone else; and he should give the brother another one if he has it and the brother is without. And let it be known that the old men of the house and those who cannot perform their duty for the benefit of their souls and of the house should act in this way. For let it be known that great harm comes to the house when a brother keeps three or four horses and his other equipment without doing his duty to the house. The old men should set a good example to the others and should zealously ensure that they do not commit any offence, not in eating, nor in drinking, nor in dress, nor in anything, so that especially the young brothers should be mirrored in them, and from the behaviour of the old men the young should learn what behaviour they should adopt.

Religious Service

340. Each brother should strive to live honestly and to set a good example to secular people and other orders in everything, in such a way that those who see him cannot notice anything bad in his behaviour, not in his riding, nor in his walking, nor in his drinking, nor in eating nor in his look, nor in any of his actions and works. And especially should each brother strive to conduct himself humbly and honestly when he hears the office of Our Lord, or says it, and he should say those prayers and make those genuflexions as are customary in the house.

341. When the brothers are in the chapel or anywhere else, and the hours are sung or the brothers themselves say them, each should make obeisance as is customary in the house every day; except such days as the nine lessons are read in the house where they are, or during the octave of the feasts during which it is customary to observe the octave in the house of the Temple, and during Advent when those antiphons are sung which are called the 'O's',[1] the brothers should not make obeisance at vespers, but at all the other hours they should do so. Neither on the eve of Epiphany[2] nor on Christmas Eve, should obeisance be made at any of the hours; and always when obeisance is omitted it should be omitted on the eve of the feast, when nine lessons are read at the nones of the day.

342. When Lent arrives, every time the priest or the deacon says *flectamus genua*, when mass is being sung, all the brothers who are not ill should kneel, and when he says *levate*, they should rise. The first Wednesday in Lent, as soon as matins have been said, the priest and the clerk should begin the seven peniten-

341.1 So-called because they begin with 'O'. The first is said on 17 December and so on until 23 December. These antiphons are O *sapientia* . . ., O *Adonai* . . ., O *radix Jesse* . . ., O *clavis David* . . ., O *oriens* . . ., O *rex gentium* . . . and O *Emmanuel*. They were sung before and after the *Magnificat* at vespers.

341.2 The French text has 'apparition', which is taken from the phrase in the office of lauds, 'The true light has appeared and gives illumination to all.'

tial psalms,[1] and while the seven psalms are being said, all the brothers should be standing; except at the end of each psalm, when *gloria patri* is said, each brother should kneel and rise immediately. And when the seven psalms are finished, the priest and the clerk should begin the litany and say all of it softly and quietly, all the prayers which are appropriate; so saying, the brothers should prostrate themselves and listen to that office with great devotion. And these seven psalms and this litany should be said in such a manner every day until the Wednesday of Holy Week, if it does not happen to be a feast of nine lessons, and each day the brothers should do as is said above.

343. And on the first Wednesday of Lent itself, which is called Ash Wednesday, all the brothers should receive the ashes on their heads; which ashes the chaplain brother should place there, or another priest if they cannot have a chaplain brother, in remembrance that we are ashes and to ashes we shall return.

344. When the middle Saturday of Lent arrives, when that antiphon which is called *media vita* is sung, every time *sancte Deus, sancte fortis, sancte et immortalis* is said, all the brothers should make obeisance, every time *sancte* is said, whether it is a feast day or not.

345. But from the Wednesday of Holy Week, after nones are called, obeisance is not made in the house at the end of the hours until the Monday after the octave of Pentecost, unless it is Good Friday, when *Kyrieleison, Xristeleison, Kyrieleison* and *miserere mei Deus* are said, for then each one should be on his knees and prostrate until the prayers are finished, at each of the hours; and that same Friday, when the deacon or priest says *flectamus genua*, when the office is sung, each brother should kneel; and when he says *levate* he should rise as is said above. And after Easter, every time the resurrection is commemorated each brother should kneel. And the brothers should make no other obeisance except as it is told.

But let it be known that the sick brothers are not required to make these obeisances until they are so recovered that they may make them without a worsening of their illness.

346. On Maundy Thursday, it is customary in the house to ring the bells at matins and the other hours until mass. But after mass has started they should not be rung until Easter Eve when *Gloria in excelsis* is begun, and at that time they should be rung loud and clear. The kiss of peace should not be given on Maundy Thursday; but when mass and vespers have been sung the Almoner should have thirteen paupers supplied with enough hot water and flasks or swathes (*gavetes*)[1] and towels.

347. And the brothers should wash the paupers' feet and dry them with the towels, and afterwards kiss their feet humbly. And let it be known that the Almoner should ensure that those paupers who are to be washed do not have

342.1 Psalms 6, 31, 50, 101, 129 and 152.
346.1 I have taken this to read *javeles*.

any vile diseases on their feet or legs; for perhaps it could bring illness to a brother's body. And while this service is performed, the priest and the clerk should wear the surplice and carry the cross, and say such prayers as are customary in the house on that day. And afterwards, the commander of the house, if there is no-one more senior, should give each pauper who has been washed two loaves of bread, a pair of new shoes and two deniers. And all this should be done on Maundy Thursday before the brothers eat.

348. On Maundy Thursday, when it is nearly time for compline, a *table*[1] should be struck and at the sound of this, the brothers should assemble in the palace just as they would if the bell were rung; and the priest and the clerk should also go to the palace, and should carry the cross. And then a priest or clerk should read the gospel to the palace, that which it is customary to read on that day, and he should read it without a title; and he may be seated while he reads if he wishes, but he should be fully dressed;[2] and when he has read for a while he may rest. And the sergeants should bring wine to the brothers, and the brothers may drink if they wish; and when they have drunk, the one who is reading should read what remains of the gospel. And when the gospel is finished, the brothers and the priest and clerk should go to the chapel; and the priests should wash the altars, and afterwards they should sprinkle wine over the altars. And then it is customary in the house for all the brothers to go and pray at the altars and kiss them, and each brother should wipe a little of that diluted wine which is sprinkled on the altars, over his lips, and he should drink it. And afterwards, when all the brothers who are present have done so, compline should be sung; and when it has been sung, the brothers should do as is told above.

349. On Good Friday, all the brothers should pray at the cross with great devotion; and when they go to the cross they should be barefoot. And on that day they should fast on bread and water and eat without a napkin; moreover, the tables should be washed before the bread is put on them; and brothers of the Temple should eat without a napkin on no other day unless it is in penance on the floor, for then he should eat on a piece of his mantle and without a napkin, as will be told below at the appropriate place.[1]

And although the brothers eat in the convent on Good Friday, at the first sitting they may rise from the table when they have finished if they wish, which they can never do any other day.

350. The other fasts which the brothers of the Temple should observe are these: that is to say they should fast every Friday, from the feast of All Saints until Easter, except the Friday which falls during the octave of Christmas. And if the feast of Christmas falls on a Friday, all the brothers should eat meat in honour of the feast of Christmas. And also if the feast of Epiphany, the purifica-

---

348.1 A piece of wood which was struck instead of the bell being rung. See §30 and note.

348.2 I.e. in his vestments.

349.1 See §§636 and 637; but these relate to chaplain brothers only.

tion of Our Lady[1] or of St Mathias the apostle[2] falls on a Friday, the brothers are not obliged to fast.

351. In addition, all the brothers of the Temple are required to observe two fasts a year; and the first fast always begins on the Monday before the feast of Saint Martin which is in November,[1] and they should fast until Christmas Eve. The other fast should always begin on the Monday before Ash Wednesday, and they should fast until Easter Eve.

352. Each brother is required to fast on the eve of Epiphany; the eve of Saint Matthew the apostle; Saint Mark's day;[1] the eve of Saint Philip and Saint James, two apostles;[2] and three days before Ascension; the eve of Pentecost; the eve of Saint John the Baptist;[3] the eve of Saint Peter and Saint Paul, two apostles;[4] the eve of Saint James the apostle;[5] the eve of Saint Laurence;[6] the eve of Saint Bartholomew, apostle;[7] the eve of Saint Mathias, apostle;[8] the eve of Saint Simon and Saint Jude, apostles;[9] the eve of Saint Andrew, apostle;[10] and the eve of Saint Thomas, apostle.[11] – The brothers of the Temple are also required to observe four fasts: the first on the Wednesday, Friday and Saturday after Ash Wednesday; another on the Wednesday, Friday and Saturday after Pentecost; the third on the Wednesday, Friday and Saturday after the Exaltation of the Holy Cross in September;[12] and the fourth and last on the Wednesday, Friday and Saturday after Saint Lucy the Virgin.[13]

353. And the brothers of the Temple should not observe any other fasts without permission, nor may they, except the Fridays and other fasts with which they are charged in chapter; and those they do not observe with the permission of, but rather by the order of, the chapter. But if they are charged with fasting on Fridays for penance, or any other fast, they should keep it, and anyone may do so without permission except the confessor.

354. But let it be known that a brother of the Temple should not make confession except to a chaplain brother, except out of great necessity and when there is no chaplain brother; but he may do so with permission.

350.1 2 February.
350.2 24 February.
351.1 11 November.
352.1 25 April.
352.2 30 April.
352.3 23 June.
352.4 28 June.
352.5 24 July.
352.6 9 August.
352.7 24 August.
352.8 21 September.
352.9 27 October.
352.10 29 November.
352.11 20 December.
352.12 14 September.
352.13 13 December.

355. And all the brothers of the Temple should know that always after nones, vespers for the dead should be said in the house, and the brothers should hear them, unless it is the vigil of any feast when nine lessons are read, for then the vespers for the dead may be omitted; and on the day before Christmas Eve, the day before the eve of Epiphany, Holy Trinity, and during the octave of the feasts which it is customary to observe in the house, vespers for the dead may be omitted.

356. And you should also know that vigils for the dead should be said every day in the Temple between nones and vespers, except in Lent when, after the first Sunday is passed, they are said between dinner and compline on fast days, and on other days at the time given above. Moreover, for the same reason vespers for the dead are omitted, the vigils may be omitted;[1] and those vigils the chaplain brother and the other priests and clerks should say for them. And the other brothers may omit to hear them if they wish; but let it be known that it is a much better thing that they hear them, if they do not have a more important task to perform.

357. It is customary in our house, every day in the chapel, before matins begin, to say the fifteen psalms,[1] except on a feast of nine lessons, Christmas Eve and the eve of Epiphany. But during the octave of Christmas, Easter, Pentecost, the Assumption of Our Lady and the feast of the saint to whom the church is dedicated, none of the fifteen psalms is said. – The hours of Our Lady should be said every day in the house of the Temple except Christmas Eve, during the octave, and the eve of Epiphany; neither on the day of the purification of Our Lady, nor during the octave, unless it is Septuagesima, is more than one service said in the house.

358. But if Septuagesima falls during the octave, it is fitting that all the hours are said every day, and the office of Our Lady, and that of the day after Septuagesima, and that the octaves are omitted. Only one office is said in the house of the Temple on the day of the Annunciation of Our Lord, Palm Sunday, Maundy Thursday, Good Friday, Easter Eve, Easter Day and during the octave, Ascension Day, the eve of Pentecost, Pentecost and during the octave, the day of the Assumption of Our Lady and during the octave, the day of the nativity of Our Lady[1] and during the octave, All Saints, the saint's day to whom the church is dedicated and during the octave, the day of the dedication of the church in whose parish they are living and during the octave.

359. And all the offices performed in that chapel that we have listed here, each brother should hear attentively if he is able, and is so obliged to do; except the vigils for the dead which they may omit as is said above.

But the sick brothers, when they cannot hear the office or make obeisance

356.1 The vigils are the matins, usually said after vespers.
357.1 The office of matins consisted of six psalms said twice, plus three canticles. They were divided into Nocturns, between which the lessons were read.
358.1 8 September.

like the healthy ones when they are in the chapel, should keep to one part of the chapel behind the other brothers and may be seated, and in such a way they should listen to the office with great devotion, and keep silence, and do and say the best they can without injury to their bodies.

360. Also, all the brothers of the Temple should know that in our house, where there is a chapel or church, we make a procession on Christmas Day, Epiphany, Candlemas, Palm Sunday, Easter Sunday, Ascension Day, Pentecost, the Assumption of Our Lady, the Nativity of Our Lady, All Saints, the saint's day to whom the church is dedicated, and the day of their church's dedication. And these processions are called general because all the brothers generally who are present in that house where the procession takes place should be there if they are well, and may not remain behind without permission. Also, if they are in the vicinity of the house, wherever they may be, they should be in the procession if they can.

361. And also other processions are made in the Temple which are called private because the chaplain brother, the priest and the clerk make them privately without the other brothers. For the other brothers are not obliged to go if they do not wish to, but if they wish to they may go. But if the processions go anywhere where the brothers may not go on other days without permission, they should obtain leave to go there, and otherwise they should not go.

362. All the brothers of the Temple should go to their chapel with great honour and great reverence; and let it be known that no brother should throw out of the chapel anything that has been put there for the performance of the office in the chapel or of those who hear their office there, if he does not throw it out with permission, neither a crook (*potence*) nor anything else that he has taken there.

363. While the office is being said, no brother should remain in that part of the chapel in which the priest and the clerk stay when they perform the office of Our Lord, if he does not do so with permission, unless he is a chaplain brother or clerk, because he may perhaps hinder them in performing their office.

All the other things which are appropriate to the office of Our Lord each one should do the best he can according to the means of the house and as our ordinance, which was taken from the ordinance of the Sepulchre, commands.

364. And you should know that in the same manner as is said above, the brothers should go to the chapel to hear the office when they are in residence; in the same way when they are in camp they should go to the chapel or wherever the office is sung, except when instead of the bell the cry is often raised. And let it be known that the brothers are required to obey the call as well as the bell or him who has the cry raised.

365. And when the call is made for the brothers to say matins in their lodgings, or their other hours, they should get up immediately and say them; and in whatever place the brothers may be where they have no priest or anyone else to say the hours for them, they should say for each hour those paternosters it is

established they should say if they are able, in such a manner that they render to
Our Lord what they should at the time which is established for them to do so.
For they should not go beyond the time if it is within their power; also it is better
that they render it to Him before the time rather than afterwards; but always, if
anyone forgets to render to God what is due to Him at the established time, he
should do so as soon as possible afterwards.

Discipline on Campaign

366. When the brothers are in camp, they should have one commander who
is in charge of the food; and he should share out and distribute the food to the
brothers, communally as it is commanded below; and this commander should be
one of the old men of the house, and such who fears God and loves his soul.
When the brothers wish to make camp, they may not erect three tents or more
together without permission, but they may erect two and no more without
permission.

367. When the brothers are in camp, if they eat in the convent they should
behave in eating, rising, reading the lesson and in everything else as is said above
they should in the other dwelling places; and if they eat in the infirmary, they
should behave just as they would if they were in their other dwellings. And if it
happens that the brothers eat in lodgings each brother should ensure that the
other brothers, especially his companions, behave well like worthy men and as it
is established, and that one does not lead a harsher life than the other, nor than
the community, unless the Rule commands it, and that the others do not let
themselves go nor elevate themselves and do things which are against the
honesty and good customs of our house.

368. When the order is given for the brothers to go to the distribution of
rations, one or two should go from each mess, and they may take from their
household those who seem to them best suited to carry the food; and the
Commander of the Victuals should give to them in line as fairly as he can, and
he should not favour anyone, unless he is ill; for thus the Rule commands, that
he should not consider the person, but the illness of the brother. But the person
of the Master should be considered, for he should be given the best and finest;
but the Master's companions and the other brothers who are in his company
should be given the same as the queue. And if gifts of food are sent communally
to the convent, they should be carried to the mess tent and the Commander of
the Victuals should share it out fairly among all the brothers.

369. And if the Commander of the Victuals wishes to make a present of
anything to the brothers he should do so equally. And let it be known that the
brothers should not search for any other food except what is given communally,
except green vegetables from the fields, or fish if they know how to catch them
themselves, or wild animals if they know how to take them without hunting, in
such a way that they do not transgress the commandments of the house. Or if
wine or any other food comes to any brother as a gift or by any other means, he

should send it to the food tent, and should inform the Commander; and if the Commander wishes to keep it he may do so, but it would not be a good thing, for it is better that he gives it back to him.

370. When the brothers are in camp, the brothers from one mess may give such food as they have to brothers from another mess, and it is good that they do so.

And let it be known that two brothers' piece of meat should be such that what remains in front of two brothers can sustain two paupers; and the ration of two brothers should be given to three turcopoles; and the ration of two turcopoles should be given to three people from another household.

And let it be known that the rations were not fixed so large and generous in order that the brothers or sergeants could fill their stomachs, for they could easily abstain, but primarily they were established so large and fine for love of God and the poor, to give to alms. And for this reason it was also established that no brother, neither in the convent nor in the infirmary, may give away any of the food in front of him, so that the alms do not diminish; that is why each one should know that, when the food ration which was established for the brothers is reduced, so are the alms.

371. And also it is a commandment of the house that the brothers, when they are served meat or cheese, should cut their piece in such a way that there is enough, and that they leave the piece complete and whole as far as possible, providing they have enough and as much as they need. And this was established so that the piece may be more worthy to give to a shameful pauper, and more worthy for the poor man to accept.

372. When the Commander of the Victuals distributes meat to the brothers, he or the one who is in his place should ensure that he does not put together two good pieces or two bad, like two haunches or two shoulders; but he should give to one and all as fairly as possible. And in the same way the convent in the palace should be served, so that two good pieces are not sent together, but always the bad after the good, so that the brothers always take turns.

373. And each brother may give some of the food in front of him to the other brothers around him, as far as he can stretch his arm, but no farther; and always he who has the best should invite the one who has the worst. And if it happens that in any mess there are one or two or more who eat food from the infirmary because of their illness, the brothers who are lodged with them may eat it in such a way as there is no shortage. And let it be known that the Commander of the Victuals should give food to that sick brother in such a way that the brother's companions may have some of it if they wish.

374. The Commander should also distribute the food of the infirmary in line like that of the convent. The Commander of the Victuals should give the best of the food he has to the sick brothers; and when the brothers who are healthy have two dishes, the sick should have three; and when they have only one, the sick should have at least two. And if he wishes to show them some favour he may

do so, and he may give them presents; and he may not do so to the healthy ones
unless it is communally, as is said above. If one or two worthy secular or religious
men pass by the camp, each brother may invite him in when he passes in front of
his mess; and the Commander of the Victuals should give to the brother who has
invited the worthy man so generously of the food he has, for love of the worthy
man, that all those in the mess may have plenty.

375. No brother should keep in his mess any other food except what he is
given at the mess tent, without permission.

When bread or wine remain in any mess from one day to the next, the
brothers from the mess should return it or disclose it at the tent when they take
their rations. And let it be known that the rations, that is to say the pieces [of
meat] and measures [of wine] should be equal, and the other rations also. And
when the brothers fast, two brothers should be given four measures of wine and
when they are not fasting, five measures; and two turcopoles should be given
three measures; and the measure of oil should be the same throughout the land
this side of the sea.

376. And when the brothers are in camp they should not go out for pleasure
without permission, except as far as they can hear the call or the bell, not even
to their dwellings, except as far as they can hear the bell. Nor may they even
carry any baggage on their horses, near or far, without permission; and it is
understood by 'baggage' everything that is found between the pommels of the
saddle or that hangs from them.

When a brother wishes to send his horses to the baggage train, or wishes to
carry anything on his horse, he should have the saddle or the saddle pad covered
with a rough cloth or something else.

377. No brother, either in camp or anywhere else, may lend his horse without
permission to a brother or anyone else to go far away for pleasure. No brother,
either in camp or anywhere else, should allow his horse or any other animal to be
lent without permission. No brother should leave his horses' fetters or muzzle
anywhere at night without permission.

378. When the brothers are given permission to groom their horses and
animals at night, none should keep the horse blanket on his horse by such
permission, unless the blanket has been expressly mentioned. And you should
know that when a brother obtains or asks for permission, for whatever it may be,
he should make known and clarify the thing for which he asks permission to him
from whom he asks permission; and he should not hide anything. And the one
who has the authority to grant the brother permission, when he has heard the
reason he asks for it, if the thing is reasonable and he can give it without harm to
the house, it is a good thing that he gives the permission.

379. When the horses eat straw communally, no brother should give grass to
his horses without permission, and especially he should not give it to the horses
which eat straw. No brother should place harness or ropes on his horses, nor

anything else in order to make them amble, without permission. And two brothers should not ride on one horse.[1]

380. And if it happens that the alarm is raised in camp, the brothers who are camped in that part where the alarm is raised should leave that area with their shields and lances and they should not go far from the camp until there has been another order; and all the other brothers who are not from that area should go immediately to the chapel to hear the order if any is given. But if the alarm is outside the camp, they should go out without permission towards the cry, for whatever reason it was raised.

381. When it is time to strike camp, and it seems good to the Master and to the other worthy men that they disperse, the Commander of the Land should indicate to the Marshal how many brothers to place in each of the houses; and the Marshal should trust him, for the Commander knows better than any other how many brothers may stay in each of the houses, and how many each of them can accommodate. And then the Marshal should organise for the brothers to disband, as is said above of other things, as equally as possible; and he should send them out into the houses if he can, just as the Commander advises him. And when the Marshal has disbanded the brothers, and has ordered them to go to their houses, each brother should look for his equipment and that of the mess in such a manner that, when they leave camp, nothing remains of his equipment, except by permission.

382. And the Marshal or he who organises it should give to each house a commander of knights; and that commander of knights, when the brothers are in their houses, should give them sleeping space and room for their horses and straw mattress; and so he should give them out in line as fairly as possible. And that commander of knights should hold chapter for them, if there happens to be no-one superior among them, and he should issue orders; and the brothers should obey him as they would the Master, for all are under his command, and they should obtain permission from him, those to whom he may give permission.

And if it happens that brothers are housed in any farm, the commander of the house or castle under whose command the farm falls [should provide] the things that the brothers need as if they were living in the house or castle of which he is commander, except goblets and bowls, which the commander of the cellar should provide for them.

383. And when the brothers are in their houses, they should strive hard to behave to the honour of God and the house, and the benefit of their souls; and each one should take care within his power not to anger his brother.

And each one should zealously take care of his brother, that he does not do or say anything, or conduct himself in deed or appearance in any way he should not.

379.1 The earliest seal of the Order showed two knights riding on one horse, presumably to symbolise the poverty of the brothers, but this custom, if it ever existed, was soon dropped.

384. And if any brother sees another brother doing anything he should not, or behaving in any wicked manner, he should chastise him alone once; and if the brother does not wish to make amends by his request or his advice, he should call another brother and he should be warned, listening to the brother. And if he does not wish to make amends even with the counsel of two brothers, the good brother should take the brother who does not wish to make amends to the first chapter to assemble, in front of all the brothers, and pass him over to the jurisdiction of the house; for this the Rule commands.

And let it be known that the brothers who are in that chapter should be against that brother who commits that fault or another; for no brother should knowingly uphold crime, and especially in chapter; for if he did so the judgement of the house could be vilely corrupted in such a way that the religious would be lost.

385. And you should know that it is a commandment of the house that wherever there are four or more brothers assembled, they should hold chapter if it is convenient, on Christmas Eve, Easter Eve and the eve of Pentecost; and they should also hold chapter each Sunday, except the Sundays during the octaves of the three aforementioned feasts, which are at the discretion of the brothers and of him under whose command they are, whether or not to hold it; and for the benefit and needs of the house, it can be permitted to hold chapter on any other Sunday, but always it should be done by the judgement of the brothers who are present, or of a group of the most worthy men.

The Holding of Ordinary Chapters

386. Each brother, when he enters the chapter, should cross himself in the name of the Father and of the Son and of the Holy Spirit, and should remove his cloth cap and his coif if he is not bald, and if he is bald he may leave on the coif; and standing he should say one paternoster before sitting down, and then he should sit down, and each one should do so. And when all the brothers or the majority have arrived, the one who is to hold chapter should say to the brothers before he begins his sermon, 'Good lord brothers, stand up and pray to Our Lord that He today sends His holy grace among us,' and then all the brothers should rise to their feet and each one should say a paternoster.

387. And the chaplain brother, if he is present, should also say his prayer as he sees fit, that is the sermon, before the chapter begins. And then they should sit, and let it be known that they should take care that no-one who is not a brother of the Temple may listen when they hold their chapter.

388. When the prayer is said, the one who is to hold chapter should begin his sermon in the name of God, and deliver it to the best of his ability, and should admonish the brothers and pray and command them to make amends.

And after the sermon has begun, no brother should move from his place to go to the back without permission, but beforehand he may go without permission.

389. When the one who holds chapter has finished his sermon, each brother who thinks he has sinned should rise to his feet and should do with the cap and coif what is said above, and should come before him who holds chapter, and should kneel once or twice or more times, and should be humble like one who confesses, and should speak in this way, 'Good lord, I plead for mercy to God and Our Lady and to you and the brothers, for I have failed in this way,' and should relate the fault wholly and truthfully as it was, and he should not lie, neither for shame of the flesh, nor for fear of the justice of the house; for if he lies it will not be a confession, and let it be known that our chapter was established so that the brothers could confess their faults and make amends.

390. After the brother has recounted everything concerning the fault he believes he has committed and has confessed it entirely, the one who holds chapter should command him to go outside, and the brother should go to such a place where he cannot hear what the brothers in the chapter say; for no brother, while he is outside the chapter, either because of sin or because he is on penance, should listen to what the brothers in chapter do or say or consider. Afterwards, when he is outside the chapter, the one in charge of that place should recount the brother's fault before all the chapter, and should ensure that he does not change anything; and when it has been told to them just as the brother con-

fessed it, so he should ask for their advice communally and do what the majority agrees.

391. And when the brothers have communally given their advice, as they see fit, and the commander has heard what the majority agrees, he should have the brother return before him, and he should indicate the fault to him and relate how it is serious and how the brothers hold him to have failed; and he should command him to do what the brothers have judged, and should relate to him the judgement of the brothers; but he should not say, 'such-and-such a brother gave such-and-such a judgement' or 'he agreed to that', for he would disclose the dealings of his chapter.

392. When a brother pleads for mercy in chapter for any fault, all those who believe they are tainted with that sin should also plead for mercy with him; and each brother, when he pleads for mercy for a fault, should do so for all the faults he believes he has committed; and for as many faults as he has committed, however many they may be, he may be given only one penance, since he has pleaded for mercy for all of them together.

When a brother pleads for mercy for a fault, no other brother should get up to plead for mercy for his failing so that it may be considered, unless he is tainted with that same fault as is said above. If a brother pleads for mercy for ten faults at any one time and it is fitting that he be pardoned for one of them, it is fitting that he be pardoned for all.

393. When the brothers are in chapter, all should be against the one who does or says anything unreasonable, and each one should be quiet and keep silence; and none should speak, unless he is asked something, or unless someone does or says something unreasonable; for each should be against the one who does or says anything unreasonable. Each one may accuse him without getting up from his place without permission; moreover he should do so immediately he does or says anything unreasonable, and each one is obliged to make him make amends; and in no other way may a brother accuse another brother in his place, except the Master. And the Master may and should accuse in his place any other brother he wishes, without moving.

394. Each brother, when he comes to chapter, should come thoughtful and mindful if he has failed in anything or broken his vow and his promise, and he should think of it in the chapter itself: whether he has heard or said his hours well, and has not angered his brother in anything, and if he has kept the commandments of the house. And if he believes he has failed in anything, he should plead for mercy for it and make amends before he leaves the chapter. For after the sermon of the chapter is finished, no brother should report his failing outside the chapter, rather he should reform in every way he can; and if he knowingly reports his failing, it will be more serious, and he will be disobedient.

395. Moreover you should know that neither the Master nor any other brother who holds chapter should do anything that he should do with the advice of chapter and the judgement of the brothers, before he has said the prayer and

the sermon as he sees fit; for at the beginning of all the assemblies of the chapter that we hold, we should ask for the grace of Our Lord.

396. No brother may be absent from chapter without permission unless he is ill in the infirmary. No brother may leave the chapter without permission, unless he thinks he will immediately return to that same chapter before the chapter disperses. From the moment the sermon is finished, no brother may show anything to another brother without permission, in such a way that he makes him rise from his place or he himself gets up; but when a brother is standing before the one who holds chapter, each one may rise from his place without permission and accuse the brother who is on his feet of the sin he knows he has committed.

397. When any brother knows that his fellow brother has done or said anything which he should not, he should make him make amends at the first chapter where they are both assembled, and should not let him go out of the chapter without making him reform; but it is a good thing if the brother who knows that his fellow brother has done this reminds the brother who has failed of it apart, before they enter the chapter, and warns him in front of one or two other brothers, in this way, 'Good brother, remember such-and-such a thing,' and he should recount the fault; and he should say to him, 'Make amends at the first chapter you attend.' The worthy men say that a brother has said enough when he says to another brother, 'Remember such-and-such a thing,' and the one to whom these words are said should consider himself accused and should make amends at the first chapter he attends, as is said above.

398. No brother should accuse another brother in front of any man unless he is a brother of the Temple; and a brother may not nor should he accuse his fellow brother either in chapter or outside, nor bring a charge against him through hearsay; but of anything he has seen or heard he may accuse him and bring a charge against him; and if he does otherwise, he is very wretched and may be held to be a conspirator.[1]

399. When a brother wishes to accuse another, he should take care not to charge him with trivial things, but if he has not accused him outside as is said above, or still if he has charged him and the brother does not wish to reform, he should do so in the same way when they are in chapter. For before he rises he should say to the one who holds chapter, 'Commander,' or 'Good sir, give me leave to speak to a brother,' and he should give him permission.

400. And when he has permission, he may get up and should call by name the brother whom he wishes to accuse, and that brother should rise to his feet and should remove his cap and coif if he is called, and should come before the one who holds chapter. Then the accuser should indicate to him calmly and quietly that thing in which he knows he has failed; for none should accuse his brother falsely. And so he should speak in this way, 'Good brother, plead for mercy for such-and-such a thing,' and he should recount the thing or fault just as

398.1 See §418.

it has been said or done. And the one who is accused should say, 'Good sir, I plead for mercy to God and Our Lady, and to you and the brothers, for the thing of which I am accused,' and he should kneel each time he is charged.

401. And if he knows the thing of which he is accused is true, the brother who is accused should admit to it before all the brothers, for none should lie in chapter. But if the thing of which he is accused is false, he should speak in this way, 'Good sir, I plead for mercy to God and Our Lady, and to you and the brothers for the thing of which this brother accuses me' – and he should kneel – 'but you should know that it is not so.' Or he may say, 'Sir, no, God forbid that I should ever do such a thing.' Or, 'Sir, it is otherwise.' And he should speak fully on the matter; for, just as it is said above, he should not lie, neither for shame of the flesh nor for fear of the justice of the house.

402. And the one who has the task of defence should not call by name the one whom he wishes to produce for the defence, nor name him without permission, but he should say to him who holds chapter, 'Sir, there is a brother who knows about this matter' once or more; and then the commander should say, 'If there is any brother who knows anything of this, come forward.' And if there is anyone who knows about it, he should rise and come before the commander, and should stand guarantee of what he has seen and heard; and he should not say anything but the truth, and that he should not hide or change, neither out of love nor ill will, on the part of one or the other, for it would be a very great sin and may be considered a conspiracy.

403. And if the brother who knows about the matter does not wish to rise, when the commander has asked once or twice in the manner given above, the commander should say to the brother who wishes to produce the brother in his defence, 'Good sir, make him come forward.' And then he may call him by name, and that one should rise and do just as is said above of the guarantee. And that brother who should stand guarantee may and should be considered guilty of a serious fault and given a harsh penance, if he knows anything of the thing for which he was called in defence, because he did not rise immediately the order was given.

404. And if the accused brother wishes to charge the one who has accused him, and he knows that he has failed in anything, he may accuse him without asking further permission, while he is on his feet; and so he should accuse him and indicate to him his fault as is said above.

405. And the one who is found guilty of his fault, the commander should send out, or both if they are convicted; but he should not send out any brother from chapter for anything of which the brother has been accused, if he is not found guilty. And when the brothers are outside, the commander should recount the thing or the fault for which they have pleaded for mercy and are found guilty just as it was related to him, and afterwards he should communally ask the brothers who are in that chapter for their advice, and do what the majority agrees. And when the brothers have said what seems fit to them communally, he

should do to those brothers who are outside as is said for that brother who voluntarily pleaded for mercy for his fault.

406. And if the brothers judge that the brothers who are outside should be immediately put on penance, the commander should do so immediately he has told them the judgement of the brothers; and yet if the brothers do not judge that they should be immediately put on their penance, the commander who holds chapter, as soon as he has told them the judgement of the brothers, may say to them, 'Go and undress yourselves,' and he may give them corporal punishment and immediately put them on penance if he sees that it is fitting; and the brothers are content for it is at his discretion.

407. One brother alone may accuse another brother in the manner which is given above, or two or three or twenty; moreover, one brother alone may not find another brother guilty, but two brothers may find another brother guilty or two or a hundred, when the two and the hundred see that the thing is not so, as long as they are in chapter, for defence (*guarentie de non*) is not accepted in our chapter unless it is not possible to find him guilty by any other means.

408. But if one or two brothers say in chapter to another brother, 'Good sir, you committed such-and-such a fault at Château Pèlerin[1] on Sunday; plead for mercy,' and the brother replies, 'No, God forbid, for I was in Beirut[2] on Sunday,' and he can prove by reference to one or more brothers that it is true, the brother who is accused should be acquitted, and the brothers who have accused him are found guilty of having lied against him, they may be charged with conspiracy; and in such a manner defence may be achieved, not by another thing or in any other way.

409. And if it happens that two or more brothers accuse another brother or two or more and the Master or the one who holds chapter suspects that the brothers brought the accusation out of malice, he may and should make the one brother leave the chapter and hear from the other of what thing he charges his fellow brother, and how he knows the thing of which he accuses him, and if he saw or heard it; and when he has enquired deeply into the matter, he should and may make him go outside, and call the other and hear from him just as he did the other, what he knows of the matter. If they both agree, the brother who has been accused is found guilty, and if they do not agree, the brother who has been accused is acquitted and cleared of that thing of which he had been accused; and so, much evil may be noted against the other two and great wickedness counted [against them] and even conspiracy.

408.1 Château Pèlerin, or Athlit, lies to the south of Acre on the Israeli coast. The pass was often the scene of encounters between the Templars and Moslems. In order to guard the pass the Order built a watchtower and in 1217/8 the castle. It was attacked often, but resisted until 1291.
408.2 Beirut was captured in 1111 by king Baldwin and lost in 1291. It was one of the most important fortified towns in the Kingdom of Jerusalem, lying to the north of Sidon.

410. And let it be known that no brother of the Temple may be convicted by any secular man nor by a man of another order, nor by two or more, except by brothers of the Temple, and in the manner given above, of anything in such a way that the justice of the house falls upon him.

411. But if any worthy secular man or religious, such as is worthy of being believed or who is a *confrère* of the house, says to the Master in truth that such-and-such a brother has brought shame on the house, the Master, with the guarantee of those worthy men, may harass that brother a great deal, and give him much hardship, and he should do it without speaking to the brothers and without their judgement. And let it be known that the good Master should separate and distance the wicked brother from the company of the good ones, and thus commands the Rule.[1]

412. When the one who holds chapter asks the brothers for their advice on anything in chapter, he should first ask those who should know most about the matter and the customs of the house, and afterwards the others communally, according to their worth and knowledge, and the goodness of their lives.

Each brother, when his advice is asked in chapter, should say what seems best to him, for it should not be omitted out of love for the one or hatred of the other, nor to appease the one or anger the other; but he should have God fully before his eyes, and he should do and say what he says and does out of love for God. No brother should accuse another brother except out of charity and with the intention of saving his soul.

413. When any brother is charged with any thing or fault which he has committed, he should not become angry, rather he should thank the one who has accused him; and if a brother accuses another of trifles, he may be given penance.

414. And all the brothers of the Temple should know that when a brother is sent out of chapter, either because he is accused of any failing or because he himself has voluntarily pleaded for mercy, the behaviour and life of the brother should be considered, and the type and gravity of the fault. And if the person is of good behaviour and the fault is slight, the brothers should pass a light sentence, and if the person is of bad behaviour and the fault is serious and vile, the brothers should give him a harsh and hard penance; and often a worthy man is given a light penance for a serious fault, and a wicked man a heavy penance for a slight fault: for just as the good man should have profit and honour in his goodness, also the wicked should have loss and shame in his wickedness.

And let it be known that for the smallest fault and disobedience by which a brother transgresses the commandment of the house, two full days during the first week should be considered, according to the behaviour of the brother; but for no failing should more be considered unless it touches on the habit or the house, from which God keep each brother.

411.1 See §46.

415. And you should know that after the one who holds chapter has sent a brother out of chapter in order to judge his fault, that brother may not return to the chapter to accuse another brother without permission; but he may and should return without permission to plead for mercy for another fault which he had forgotten.

Each brother should voluntarily do the penance which he is given by chapter.

Penances

416. And these are the penances which the brothers may be given, those who have deserved them. The first is to be expelled from the house, from which God keep each one. – The second is to lose the habit. – The third is when a brother is allowed to keep the habit for love of God. – The fourth is two days and a third during the first week. – The fifth, when what may be taken from a brother except the habit is taken from a brother, that is two days. – The sixth is one day. The seventh is Fridays. – The eighth is by the judgement of the chaplain brother. – The ninth is acquittal. The tenth is deferred.[1]

417. The first is to be expelled from the house for ever.

Moreover, it may and should be given to any brother for nine things,[1] of which the first is simony. That is to say, when a brother enters the house through a gift or promise he has made, or another for him, to his knowledge, which please God it is not so: for he who enters the house in such a manner will be expelled from the house if he is proven guilty of it; and he who gave him the habit in such a way should lose his own habit, and should never have any brother under his command, nor have the authority to give the Temple's habit; and all the brothers who are agreed that the habit was given in such a way, if they knew that they should not do so, should lose their habits, and they should never be asked to make anyone a brother.

418. The second is if a brother discloses his chapter to any man, a brother or any other, unless he was there.

The third is if a brother kills a Christian man or woman.

The fourth is if a brother is tainted with the filthy, stinking sin of sodomy, which is so filthy and so stinking and so repugnant that it should not be named.

The fifth is if a brother conspires against another brother; and conspiracy is committed by two or more, for one man alone cannot conspire.

419. The sixth is if a brother flees from the field [of battle] for fear of the Saracens, while the piebald banner is aloft, and leaves the banner. And this includes knight brothers and sergeant brothers while they are armed with swords. But if there is any sergeant brother who is not armed with a sword, and his conscience tells him that he cannot be of assistance, nor do what is necessary there, he may retreat to the rear without causing harm to the house if he does

416.1 The order of the last two is reversed. The ninth should be deferment, the tenth acquittal.

417.1 Cf. the list given in §§224–32. In §418 sodomy replaces leaving a castle except by the prescribed gate, a failing which is incorporated into the explanation of theft given in §423.

not fall short in any other way. But a knight brother may not act in such a way, whether he is armed with a sword or not; for he should not leave the banner for anything without permission, neither because of a wound nor for anything else.

420. But if the knight brother or sergeant brother is wounded in such a way that it seems to him that he cannot do what is necessary, he may obtain permission to retreat or have it obtained for him; and the Marshal or the one who is in his place should give it to him if he asks him, or to another for the wounded brother, and with this permission the wounded brother may retreat without causing harm to the house. And if it happens that the knight brother and sergeant brother are both without swords, they should remain in this way with the banner all together, both knight brother and sergeant brother, for none should leave while there is a piebald banner aloft. And if anyone does so, he will be expelled from the house, if he is a sergeant; for from the moment they are all armed together, they should all together take what God wishes to give them.

421. But if it happens that there is no piebald banner aloft, and there is another Christian banner aloft, they should go to that one, whether they are armed with swords or not, as is said above, and especially to that of the Hospital. And if there is no Christian banner, each one may go to the garrison which God will direct him to and indicate without causing harm to the house; but it is a good thing if our brothers keep always together if they can, either with a banner or without.

422. The seventh is if a brother is found to be a heretic, that is if he does not believe in the articles of faith in which the Church of Rome believes and commands him to believe.

The eighth is if a brother leaves the house and goes to the Saracens.

423. The ninth is if a brother steals things from the house; this sin has so many branches, and whoever does not studiously guard against it may fall in so many ways; nonetheless, for each way, when a brother commits it, he will be expelled from the house because of it, if he is proven guilty of it. And let it be known that it is called theft when the brother removes things from the house. And if a brother leaves a castle or other fortified house at night except by the gate, he is considered a thief. If the Master or a commander asks a brother who is under his command to show him the things of the house that are under his command and authority, the brother should show them all; and if he keeps anything back and does not show it, he will be considered a thief.

424. If a brother leaves the house and in going takes anything he should not, and in the same way with that thing spends two nights outside the house, he will be considered a thief. If a brother places the alms outside the house by giving or lending them or pledging them, he should not deny them if anyone asks, rather he should gather them together. For if he denies them and afterwards is proven to have them, he will be considered a thief. And for all the above-named things, all the brothers who do them will be expelled from the house without re-entry.[1]

424.1 An example of this is given in §566.

425. And all the brothers of the Temple should know that when they have a brother who, by his sin or by his great misfortune leaves the house and goes away, that brother should studiously ensure that he does not take anything other than what we will name hereafter. He may go just as he goes to prime in the chapel, except that he should not wear two of anything, nor an arming dagger; but he may wear his shirt, his breeches, his tunic, his hauberk, his *garnache*, his belt, his hose and his shoes; and he may wear a mantle or his cope, but if he wears one he may not wear the other. Moreover, if the mantle is asked of him, he should return it and should not keep it under any circumstances. The second night he will be expelled from the house for ever.

426. Let it further be known that whatever is asked of him, the brother will be expelled from the house if he keeps it, since he has been outside the house two nights or more; and so he will be expelled for two nights just as for a hundred. But you should know that it is a very good thing, and is an act of charity and mercy if the mantle is asked of him. And so he may take a coif and a pair of breeches. And all the above-named things are to include those that he is wearing on his body when he goes outside the house, but he should not take them from another brother.

427. The things he should not take are these: that is to say neither gold nor silver nor any arms. That is, *chapeau de fer*, surcoat, arming jacket, hauberk, sleeveless coat of mail, sword, lance, shield, Turkish mace, arming dagger, iron hose, crossbow, Turkish arms, and briefly everything included in these words, 'nothing that appertains to arms'. And if he takes away any of the above-named things, he will be expelled from the house without re-entry.

Each brother should ensure that he does not put his hand into the money or trunk of another brother without permission from the one who may give it, and if he does so he may be considered a thief, and even more so if the brother who does it is badly behaved.

428. And if a brother does anything for which he should be expelled from the house for ever, before he is given leave from the house he should go naked in his breeches, a rope round his neck, to the chapter in front of all the brothers; and he should kneel before the Master and should do just as is commanded of one who is put on penance for a year and a day; and afterwards the Master should give him a letter of dismissal so that he may go and save himself in a stricter order.[1]

429. And some of our brothers say that he should enter the order of St Benedict or St Augustine, and that he should not enter any other order; but we do not agree with this, for he may enter any stricter order in order to save his soul, if the brothers of that order wish to consent to it, except the order of the Hospital of St John, of which it was established in this way with the agreement of the brothers of the Temple and of those of the Hospital, that no brother who leaves the Hospital should come to the Temple in such a way that he takes the

428.1 I.e. Cistercian, Benedictine, Carthusian.

habit of their house.[1] Nor may any brother of the Temple enter the order of St Lazarus unless he becomes a leper;[2] nor may a brother who leaves the house of the Temple enter a more lenient order without the dispensation of the one who has the authority.

430. You should further know that there are some other things for which a brother of the Temple may be expelled from the house. For it is established in our house that when the Master or another who has the authority to give the habit of the house to any man wishes to do so he should make him swear on the Holy Gospel that he will tell the truth about everything he will ask him; and when he has sworn and promised, the one who is to make him a brother should say to him, 'Good gentle friend, take care to tell the truth about everything we will ask you, for if you lie and afterwards it is proven that you have lied, you will be put in irons and you will be severely put to shame and will be expelled from the house because of it.'

431. Afterwards, if he is to be a knight brother, the one who makes him a brother should ask him, 'Good gentle friend, have you, or any man for you that you know of, given or promised anything to any man for which he will help you to enter our Order, for that would be simony, and you would not be able to save yourself. Are you a knight and son of a knight or are you descended from knights through your father, in such a way that you should and may be a knight? Were you born in legal wedlock? Have you made a vow or promise or worn the habit of any other order? Have you a woman for a wife or fiancée or betrothed: tell the truth, for if you lie and are found guilty, your habit will be taken away and you will be severely put to shame, and afterwards you will be sent back to your wife. Do you owe any debt through which the house may suffer: for if you do your habit will be taken away and you will be severely put to shame and you will be sent back to your creditor. Have you any secret illness? Are you a priest or in holy orders?'

432. And he who wishes to be a brother should reply briefly, yes or no, to each of the above-mentioned questions; moreover he should tell the truth every time, for if he lies and afterwards it is proven that he has lied and perjured himself, he should be put in irons and severely put to shame, and then dismissed from the house; also if he has a wife; and if he is in debt he should be sent back to his creditor.

433. But the worthy men of our house so agree that, if the one who would be sent back in this way can arrange for his wife to enter another order and become a nun, or if it happens that she dies and he has in every other way led a good and

429.1 This agreement was made during the mastership of Roger de Molins for the Hospitallers and Eudes de Saint-Amand for the Templars.

429.2 The Order of St Lazarus was founded in the East probably in the 1130s. It followed the rule of St Augustine and received, like the Hospitallers and Templars, numerous privileges and donations. However, it was not confirmed by the papacy until 1255. The knights wore a green cross on their mantles.

honest life, without the customs of the house being broken, he may return to the house if it please the brothers, without doing penance; but he should make his vow and promise just as before at the beginning. And of the one who should be sent back to his creditor, our worthy men say that he may act in the same way, when he is rid of the creditor in such a way that he cannot ask anything of him, nor of the house for him.

434. But if they are priests or in holy orders, that is deacons or sub-deacons, they should not be put in irons, nor should they be put to any shame except having their habits taken away from them, and afterwards should be sent to the patriarch or the archbishop. And they should not allow that brother to remain in the habit of a knight, for our Rule[1] forbids any brother to wear a white mantle if he is not a knight; nor was it ever the custom or seen that a chaplain brother wore a white mantle in the house of the Temple, unless he was called to the service of a bishopric or archbishopric. But when it happens that any chaplain brother is elected archbishop or bishop of any church, he may wear a white mantle; but before he wears it he should ask both the Master and the convent very humbly and devoutly that they grant him the habit of a knight brother, and they should grant it to him with good will and voluntarily for love of the dignity which he has attained and so that great honour comes to the Order.

435. A knight should not be asked if he is the serf or slave of any man, for since he has said that he is a knight through his father, born in legal wedlock, if it is true he is naturally free.

436. But if he says he is a knight and such a one as may and should be a knight as is said above, and it is not true, the white mantle should be taken away and he should be dismissed from the house, and he may be severely put to shame. But nevertheless, the worthy men of the house say that if the brother has lost the white mantle in this way and asks with great devotion that, for love of God and Our Lady and out of pity and mercy, he be granted the habit of a sergeant brother, and he promises to serve God and the house of the Temple in the habit of a sergeant brother, well and humbly and loyally as any other good sergeant brother, and to obey the commandments of the house, and keep his vow and promise just as he promised to God and Our Lady and the house, they may allow it in this way, and grant and give him the habit of a sergeant brother.[1] And the Master, or another who has his authority as if the Master were there, should give him the habit of a sergeant brother round his neck and should ask him, before he gives him that habit, if he promises as is said above; and if he agrees, then he may put the mantle round his neck, and should grant him the bread and water of the house and the other things that the brothers are promised just as it was done at the beginning. And thus may our worthy men act if it please them, but it should be done with the advice of the brothers.

437. But you should know that if it does not seem fitting to the brothers that

434.1 See §17.
436.1 An example of this is given in §586.

this brother remain in the house, they may dismiss him for ever, and let it be known that any brother who has been dismissed from our house should go as soon as possible to a stricter order. And in any case he should do this within forty days if he can, and if he does not wish to enter an order, and the brothers can find him, they should take him and put him in irons, and give him his subsistence, and they should keep him in this way until he has thought, or another for him, of his arrangements as is described above. And it was established in this way because any wicked man, when he left the house, could go about the world and live shamefully and improperly and cause much harm and shame to the house, and for this reason it was established that it could never happen.

438. When the one who wishes to be a brother is asked if he has any secret illness, he should tell the truth; and if he has the illness and denies it – for when he is made a brother he is asked it in chapter – and afterwards, when the habit has been given to him, it is proven that he has lied, he may be put in irons and expelled from the house, if the illness is such that his whole body is affected or any of his limbs, or if it is believed that he may never be cured of it in truth. But if the illness is slight and such that he should recover in a short while, it would not be a good thing for him to be expelled from the house, for it does not include these slight illnesses, rather they should treat him with pity and mercy.

439. And yet if the brother is afflicted, the brothers may allow him into their house, if it please them, with his habit, if the illness does not in itself lead to any other disfigurement; but this permission should be given with the advice of the brothers. But let it be known that it would not be a good thing for it to be customary in the house to allow them to stay in this way, since they would be perjured if the illness touched the body and the limbs. And moreover all should know that if the illness touches on leprosy or that evil disease called epilepsy, or if it is another infectious disease, he should be dismissed from the house for ever, for under no circumstances may and should one who has been dismissed from the house be kept in the company of the brothers. The house is not obliged to prove anything because he denied it when he was asked about it on oath and perjured himself.

440. But if the one who is ill in this way confesses it before the one who is to give him the habit and before all the chapter in the hearing of all, when the one who is to make him a brother asks him, and afterwards the one who has asked him gives him the habit, if it is done with the agreement of the brothers in front of whom the sick person has confessed and revealed his illness, his habit should not and may not be taken from him, nor should he be dismissed from the house unless he requests it; but he may be put in any private place away from the company of the brothers, and in that place he should be given what he requires like any other sick brother.

441. But the one who has given him the habit and all those who were in agreement in this way deserve to have their habits taken away, for they should not nor may they keep them, in reason, because the habit was given with their

consent to such a man who was not worthy of it. And you should know that the brothers who were in agreement have troubled their consciences to such an extent and so seriously that they should never again be asked their advice in making a brother; and the one who has knowingly given the habit to such a man, or to another who was not worthy, should never again have the authority to make a brother, rather he should have lost it for ever.

442. And if any vile disease befalls a brother after he has received our habit, that brother should be put in any private place, just as is said above, and be well provided with what he requires for his illness while he lives, if the disease does not touch upon leprosy, for that should be dealt with otherwise and in another manner.

443. When it befalls any brother that by the will of Our Lord he contracts leprosy and the thing is proven, the worthy men of the house should admonish him and ask him to request permission to leave the house and go to St Lazarus, and take the habit of a brother of St Lazarus; and the sick brother, if he is a good man, should obey them, and yet it would be better if he requested the said permission himself before being admonished and asked. And if the brother asks for the said permission, the Master or the one it concerns should give the said permission, but he should do so with the advice of the brothers; and afterwards the Master and the worthy men of the house should look after him and help him until the habit of St Lazarus is given to him. And so they should studiously take care of such of our brothers, that he becomes a brother of St Lazarus in such a way that he does not lack any of the things he requires for his meagre upkeep for as long as he lives.

444. However, let it be known that if the brother who contracts leprosy in this way is so stubborn that he does not wish to request the aforementioned permission nor leave the house, the habit should not nor may it be taken from him, nor should he be expelled from the house, but, just as is said above of the others who have vile diseases, he should be placed apart from the company of the other brothers and in that place should be maintained.

445. And let it be known that all the things a knight brother is asked when he is to be a brother, all those same things and in the same way a sergeant brother is asked when it is wished to give him the habit; and that same justice should be exacted if he lies. And furthermore a sergeant brother is asked if he is the serf or slave of any man; and if he is, and confesses it before the brothers, he should not be given the habit; and if he denies it when he is asked in the chapter where he is to be made a brother, and afterwards when he is a brother it is proven that he has lied, the habit should be taken from him and he should be sent back to his lord forcibly.

446. If the one who is a sergeant brother is a knight and he denies it also in chapter when the one who is to make him a brother asks him, and because of this the habit of a sergeant brother is given to him, and afterwards he is found guilty of being a knight, the habit should be taken away from him and he should

be put in irons, and should be severely put to shame and be dismissed from the house; for if he is a knight and such a one as should be, he cannot remain in the house in the habit of a sergeant brother, for just as one who is not should not be, nor wear a white mantle in the house, so one who is a knight in the same way as he should be should not wear a brown habit in the house.

447. Some say that if it please the Master and the brothers to grant him the white mantle through pity and mercy, in this way they may keep him in the house, but he may not remain without a white mantle. But we do not agree that such a man should ever remain in the house, for by such dissemblance, betrayal and harm may be caused and brought to the house and the brothers.

448. No brother of the Temple, for as much as he is a gentleman, if he is not a knight before he is given the habit of the Temple, may ever be a knight or wear a white mantle after he has received the habit, unless he is made a bishop or better, as has been recounted above.[1]

449. When it is wished to make a chaplain brother a brother, he should be asked everything as is said of the knight brother or the sergeant brother in the same way, except that he is not asked if he is the serf or slave of any man, for since he is a priest he must be free, nor if he has a woman as wife, fiancée or betrothed. And in the same way the one whom it is wished to make a chaplain brother should tell the truth when he is asked like the one whom it is wished to make a knight or sergeant brother. And if he lies and afterwards it is proven that he has lied, he may be treated just as is said above of any other brother, except that he is not put in irons nor put to any shame, but the habit is taken from him and he is sent back to the patriarch or archbishop.

450. And so there is yet one other thing for which a brother may be expelled from the house; that is to say if any man enters the house as a layman and is given the habit of the house as a layman, and afterwards he has himself ordained in holy orders without the permission of the one who may give it, he may be dismissed from the house if the Master and the brothers agree. But they may allow him to stay in the house if they wish in the habit of a chaplain brother; but he may not remain in the habit of our house in any other habit or in any other office, after he is ordained in holy orders in our house. But whatever is done should be done with the advice of the brothers. And if the Master and brothers allow him to remain in the house, they should make him plead for mercy for the disobedience he has committed, for he had himself ordained without permission, and they should give him a severe and harsh penance, according to the discretion of the brothers and according to his other behaviour. But it would be a more beneficial thing if he were dismissed for ever, as a warning to others.

451. The second penance that may be given to a brother is the hardest and harshest after being expelled from the house; that is to lose his habit, from which God keep each brother; and this penance may be given to a brother for numerous misfortunes which may befall him. For a brother may lose his habit if he has

---

448.1 See §434.

knocked down and struck another brother in anger or wrath in a manner which has caused his feet to move from their position, or if he has broken in wrath the laces of his mantle. And that brother who acts in such a way will be excommunicated and should receive absolution. And as soon as the brother is without his habit, his armour should be returned to the saddlery in the caravan, and so it may be given to the brothers when they have need of it, and his horses also should be returned to the Marshal's caravan, and so he may give them to the brothers who need them.

452. And if a brother strikes any Christian in anger with anything a blow from which could kill or maim, he should not keep his habit.

If a brother is proven to have lain with a woman, he should not keep his habit and should be put in irons. And he should never again carry the piebald banner or seal, nor should he have brothers under his command, or be involved in the election of a Master in such a way that he is one of the thirteen electors.

453. If a brother lies, he should not keep his habit.

If a brother says that another of his brothers has said or done anything for which he should or may be expelled from the house if it were proven, and he does not succeed in having him convicted, and he has done all in his power to have him found guilty, and he does not wish to repent or retract, but rather remain for ever in his folly, he may not keep his habit.

454. For let it be known that when a brother accuses another brother in his chapter of something for which the brother who is accused of the thing may be expelled from the house if it were proven, and the brother does not succeed in having him found guilty, he should lose his habit if he does not wish to retract, and speak in this way, 'Good lord brothers, before all in the chapter I make known to you that the evil I spoke of him is all lies, for truly I know only good.' The habit is at the discretion of the brothers, whether to take it from him or let him keep it. And let it be known that such a brother who in this way has retracted in his chapter should never again be believed against any brother, in anything which touches on the house or the habit, nor should his advice be asked, for he has proven himself guilty of wickedness, and no-one, after he has been proven guilty of wickedness should ever be believed against any good man.

455. If a brother kills or loses a slave through his own fault he should not keep his habit.

If a brother says for certain, or says in anger or wrath that he is going to the Saracens and some brothers hear him, and the brother who has said the words is not of good behaviour, he may not keep his habit; but if the brother is of good behaviour, the habit is at the mercy of the brothers, whether to take it from him or let him keep it.

456. If a brother kills or maims a saddled animal in anger or wrath, or through his own fault, the habit is at the discretion of the brothers.

If a brother carries anything belonging to secular people or anyone else not of the Temple, and says that it belongs to the Temple and it is not true, and the lords of the lands may lose their rights and tolls to it, he may not keep his habit.

If any brother who does not have the authority gives away a live, four-legged animal, except a dog or cat, outside the house, the habit is at the mercy of the brothers.

457. If any brother rebels against the commandments of the house and refuses to obey them without repenting and remains in his folly, and does not wish to make amends despite prayers and warnings, his habit may be taken from him and he may be put in irons and kept in this way for a long time. But it is better, when it happens that a brother, either in anger or wrath, says that he will not carry out the commandment of the house, that his anger is left to cool down; and afterwards someone should go to him and say to him quietly and calmly, 'Good brother, for love of God carry out the commandment of the house.' And if he does it and no harm has been caused, he should be tolerated for love of God and should be shown pity, and may be shown great goodness and mercy; and this way is better according to God. And if he does not wish to do it, his habit should be taken away and he should be put in irons as is said above.

458. If the Master or another commander who holds chapter orders a brother who is under his command to plead for mercy for anything, and the brother does not wish to plead for mercy, but rather remain in his folly, he should not keep his habit. But it cannot be done in this way if an ordinary brother accuses another ordinary brother; for if an ordinary brother does not wish to plead for mercy for another brother who is not his commander, he should not lose his habit; but he may be given a severe, harsh and heavy penance. For immediately a brother says to another, 'Plead for mercy for such-and-such a thing,' the brother should plead for mercy if he is in the place, and do as is said above.

459. If a brother asks for permission to leave in his chapter, and they do not wish to grant it, and thereupon he says that he is going away and leaving the house, he should not keep his habit.

If a brother breaks the Master's seal, he should not keep his habit.

And some of our old men say that if any brother breaks the seal of the one who takes the place of the Master, his habit may be taken away from him for the same reason, although the fault is not so serious, because of the harm that could come of it.

460. If a brother gives the habit of the house in a way he should not, or gives it to such a man as is not worthy of it, he may not keep his habit, and the one who gave him the habit in this way should never again have the authority to make brothers.

If any brother lends the alms of the house without permission to such a man or in such a place as the house may lose them, he should not keep his habit. If a brother who does not have the authority, gives the alms of the house to secular people or to an order other than the Temple without permission, he should not keep his habit.

461. If a brother for whom it is not fitting builds a new house of stone or lime without permission, he should not keep his habit. Other ruined houses he may

repair and equip without harm coming of it, rather he should be shown much gratitude.

462. If a brother leaves the house in anger or wrath and sleeps one night outside without permission, his habit may be taken away from him if it is wished and if it please the brothers, and he may be allowed to keep it if it please the brothers. But let it be known of this thing that the brother and his behaviour should be considered: if he is of good behaviour and leads a good and honest life, the brothers should show him more goodness, and all the better, they may let him keep his habit, and more boldly and easily they should and may agree to let him keep it. But if he sleeps two nights outside without permission, and has returned in their entirety the things he should return, and has taken away nothing he should not, he may recover his habit when he has done penance for a year and a day; but before he has done penance for a year and a day he may not recover it. But if he takes away anything he should not, and sleeps two nights outside, and that without permission, he is lost to the house for ever. And let it be known that it is certain for a brother who leaves the house, if he does not wish to return immediately within the two days, that on the second day he sends his mantle to the house; for if he keeps it for two nights, he may be expelled from the house as is said above.

463. If a brother throws his habit on the ground in anger in front of other brothers, and the brothers beseech him to pick up his habit, and he does not wish to, and any brother removes it before he has picked it up, he may not recover it for a year and a day; but if any brother takes the habit of the brother who has thrown it down and puts it round his neck, that brother who in this way has returned the habit to the brother who threw it down will lose his own habit, and the other brother who in this way recovered it will be at the mercy of the brothers, whether to take it from him or let him keep it. And you should know that the one who in this way returned the habit to the brother who threw it down will lose his habit for this reason, for no brother who cannot give the habit may return it, and whoever does so will lose his own. And just as the habit is given in chapter, so it should be returned in chapter, and for this reason each brother should know that no commander may take the habit from a brother who refuses his order, although the brother is under his command, for no commander who cannot make a brother should take the habit from a brother.

464. But if it happens that any commander who cannot make a brother has brothers under his command, and any of those brothers refuses to carry out his order, he should admonish him as is said above; and afterwards, if he does not wish to carry out the order, he may immediately sound the bell and assemble the brothers. And when the brothers are assembled, he should hold chapter and make the brother plead for mercy because he has refused to carry out his order, and he should send him outside; and the brothers should all agree that sentence be deferred, either before the Master or before that commander who has the authority to take away the habit.

465. And no failing for which a brother may lose his habit should be considered or judged before such a one who does not have the authority to take away the habit, nor should the one who holds chapter allow it, or the brothers agree to it; and if any agrees to it, he may be considered to have failed and given a heavy penance, for it would not be reasonable for the brothers to make their judgement on a brother before such a person who may not take from the brother what the brothers have judged, whatever may be the sentence of the brothers, heavy or light. And for this reason it was established in the house, according to whether the failing is serious or slight, that it should be considered before the Master or before such a commander who has the authority to carry out the sentence of the brothers whatever it is, heavy or light.

466. And let it be known that often it happens in the Temple that a commander may make a sergeant brother and not a knight brother, and that commander who cannot make a knight brother should not, nor may he take the habit from a knight brother, for none should take nor may he, except such habit as he may give to a brother. And just as each one should ensure that he does not give the habit in a way he should not, so he should ensure that he does not take it from another brother in a way he should not; and if he does, he should be subject to the same justice. And so that the habit is not taken away in a manner in which it should not be, it was established that it should be taken away before the Master or such a one who takes the place of the Master. And no-one has the authority to make a brother or to take away the habit privately, unless he takes the place of the Master or unless the Master has given him permission specially to do so.

467. If a brother tears or gives back his habit willingly, he should not recover it for a year and a day.

And you should know that, whatever has been said above, for all the things which have been recounted for which a brother may lose his habit, always it is at the mercy of the brothers, whether to take it from him or let him keep it, except for these last three: that is to say the one who throws it down, if another brother has removed it before he has picked it up, and the one who gives it back willingly, and the one who has slept two nights outside without permission, just as is said above.

468. And let it be known that while a brother is without his habit, he should remain outside the door of the chapel and on Sundays should come to corporal punishment after the Gospel to the chaplain brother if he is present, and if the chaplain brother is not there, to that priest who takes the office, and should come to his punishment with great devotion and receive it with patience before all the people who are in the chapel. And when that brother comes to punishment, he should be completely naked except for his breeches, which he should have pulled on, and his feet should be covered in hose and shoes. And when he has received the punishment, he should go outside the chapel again, there where his clothes are, and should dress himself in his clothes and hear the office of Our Lord quietly and in silence like any other brother; for every brother who is on

penance without his habit is required to hear the office of Our Lord in its entirety, like any other good brother; and when he wishes to be absent from the hours, he should obtain permission or have it obtained just like any other brother.

469. But if it happens that any brother who is on penance for a year and a day is ill in such a way that it is fitting that he remains all that year or a great part of the year in his place without going to the chapel, at the end of the year he should be given back his habit. And the time he has remained ill in his place should also be counted as served, like that time which he has served of all his penance, and as if he had come each day to the chapel and each Sunday to his punishment; because it has not rested with him that he has not done his penance, and when God wishes to give health or illness to a man, no-one can refuse it. And if the brother dies doing his penance, he should be treated like any other brother, and the cross should be sewn on him as on any other brother.

470. While a brother is on penance, he should sleep in the hospital, and if he is ill, the Almoner should see that he has the things he requires for his illness; and while he is ill he may eat in the hospital. And while he is healthy, he should work with the slaves, and when he eats he should sit on the ground before the household and eat of their food, and always he should wear a cope without a cross.

471. And if the Almoner at any time augments any of the household's portion in front of the brothers, he should not give anything at all to those brothers who are on the ground, whether they are without habit or have all their habit, for they should not have any of it at all. But if the Master eats in the convent, he may send some of the food in front of him to the brothers who eat on the ground, but no-one else may give them anything; not even the Master himself may give them anything if he eats in the infirmary or anywhere else except in the convent. And thus may the Master act towards a brother who is on penance with all his habit.

472. And each brother who is on penance without his habit should fast three days a week on bread and water, until God and the brothers release him from any of the days; and the brother, if he does his penance well, they may release from one or two days when it seems good to them. And these are the days he should fast for as long as he is without his habit: Monday, Wednesday and Friday. And when the brothers release another brother who is without his habit from a day, the first from which they release him should be understood as the Monday, and the second the Wednesday; and neither the brothers nor anyone else may release him from the third, that is from the Friday. For it is fitting that every brother who eats on the ground by judgement of the brothers fasts on Friday, whether he is without his habit or has all his habit; but as soon as he is raised from the ground, he is free of the Friday and of all the other days as long as it appertains to that penance for which he was put on the ground that time.

473. And when the habit is returned to a brother who has been on penance

without his habit, he should not be raised immediately from the ground, rather he should eat on the ground with all his habit at least once or more. And while he is on the ground, after the habit is given back to him, he remains there on the Friday; but after he has eaten once on the ground with all his habit, he may be raised when it pleases God and the brothers; and so he may be kept there for a long time if it please the brothers and he has not done his penance in the way he should.

474. And no brother should leave the house in order to enter another order without the permission of the Master and of the convent, and if he does otherwise, and does not have the permission of the Master and of the convent, and he wishes to return to the house, he may not regain entry to the house for a year and a day, during which time he will be on penance just as is said above; and this is customary in the house. And yet some say that after the brother has asked permission to enter another order, and the Master and the convent have given it, and the brother has entered it with this permission, that brother should never return to our house, nor should the convent allow it.

475. And let it be known that [if] our father the pope, who is master and father of our Order above all others after Our Lord, requests the house on behalf of anyone who in this or any other way has left the house, he does so saving the justice of the house; for he does not nor wishes to lightly make a request by which the justice of the house is lost, rather he wishes and commands that it be meted out to those who have deserved it according to the customs of the house.

476. And every brother, after his habit has been taken from him by the judgement of the brothers, is free and quit of all the other penances that he had to do at that time when his habit was taken from him; and it was established in this way because the penance is very heavy, and harsh the great misfortune and the great misery and shame that he suffers when he loses his habit, and all the honour that he will never have in the house. But for the one who is on a year and a day the penances that he had to do when he left the house are not pardoned, rather he is required to do them when he recovers his habit, because he has not been put to shame nor had his habit taken from him in front of the brothers, rather by his own wickedness he has shamed firstly his body and then God and the brothers and the house of the Temple; for he has left such a good and holy company as is the house of the Temple, or because he rid himself of such an honoured and fine thing as is the habit of the Temple. He should not benefit from his folly nor from his wickedness, rather he should suffer.

477. And no brother who has lost his habit by the judgement of the brothers or in any other way through his folly, as is said above, should ever give his advice in chapter against a brother, on a fault which could lead to expulsion from the house or loss of the habit, nor should the one who holds chapter ask him anything about it. No brother who has lost his habit through his wickedness should ever nor may ever bring a charge against another brother of anything which touches on the habit or the house, nor should anyone believe him; but as

long as it incurs a penance of two or three days or less he may bring a charge and give his advice.

478. No brother who has lost his habit through his wickedness should ever carry the seal or purse of the Temple, nor should he nor may he be a commander of knights, nor carry the piebald banner, nor have brothers under his command; neither should the Master or any other who holds chapter ask the advice, on anything which is done by the judgement of the brothers, of any brother who has troubled his conscience in chapter if he is found guilty of it, nor should he give it.

479. Neither the Master nor any other may in reason acquit a brother of a fault which leads to expulsion from the house or loss of the habit, nor should he allow him to be acquitted; and if he does so he acts against God and against his promise, for justice should be meted out to each brother when he does what he should not, and thus it should be meted out to the greater as to the lesser; for the higher the position the person holds the more odious is the act, if he does what he should not, and the more serious and odious the failing, the better it is that justice is meted out.

480. And if a brother does anything for which he may be expelled from the house, and sentence for that thing is deferred, he may not nor should he bring a charge against another brother, of a serious or slight failing, while that sentence is deferred.

481. No brother who has done anything for which he should be expelled from the house, and for which a brother may have him convicted, even if sentence is deferred, which may and should not be done, should ever bring a charge against a brother for either a serious or slight failing, neither should he nor may he give his advice, nor should the one who holds chapter ask him for it; neither should he nor may he accuse a brother of anything that he has done, even if he has seen it. For he should not be believed against a brother in anything; for none who has done anything for which he should be expelled from the house is a brother of the Temple, and especially if he can be convicted of it by two or more brothers who know him.

482. And let it be known that the brothers who know that any brother has done anything for which he should be expelled from the house, fail seriously if they conceal it, for since he has done something for which he should be expelled from the house, he does not remain in the house in the manner in which a good brother should remain there, from which he will never profit and great harm could come to the house. – And for no failing for which a brother should be expelled from the house after he is found guilty, may a brother be given any other penance except expulsion from the house, unless it is as is recounted above, one of the things he is asked when he comes to chapter to be made a brother, and afterwards it is proven that he has lied.

483. If the Master or another who does or does not hold chapter acquits a brother of a failing which leads to expulsion from the house, even if he does so in

front of the brothers, the brother who is acquitted is not free, for each brother who knows the truth of the matter may and should accuse him of it, every time they are assembled in chapter; and he may be subjected to the justice of the house if he is found guilty. And no brother who cannot make brothers should allow a failing which touches on the house or the habit to be judged before him if he holds chapter.

484. And all the brothers of the Temple should know that if the habit is taken from a brother in chapter, and in that same chapter it is returned to him at the request of the brothers and through his great repentance, after he has gone outside the gate of the house when that same chapter is held, he remains without his habit for two days, for he is pardoned of the third when the habit is returned to him, because of the great shame and great anguish he has received before the brothers. Yet even if in that same chapter, before he has passed through the door, the habit is returned to him at the request of the brothers, but it has been taken from him, he will remain on two days, and he will be pardoned the third as is said above. But it may not be customary for the habit to be returned in this way without going out of the door; when the habit is taken away, it is taken by the common request of the brothers, and it should be returned by common judgement and by common request of the brothers who are in that chapter.

485. Yet the old men of our house say that when a brother is sentenced to lose his habit, he may keep it if he shows great repentance and is of good behaviour; but let it be known that according to the establishments of the house, after it has been judged that the habit should be taken from a brother, it should be taken from him; and afterwards if the brothers wish to let him keep it because of the great repentance that they see in the brother, it is fitting that he be sent outside again, and the request made once more to all communally; and then if the brothers agree to let him keep it, they may let him keep it. And if the brother who has lost his habit eats one meal in the palace without his habit the same day, when the habit is returned to him he remains on one day, for he is pardoned the two days because of the shame he has received, firstly before the brothers, and afterwards before the same brothers and secular people. And if he has thus eaten in the palace twenty or thirty days, when the habit is returned to him, he will remain on one day, for he may not be pardoned that one until chapters are held by the one who specifically has the authority to put him on penance. And none who may neither make a brother nor take away his habit may put a brother on penance without his habit; for it is necessary that the one who puts a brother on penance without his habit has the authority to give him permission, both for himself and for his chapter, to go to another order to save his soul if he asks for the said permission.

486. And when the Almoner wishes to remember him before the brothers, he should speak in this way, 'Good lords, this man, or this sergeant, or this knight' – and he names him – 'who was our brother, is at the main door and requests entry to the house which he left through his folly, and awaits the mercy of the house.' And the one who holds chapter should say, 'Good lord brothers,

do any of you know if this man who was our brother has done anything or taken anything out of the house for which he may not and should not return and regain entry to the house?' And then, if there is any brother who knows anything he should say so, and none should say but what he knows to be true.

487. And if he has done nothing for which he should be expelled from the house as is said above, and that foolish brother has been at the door for a long while in order to better confess his folly, and when it seems good to the worthy men that he should come before them in chapter, he should undress to his breeches at the main door there where he is, and so he should come to chapter with a rope round his neck before the one who holds chapter and before all the brothers, and kneel before the one who holds chapter, and from that place he should beseech and entreat with tears all the brothers communally, and ask them with great humility to have pity on him. And then the one who holds chapter should say to him, 'Good brother, you have behaved foolishly in that you have left the house and your order.' And the one who wishes to regain entry to the house should say that he repents greatly, is very unhappy and very vexed that he has behaved so foolishly, and that he is very willing to make amends just as is established in the house.

488. And if the brother is known to be of bad behaviour and will [not] do his penance well, the one who holds chapter should speak to him in this way, 'Good brother, you know that you have to do heavy and long penance, and if you were to ask leave to go to another order in order to save your soul, I believe you would benefit.' And if he asks for the said leave just as is said above, the one who has the authority to put him on penance also has the authority to give the said leave, with the consent of the brothers who are in the chapter at which he asks for the said leave. And if he does not ask for the said permission, he may not nor should he be given leave, nor should he be denied re-entry into the house for this reason, for he has done nothing for which he should be expelled from the house; but before he comes to chapter in order to plead for mercy, sentence may and should be long deferred and he should be made to wait for a long time at the door in order to well recognise his folly and his misfortune.

489. But, however, if the brother who wishes to regain entry to the house is known to be of good behaviour, the brothers should immediately make him go out of the chapter and should make him dress in that habit which befits him, and he should have a cope without a cross, which he should take possession of from that day. And the one who holds chapter should tell and command the Almoner to take care of him and make him sleep and lodge in his house, for in this way it is established in the house, and to teach him the things he should do. And from the moment he is on penance, the Almoner should teach him what he should do, and should put in writing the day that he commenced his penance, so that it is remembered. And when he has finished his term, that is a year and a day, his habit should be returned to him immediately, and so it should be returned to him by chapter, and he should be treated just as is said above. And every brother who

is on penance without his habit is quit of the year of service which is incumbent upon him, but he should not touch any arms.

490. And let it be known that when a brother who has left the house comes to regain entry to the house, if he leaves the house this side of the sea, he should be sent to where he left the house, and there he should be put on penance and should do just as is said above of regaining entry to the house, if he has done nothing for which he should be expelled from the house. But if he leaves the house overseas and comes this side of the sea in order to plead for mercy and to regain entry to the house, he may be put on penance this side of the sea, if it please the brothers and if it is certain that he has done nothing nor taken anything out of the house for which he should be expelled from the house.

491. And you should also know that when a brother goes away with the intention of leaving the house, the Almoner should call a brother or two worthy men and should go to the place of the brother who has gone away and should put in writing all that he finds of the brother's equipment, neither more nor less; so that, when the brother returns by the will of Our Lord in order to regain entry to the house, it is known if he has taken anything he should not take, and particularly so that it is known if his equipment is found or not when he has gone; and henceforth it should be done just as is said above of giving leave, or putting on penance, or returning the habit.

492. And when his habit is returned to a brother, the one who returns it should speak in this way, 'Good brother, if while you have been on penance you have transgressed the commandment of the house in any way, plead for mercy at the first chapter you attend.' And that brother who has recovered his habit should do just as he has commanded. For let it be known that every brother who is on penance without his habit should guard against transgressing the commandment of the house, and do just as he should do and better as if he had all his habit; and if he sins in anything, he should make amends just like any other brother, when he has recovered his habit, at the first chapter he attends. And no-one's habit should be judged or discussed unless he has committed such a sin for which he may lose it; for it would be a very serious thing to give a brother a penance which he has not deserved, or such justice which should not and may not be meted out according to the establishment of the house.

493. The third and next greatest failing for which a brother may be judged, is when a brother is allowed to keep the habit for love of God, and that brother is on three days[1] until God and the brothers show him mercy and release him from any of the days; and that brother should immediately be put on penance without delay, and should lead an ass or do any other of the basest duties of the house, that is to say wash the bowls in the kitchen, or peel garlic and chives, or make the fire – and the one who leads the ass should be there to help in loading and unloading – and he should wear his mantle laced up tightly, and should go about as humbly as he can.

493.1 I.e. on penance three days a week.

494. And no brother should be ashamed of penance so that he omits to do any of it; but each one should indeed be ashamed of committing the sin, and the penance should each one do willingly. And that brother who is allowed to keep the habit for love of God should do that penance first, before any other that he has to do. And if he is taken ill, the Almoner may give him the broth of the infirmary; and if he is so ill that it is fitting for him to enter the infirmary, he should inform the Almoner of his illness; and he should inform the Master or the one who holds that office, that is the Marshal or the Commander of Knights. And these should assemble the brothers and inform them of the brother's illness and ask their advice, and if, when the brothers have heard the brother's illness, they agree to raise him, he should ask them if they agree that he should be put in the infirmary; and they should agree if the brother is so ill that he has great need of it.

495. And then the brother may enter the infirmary, and there he should conduct himself like any other sick brother and make himself comfortable and eat everything he believes to be good for him like any other brother. But as soon as he is commanded, he should return to his penance without speaking to the brothers, and should not eat in the palace except on the ground, until God and the brothers show him mercy and raise him from the ground; but he may remain in the infirmary until he is able to tolerate the food of the convent.

496. And let it be known that just as the brother who is on penance should be raised by judgement of the brothers, so also should he enter the infirmary by judgement of the brothers if illness befall him, remaining on penance according to the customs of the house, if the brothers do not agree that he should be raised for love of God and because of his illness; and so the brother should do some penance, either three whole days or two days and the third, or two days or one day. And such penance as allowing a brother to keep the habit for love of God is given to a brother who has done something for which he could and should lose his habit, and it may be taken from him with good reason if it please the brothers. And for such a failing which leads to loss of the habit the brothers should not be sentenced to any small penance, for much goodness is shown to a brother after he has done something for which his habit should and may be taken from him and removed: if it is left to him for love of God, so much is at the mercy of the brothers. No brother may be given three whole days unless he has done something for which he may lose his habit.

497. The fourth and next greatest penance which may be given to the brothers is two days, and a third during the first week, if the third is named; but if the third is not named, it should be two days and no more, and this penance may be given to a brother for the slightest failing by which he transgresses the commandment of the house. And if the third day is simply named without determining which should be the third, that third day should be Monday. But if the brothers speak in this way, 'We agree to two days and to the third during the first week on the same day he committed the sin,' he should fast on the third day whichever day it may be, except Sunday. And if he committed the sin on a

Sunday, he should fast on the Monday in place of the Sunday; and if he committed the sin on a Wednesday or Friday, he should fast on Monday for the third day; and on whichever other day he committed the sin, he should fast on that day he committed the sin.

498. The fifth and next greatest penance that may be given to a brother is no more than two days; and a brother who is on two days or on a third for the first week, or on three whole days, should lead an ass and do one of the basest duties of the house. And he should do the penance just as is said above, and should go to corporal punishment on Sundays at the beginning of chapter, before the prayer is said. And when a brother is sentenced to have taken from him what may be taken except his habit, it should be understood as two days and no more; and this should customarily be the greatest penance given to a brother except loss of the habit. But afterwards, because of the wickedness of some evil brothers, one was given the third for the first week because he did not wish to make amends nor keep from doing what he should not do.

499. And that brother who is on two days, or on two and the third, or on three whole days, or on one day, may be told when he is put on penance, if he is a knight brother or a sergeant brother of the convent, that he may take care of his equipment, and if he is a craftsman brother that he may carry out his work or his office.

500. The sixth penance is one day and no more, and that brother who is on one day is not to lead an ass or work, as is said above of those who are on two days, or on two and the third, or on three whole days.

501. And no brother who is on penance on the ground should touch arms unless they are falling into disrepair somewhere and he cannot otherwise repair them. And let it be known that each brother, when he is on penance, should remain quietly in his place from daybreak, and if he knows carpentry or any other skill, he should do it. And all brothers who are on penance should behave in this way.

And no brother, while he is on penance, should answer any call or any command which is made for an assembly of brothers, but privately he may be asked his advice if necessary. And if one brother or two or more are on penance and the alarm is raised, and the brothers are needed, the chapter may lend them horses and arms without raising them from the ground and without showing them great mercy; but as soon as they have returned from the alarm, they should return to their places, as they were before, and behave as they did before. But neither the Master nor anyone else may lend them horses or arms, nor give them permission to take them, without the agreement of the brothers, neither their own nor others', for they may not take their own horses or arms any more than those of the other brothers without permission, while they are on penance.

And let it be known that a brother who is on one day does not go to corporal punishment on Sundays like those who are on two days or more.

502. When the Master or the one who has the authority wishes to put a

brother on penance, he should say to him, 'Good brother, go and undress if you are well.' And if he is well, he should undress and afterwards come before the one who holds chapter, and should kneel. And then the one who holds chapter, or who should give the punishment, should say, 'Good lord brothers, see here your brother who comes to his punishment, pray to Our Lord that He pardon his sins.' And each brother should do this and say one paternoster, and the chaplain brother, if he is present, should also pray to Our Lord for him in such a way as seems good to him. And when the prayer has been said, the one who holds chapter should give the brother his punishment with a whip if he wishes, as he sees fit, and if he does not have a whip he may use his belt if he wishes.

503. And let it be known that when the brothers say this prayer in chapter or anywhere else, they should be standing unless it is such a day as obeisance is made in the chapel; but on all the days when obeisance is made in the chapel, if chapter is held, all the brothers should kneel for all the prayers that are said in chapter communally, for the one at the beginning and the others; and above all on the day nine lessons are read they should kneel for the prayer which is said at the end of chapter, except the one who holds chapter, who should be standing while he says the prayer, but afterwards he should kneel when the chaplain brother gives absolution or when he says his paternoster. And for this reason it was established that the brothers should kneel for that prayer, for the Master or the one who holds chapter frees them from the authority that he had before he commenced his prayer.

504. And after the prayer of the one who holds chapter, each brother should say his confession, and the chaplain brother, after the brothers have said their confessions, should give absolution as he sees fit. And if the chaplain brother is not there when the one who holds chapter has said his prayer, each brother who is kneeling, just as is said above, should say one paternoster, and then he may go if he wishes, if there is no other order.

505. But if the brother who is to be put on penance says that he is not well, the Master or the commander should not force him to enter into his penance unless it is a brother who has been allowed to keep the habit for love of God, for that brother should immediately enter into his penance, be he well or sick, if the illness is not so serious that manifestly he is in great danger; and if it is so, he should be put in the infirmary apart from the brothers immediately, and as soon as he is recovered he should enter into his penance without delay. And if the brother who should enter into his penance says that he has any illness because of which he cannot attend punishment in chapter, the one who holds it may send him to the chaplain brother, who should give the punishment; and every brother who has a secret illness should be treated in the same way, when it is wished to put him on penance, or if he is sentenced to Fridays. And every brother who is to do penance should take his punishment before he commences his penance.

506. And let it be known that each brother should do his penances one after the other in order, just as they are given to him, the one which was given to him

first, and then the others in the same way; except a brother who is allowed to keep the habit for love of God – for that brother who is allowed to keep the habit should do that penance first, even though he has others to do, and should immediately be put on penance without delay, just as is said above – or except if the brothers sentence any brother expressly to do first that penance which they have given him last. For often a brother is sentenced, because of his bad behaviour, or because his failing is so serious, or because he is in the habit of failing, to be immediately put on the penance that he has been given last, first. And it should be done just as the brothers have judged.

507. And that one should immediately be put on penance if he is well; but if he is not well, it should wait until he is recovered. But the one who holds chapter may not release him from entering immediately into his penance, neither because of illness nor for anything else, without speaking to the brothers and asking them; but the brothers should give him respite until he is recovered. But as soon as he is better, he should inform the one who has the authority to put him on penance; and he should assemble the brothers after prime in any private place, except on a day when chapter is to be held, and when the brothers are assembled, that brother should undress just as if he were in chapter, and afterwards he should come before the one who has the authority to put him on penance, and he should kneel. And then the one who holds that office should say to the brothers, 'Good lords, see here your brother who comes to his punishment, pray to Our Lord that He pardon him.' And henceforth they should say the prayer and give the punishment just as if they were in chapter.

508. And every brother who is to receive corporal punishment from the Master or from another who holds chapter, should have his mantle fastened, except that he should keep the hooks outside his collar when he receives the punishment. And all the brothers who are put on penance on the day of chapter, should be put on it at the end of chapter, except a brother who should be put on it immediately his failing has been judged, just as is said above.

509. And when the Master or another who has the authority wishes to give a brother corporal punishment, he should say to the brother, before he gives it, when the prayer has been said for him, 'Good brother, do you repent of having failed in this way?' And he should reply, 'Sire, yes very much.' And the Master or the one who takes his place should say to him, 'Will you take care in future?' And the brother should say, 'Sire, yes, if it please God.' And then he may give such punishment as he pleases and as is customary in the house.

And when he has given it in this way he should say, 'Go and get dressed.' And when he is dressed, he should return before him, and he should say to him, 'Go outside.' And if he wishes, the commander may tell him to take care [of his equipment], if he is a brother of the convent, and he may let him if he wishes; and if he is a craftsman brother, he may order him if he wishes, to see to his work.

510. And the brother who is on penance should not take care of his equipment nor of his work unless he is ordered to, but he should say to a brother,

'Good brother, take care of our equipment.' And the brother to whom he has entrusted his equipment should take care of it like his own; and every brother to whom equipment is entrusted should act in the same way. And it is better for the brother who is on penance to entrust his equipment to another brother, than for him to look after it himself; because if the Marshal or Commander of Knights has need of equipment for the requirements of the house, and draws up ranks in order to take the equipment of sick brothers, the one to whom is entrusted the equipment of the brother who is on penance should get into line for that equipment which he has in his care: and thus should a brother get in line if he is asked, for the equipment of another brother that he has in his care, as he would for his own if he were ordered. And let it be known that when the brothers who have the care of a sick brother's equipment are ordered to line up, those brothers who are on penance should line up, so that it may be taken from those brothers as it is from those who are in the infirmary.

511. And let it be known that the one who holds chapter should give corporal punishment to all the brothers who are on penance, none taking precedence over him, unless they are ill; and if the sick are there the one who holds chapter should send them to the chaplain brother just as is said above. Or if a brother is put on penance during the octave of Christmas or Easter or Pentecost, the chaplain brother should give him that punishment privately. And if a chaplain brother is put on penance, another chaplain brother should give him his punishment. And the chaplain brother should give all the punishment that he gives to the brothers, privately, except that which he gives on Sundays after the Gospel, to a brother who is on penance without his habit.

512. And each brother who is on penance on the ground[1] with all his habit, should eat from a piece of his mantle; and if a dog or cat eats with the brother while he remains on the ground, he should chase it away. And for this reason it was established that when the brothers eat on the ground, a bench or some other thing should be put in front of them and a sergeant should look after them, so that the household, neither animal or other nuisance, may annoy them. And while a brother is on penance and eats, he should behave as quietly and humbly as he can, and should not laugh or joke.

513. When any brother is on penance, the conduct of the brother should be studied; and if he is of good behaviour on penance and off, the brothers should show mercy to him rather than to another who behaves otherwise.

But you should know that neither the Master nor another who has the authority to put a brother on penance, should give corporal punishment to the brothers during the octave of Pentecost; but if it happens that chapter is held during the octave of the said feast, and a brother is sentenced to Fridays in that chapter, the Master or the one who takes his place should tell that brother, when he has recounted the judgement of the brothers, to receive his punishment from the chaplain brother when the octave is over.

512.1 I.e. eating on the floor and not at the community table.

514. And if the brothers sentence a brother to one day or to two and the third, or to be immediately put on penance, it should be delayed until the Monday after the octave, and the one who judges him should have the same understanding. And then the one who has the authority should assemble the brothers after prime, and should have that brother put on penance, just as is said above of the brother who is put on penance on a day when chapter is not held. And all this was established in this way in honour and reverence of the body of Our Lord which the brothers have received.

515. However, if the brother to whom penance has been given is of very bad behaviour, or if his failing is very serious, or if he has been allowed to keep the habit for love of God, he may and should indeed be put on penance during the said octave, if the brothers agree; but the chaplain brother should give corporal punishment privately, for on feast days and every day the wicked brother should be compelled to do his penance, and prevented from doing evil.

516. And let it be known that when a brother pleads for mercy for his sin in chapter, the one who holds chapter should not and may not make him return to his seat nor keep him there, rather he should send him outside just as is said above; for the Rule commands that the brother who has failed should be submitted to a judgement of the Master or of the one who takes his place and of the brothers once, provided that the failing is slight or in order to avoid a dispute; and he is made to return to his seat even though it may be unreasonable.

517. But let it be known that if the Master or another who holds chapter wishes to make him return to his seat, the brothers may send him outside, and the one who holds chapter should obey them, be it the Master or another. But when the Master puts a brother before him on penance, none may raise him from the ground except the Master, unless he does so with the Master's permission, nor may he make him neglect his duties while the Master is present in that house or the brother does his penance without his permission. But if the Master leaves that house the brothers may release him from the work and the fasts, except on Fridays, when he should fast while he remains on the ground; but he may not raise him from the ground without the Master's permission.

518. And if the brothers are in camp and do not eat in the convent, the brothers who are on penance should eat in the Master's tent if he is there, but if the Master has not pitched his tent, and the Marshal has pitched his, the brothers on penance should eat there or in the tent of the Commander of the Land, if the other named tents are not there.

519. And each brother who is on penance should come to lunch when the convent lunches and to dinner when the convent takes dinner, except on days when he fasts and the convent eats twice, for on such a day he should not eat until nones have been sung. And when the brother who is on penance comes to the palace to eat, he should come early so that he is in the place where he is to eat when the blessing is begun. And if the brother who is on penance wishes to drink at nones or at compline, he should come to drink like the other brothers,

and then he may drink the same wine as the other brothers who are not on penance; but when he eats in the palace he should drink the household's wine. And while the brothers are on penance, they should drink two to a cup unless one brother is a turcopole; and if it happens that one brother cannot tolerate such strong wine as the other, some say that each one may indeed be given a cup.

520. And when a brother does his penance well, and has remained [on the ground] for as long as it seems reasonable to the one who should raise him because of his good behaviour or at the request of any worthy man or for any other good reason, the one who has the authority should assemble the brothers when he sees fit, and should say to the brothers, 'Good lords, such-and-such a brother has been on penance for a while, and it seems fitting to me that he should be raised if it please you.' And if he has been asked by any worthy man, he should say so before the brothers, and should name the worthy man who has made the request. 'Always the justice of the house is up to God and you, and while you uphold it God will sustain you; I will ask you, and you will say what seems best to you.' And afterwards he should ask them all communally, and firstly those who are most worthy and most knowledgeable; and if the majority agree to raise him, all the brothers should kneel before he is made to come, and should say together a short prayer for him, that God give him grace that henceforth he may keep from sin.

521. And afterwards they should rise, and the one who is in charge of that place should make him come before the brothers, and should say to him before all, 'Good brother, the brothers show you great kindness when they may keep you on penance for a long time if they wish, according to the customs of the house, and they raise you now from the ground, and for love of God keep from [doing] what you should not do as if you had been kept there for a long time.' And then that brother who is raised from penance should thank all the brothers, and henceforth he should do with himself and his equipment and everything else just as he did before he was put on penance, and better if he can. And often it happens that when brothers are raised from penance at the request of any worthy secular man, knight, or bishop, or any other great personage, the brothers who have been raised are commanded to go and thank him; and indeed they may do so if they wish, or they may omit to do so if they wish, and it seems a more honourable thing to me to omit to do so than to do so.

522. But let it be known that neither the Master nor any other has the authority to raise a brother from penance without speaking to the brothers and without their judgement; and if the brothers agree to raise him, may he be raised for love of God, and if all or the majority do not agree that he should be raised, the brother should remain on penance until it please God and the brothers; and otherwise he should not be raised.

523. The seventh is Fridays and corporal punishment; and that brother whom the brothers have sentenced to Fridays should receive his punishment in that same place, as soon as the one who holds chapter has recounted to him the

judgement of the brothers, before he returns to his seat, unless he is ill or it is during the octave of Christmas or Easter or Pentecost; for then the one who holds chapter should send him to the chaplain brother, and the chaplain brother should give him his punishment. And that brother who is sentenced to Fridays by chapter, should fast on bread and water the first Friday he is able, and should eat in the convent of the same bread which the convent eats, unless it is the Friday of the feasts named between the octaves; for he should not fast on these, but the first which comes after he should fast if he is able. And if he is in a place where they do not eat, he may eat bread and water at the time established for the brothers who fast to eat.

524. And if the brother who is sent to the chaplain brother is in a place where he cannot find a chaplain brother, the commander who is over the brothers and who has the authority should assemble the brothers after prime, and before the brothers he should give the punishment when the brother has made amends. But the commander and all the brothers who are present should give the punishment and say the paternoster and the other things just as is said above should be done to the brother who is put on penance, except that this brother should not fast except on the Fridays which he has been given by chapter, just as is said above. And let it be known that all the punishment which the Master or another brother who is not a chaplain brother gives, should be given in front of the brothers, except to a brother who has a secret illness, which, if there is no chaplain brother, may be given by the Master or another commander; but they should not give it privately.

525. And they say that no secular priest, who serves the house out of charity, may give corporal punishment to a brother, unless he is a chaplain brother; but although it may be done in this way, it seems better to us for the Master or another commander to give it privately, just as the chaplain brother does, particularly if he is a knight, except the punishment that the chaplain brothers give in penance to the brothers, for this the chaplain brother should give if he is there, and if he is not, another worthy priest who serves the house may give it privately after matins or when it seems good to the brother who gives the punishment.

526. The eighth is by the judgement of the chaplain brothers; and after the brothers have sentenced a brother to be under the judgement of the chaplain brother, he is subject to the justice of the chaplain brother and should do in his power what the chaplain brother commands him, for otherwise he does not carry out the sentence of the brothers or the convent.[1]

527. The ninth is when judgement is deferred until the brother is brought before the Master or before any other worthy man of the house. And all the brothers of the Temple should know that when any failing comes to chapter, and the failing touches on the habit, or if it is new, or if it is serious, or if it is such

526.1 Brothers were sent to the chaplain brother if they were judged to have sinned but not to have committed an infringement of the Rule.

that the brothers are not certain what they should do about it, they should defer judgement, until it is brought before the Master or before such other worthy brother of the house who has the authority and the knowledge to address it and treat it in such a way as they should according to God and the customs of the house.

528. And let it be known that a brother who is of bad behaviour may and should have sentence deferred until he is brought before the Master and before the other worthy men of the house for a slight failing, so that he is more ashamed of it and better makes amends, and so that the failing may be brought to his attention more closely. For let it be known that the Master is required, above all others, to bring the failing more closely to the attention of a foolish and rash brother than to any other brother, and to make a slight failing serious, just as is said above, up to two days and the third; but beyond that he should not do anything, unless the failing touches on the habit as is said above, to treat him harshly if he has deserved it, which the Master himself may do.

529. And if the brother has his sentence deferred by judgement of the brothers until he comes before the Master, for any failing, the brother whose sentence is deferred should plead for mercy for that failing at the first chapter which the Master attends, if the brother is present. And let it be known that the Master, when he has heard the brother's failing, be it serious or slight, should send him outside, for he should not nor may he make him return to his seat without the judgement of the brothers, since his sentence was deferred by judge-ment of the brothers; for the first judgement of the brothers should not be carried out, unless the brother's failing is considered before the one in front of whom the brothers have decided that he should be judged.

530. And if any brother has his sentence deferred for any failing in the land of Tripoli or Antioch, as long as it is before the Grand Commander of that same land, that failing should not be judged before any *bailli* of the Temple except him, or before the Master, in front of whom the brothers have decided that the failing should be judged; and all the failings for which sentence is deferred before all the other *baillis* who take the place of the Master in their provinces, should be treated in the same way, because they take the place of the Master.

531. The tenth is when a brother is acquitted; and this judgement may be given to a brother when it is the opinion of those who judge the failing, or of him to whom the brother has pleaded for mercy, that he has not failed in anything, neither small nor great. It cannot then be agreed to acquit the brother who holds that the other has failed, for at the same convent he is sent to the chaplain brother, for no sin should be without its penance, great or small; but they should and may agree to acquit the one who they hold has failed in nothing, for it would not be a good thing to give him a penance without sinning, and since they have judged that he has not failed in any way.

532. After the brothers have made amends for their sins just as is said above, and their penances have been given to them according to the customs of the

house, and the chapter is near its end, the Master or the one who holds chapter, before he leaves there, should instruct the brothers and teach them how they should live; and he should teach them and recount to them a part of the rules and customs of the house, and should ask and command them to be wary of evil thoughts and even more of evil deeds, and to strive and take care to conduct themselves in such a way in their riding and in their speech and in their judgement and in their eating and in all their actions, so that no excess or folly may be noted, and to take special care in their haircut and their clothing, so that there is no untidiness.

533. Afterwards, when he has instructed the brothers as he sees fit, if he wishes to put brothers on penance before he leaves his chapter, he may indeed put on it those brothers who have penances to do, and he may omit to do so if he wishes and if he has need of the brothers; but let it be known that it is a very good thing to do penance.

534. And if he wishes to put brothers on penance, he should speak in this way, 'All those who have to do three penances or two,' or as many as he sees fit, 'come forward if you are able to do your penance.' And all those who have to do as many as he says should come forward in front of the one who holds chapter; and the one who holds chapter should then tell the brothers who have in this way come before him to do penance, all together, if it seems fitting to him for all of them to be put immediately on penance, or to some of them, if there are too many, or if it seems fitting to him to keep some back for the benefit of the house, to go and undress; and they should do so. And when they have undressed in the manner which is customary in the house, they should return before the one who holds chapter and should kneel humbly and with great devotion; and immediately afterwards the commander and the brothers should say the prayer and give corporal punishment, just as is said above of the brothers who are put on penance.

535. And if the one who holds chapter wishes to keep back some of the brothers who have come forward to do penance, he may indeed do so, and if the commander of the house with another who has brothers under his command says to the one who holds chapter,[1] 'Good lord, for love of God, will you allow such-and-such a brother to be put on penance at another time, for I have need of him for the benefit of the house,' he may allow it if he wishes, and may also put him on penance if he wishes. But let it be known that each one should strive for the benefit of the house while he may without harm to his soul, but none should knowingly harm his soul for anything.

536. And let it be known that always those who have more penances to do should be put on penance first if they are well; and after chapter has begun no other brothers should be put on penance, except those who are put on it by judgement of the brothers immediately the decision of the brothers has been

535.1 The commander of a Templar house ceded his place to a superior for the holding of a chapter.

recounted to them, for it is fitting for these to be put on it then because the brothers have judged them, just as is said above.

537. And let it be known that when a brother goes overseas by order of the house, it is customary in our house that before he gathers together his belongings, he should ask the Marshal or the one who is in his place to assemble the brothers, and he should do so; and when the brothers are assembled, the one who is to go overseas should come before them and should ask and request them humbly for love of both God and Our Lady, if he has done anything against them which he should not, to pardon him, and for love of God and out of mercy they should do so, and release him from the penances that he has to do, because of the anguish and the suffering which he must undergo both at sea and elsewhere by commandment of the house. And our old men say that the brothers may and should release that brother from all the penances which he has to do; and they say that if the brothers pardon him he is quit of all these penances, and if they do not pardon him he is not quit of them.

538. Afterwards, when the one who holds chapter has put the brothers on penance, just as has been said above, if there is nothing else to say or do, he may disperse his chapter in this way, and he should say, 'Good lords, we may disperse our chapter, for by the grace of God there is nothing but good; it pleases God and Our Lady that it be done in this way, and good increases for all the days of Our Lord.' And he should say, 'Good lord brothers, you should know about the forgiveness of our chapter, and who shares in it and who does not, for let it be known that those who live as they should not and avoid the justice of the house, and neither make confession nor make amends in the manner which is established in our house, and those who take the alms of the house for themselves or in a way in which they should not, and those who in their own name expel them from the house wrongfully and sinfully and unreasonably, do not share in the forgiveness of our chapter, nor in the other good things which are done in our house.

539. 'But those who confess their faults, and omit neither to tell nor to confess their failings out of shame of the flesh or for fear of the justice of the house, and who are truly repentant of the evil things which they have done, share in the forgiveness of our chapter and in the other good things which are done in our house; and to those I give such pardon as I may on behalf of God and Our Lady, and on behalf of my lord St Peter and my lord St Paul, the apostles, and on behalf of our father, the pope, and on behalf of you who have given me the authority, and I pray to God that He, through His mercy and for love of His sweet mother, and for the merits of Him and of all the saints, forgives your sins just as He forgave the glorious St Mary Magdalene.

540. 'And I, good lords, plead for mercy to all of you together and to each one separately, that if I have done or said anything against you which I should not, or if I have by chance angered you in any way, you should forgive me out of love for God and His sweet mother; and pardon each other for love of Our Lord,

so that neither anger nor hatred may remain among you.' – And thus Our Lord grants through His mercy, and the brothers should all act in the way he asks and commands them.

541. Afterwards he should say, 'Good lord brothers, you should know that every time we disperse our chapter, you should pray to Our Lord for peace.' And he should commence his prayer as best as God instructs him, and he should pray especially for peace and for the Church and for the holy Kingdom of Jerusalem, and for our house, and for all religious houses, and for all other religious men, and for our *confrères* and our *consoeurs*,[1] and for all the benefactors of our house, living and dead; and finally he should pray for all those who have departed from this world and who await the mercy of Our Lord, and especially for those who lie in our cemeteries, and for the souls of our fathers and mothers, that Our Lord through His kindness may pardon them their sins and lead them soon to the place of rest. And we should say these prayers always at the end of our chapters; and if it seems fitting to the one who holds chapter to say more prayers, it is at his discretion.

542. Afterwards, if the chaplain brother is present, he should say, 'Good lord brothers, say your confessions after me.' And they should say what the chaplain brother instructs them; and when all have said their confessions, the chaplain brother should give absolution and absolve all the brothers just as he sees fit and as is the custom in our house. For let it be known that the chaplain brother has great authority on behalf of our father the pope to absolve the brothers always according to the type and gravity of the sin. But if the chaplain brother is not there, after the prayer each brother should say one paternoster and one Hail Mary.

543. In what way the prayers of the chapters should be said and in what way the brothers should behave while the prayers are said, both when they should kneel and make obeisance and when not, it has been well recounted above: for this reason we henceforth remain silent on it.

541.1 Female equivalents of *confrères* (see note 69.1).

Further Details on Penances

These are the Things for which a Brother is Expelled from the House For Ever

544. The first thing for which a brother is expelled from the house for ever is simony, for a brother who enters the house through simony cannot save his soul and is lost to the house; and the one who receives him loses his habit. For simony is committed by a gift or promise made to the brothers of the Temple or to another who may help him enter the house.

545. It so happened, during the time of Master Brother Hermant de Pierre-gort,[1] that there were worthy brothers who searched their consciences and consulted wise men, and found that they had entered through simony.[2] So they were very sick at heart, and came before Master Brother Hermant de Pierregort and told him with many tears and in great sadness of heart, and disclosed all their deeds. And the said Master was in great distress, for they were worthy men who led lives of goodness, religion and purity. And the said Master took council privately with the old and wisest men of the house and those who knew most of this matter; and he commanded them in virtue of obedience not to speak to any man of this matter, and to advise him in good faith and to the benefit of the house.

546. And they advised him in this way, and considered that the worthy men were so wise and led such good lives that great harm and serious scandal could come to the house if they were expelled from the house. They did not want to take matters further, and sent to the pope[1] in Rome a brother who recounted the whole matter to him, and they beseeched him to send his authority to the archbishop of Caesarea,[2] who was a friend and confidant of the house. The pope did so willingly and sent letters to him.

547. And when they arrived with the Master, the Master took the letters and the brothers, and sent them to the archbishop of Caesarea, and sent with the said brothers the brothers who had been in the Master's private council; and one

545.1 Armand de Périgord, Grand Master 1231/2 to 1244. He died in the battle of Gaza.

545.2 This passage suggests that it was difficult to define simony and that it could be committed almost by accident. (See Introduction for a discussion of this.)

546.1 Gregory IX (1227–41), Celestine IV (1241–3) or Innocent IV (1243–54).

546.2 Possibly Peter of Limoges (1199–1237). He seems to have been on friendly terms with the Templars. This is in direct opposition to the impression of the relationship between the Order and the secular clergy given by William of Tyre, who vehemently opposed the autonomy of the Order. It was probably he who, at the Lateran Council of 1179, led the attack upon their special privileges with regard to the secular hierarchy. Caesarea, which lies on the Israeli coast between Haifa and Tel Aviv (Jaffa), was conquered by the Christians in 1101. Several General Chapters of the Order were held there between 1245 and 1278.

was made a commander, and he gave him the authority to make brothers with their advice. They came before the archbishop with the brothers who were in the house through simony and delivered to him the pope's letter; and the letter explained that he absolved the said brothers in the form in which simony should be absolved;[1] and the brothers deliberated together and he told them that it was fitting they should leave off their habits.

548. So they returned their habits to the one who was their commander. And he took them, and the archbishop absolved them, and the said commander and the other brothers who were in his company entered a chamber and held chapter. There the brothers who had left off their habits came and requested the company of the house for love of God and Our Lady; and the commander sent them outside and asked the brothers their advice, and they agreed to the request of the archbishop who had asked them, and to the request of the brothers. And he made them brothers again, just as if they had never been brothers.

549. And these things were done because they had been brothers of the house for a long time, and were wise and worthy men, who led good and religious lives; and then one became Master of the Temple.[1] – And these things I have heard recounted by the worthy men of that time, for I know it only from them. And if the brothers had been of bad behaviour, this kindness would not have been shown to them. And the same thing happened later to a worthy man of the house because of his goodness.

550. The second is if a brother discloses his chapter to any brother of the Temple or to another who was not in that same chapter.[1] But if a failing is considered in chapter, he may indeed recount it, but he may not name any brother; for if he names the one who has pleaded for mercy or the one who considered the failing, he will be expelled from the house; but if the brother is dead or has been expelled from the house, he may indeed recount it and name him without causing harm. And also when *baillis* are made by chapter, they should not recount or tell to what one agrees nor to what the other, for that would be disclosure of chapter and great hatred could arise from it.

551. And also when they are in the Master's council, they should take care when *baillis* are made, but if it is heard that a worthy man makes a ruling in chapter, he may indeed be named, but it should not touch on the failing of a brother who is in the house. But if a change is made in chapter and the Master knows of it by any means, the Master may say in chapter, 'I have heard that such-and-such a change has been made, and I command that such things are revealed.' And in this way it may be said; but the Master should not command to

547.1 A special ceremony similar to that for the lifting of excommunication, an extract from the decretals of pope Gregory IX.

549.1 This may refer to Guillaume de Sonnac, Grand Master from 1247 to 1250.

550.1 This clause seems to be aimed at preventing gossip and ill-feeling between the brothers. The secrecy lent the chapter the nature of a confessional.

be told outside chapter anything that was done by chapter, but in chapter he may order it, and the other may also tell of a change if it has been made.

552. For it happened at Château Pèlerin[1] that Brother Pierre de Montagu,[2] who was Master, put brothers on penance and then went away to Acre. And the brothers of the castle raised them from the ground; and when the Master found out, he turned back, and held chapter, and accused all the brothers who had agreed to raise the brothers from the ground, and they were judged to have failed seriously because they did not have the authority to raise them: for the Master had put them there.

553. The third is if a brother kills a Christian man or woman, or causes them to be killed, he will be expelled from the house.

554. For it happened in Antioch that a brother who was named Brother Paris, and two other brothers who were in his company, killed some Christian merchants; so was the thing known by others, and they were asked why they had done such a thing, and they replied that sin had made them do it. And the commander made them plead for mercy, and their sentence was deferred; and the failing came before the convent, and they were sentenced to be expelled from the house and flogged throughout Antioch, Tripoli, Tyre[1] and Acre. Thus they were flogged and cried, 'See here the justice which the house exacts from its wicked men,' and they were put in perpetual imprisonment[2] at Château Pèlerin, and died there. And then in Acre a similar thing happened to another brother.

555. The fourth is theft, which is understood in several ways: the one who steals is held to be a thief, or the one who leaves a castle or fortified house, by night or day, by any other way but the prescribed gate which is open, neither above nor below should he leave. Or the one who steals the keys or makes duplicates in order to open the gate, he will be considered a thief because of it; for no brother should open the gate except as is customary in the house. And if a commander asks a sergeant brother who is under his command to show him the things which are in his charge and under his command, the brother should show them all to him or say where they are, and if he does not do so and keeps a sum of more than four deniers, he will be expelled from the house because of it.

556. For it happened at Château Blanc[1] to a brother who was in charge of the sheepfold, that his commander told him to show him all the things that he

552.1 A castle built by the Templars in 1217–18, on the coast between Haifa and Caesarea.

552.2 Grand Master 1219 to 1230/1.

554.1 The Templars had possessions near this town, which was conquered by the Christians in 1110.

554.2 This suggests that the Order had its own prisons, presumably in the larger castles. Imprisonment was a common form of punishment in monastic orders, but the building of prisons in each Cistercian abbey was permitted only after 1206. By the second half of the thirteenth century prison sentences, often for life, were given to 'incorrigible and habitual criminals, thieves, incendiaries, forgers and murderers'. L.J. Lekai, *The Cistercians* (Kent State University Press 1977), p. 366.

556.1 This stronghold at Safita, in the County of Tripoli, now lies in Syria. It was

had under his command, and the brother showed him everything except a jar of butter and said that he had nothing else. And his commander knew that the jar was there and accused the brother. And the brother could not deny it, so he conceded it; so he was expelled from the house because of it.

557. If any brother through anger or wrath leaves the house and takes things which he should not take, he is expelled from the house, for he is a thief. – And all brothers of the Temple who leave the house should know that they should not take two of anything. And they should take neither gold nor silver, nor lead a horse, nor any arms: that is to say *chapeau de fer*, nor coat of mail, nor iron hose, nor crossbow, nor sword, nor arming dagger, nor surcoat, nor arming jacket, nor mace, nor lance, nor Turkish arms. And briefly, anyone who takes anything apperraining to arms will be expelled from the house because of it.

558. (These are the things which they may take.) That is to say a tunic and a *garnache* with fur, or a tunic, and a shirt, and one pair of breeches, and one pair of hose, and one pair of shoes, or hose without shoes, and a cloth cap, and the coif, and a belt, and a knife with which to cut bread; and all these things are to include what he wears to prime. And he may wear a mantle or cope, but if he is asked to he should return it, and if he keeps it he will be expelled from the house; and if he is not asked, he should return it afterwards, for if he keeps it for more than two nights, whether asked or not, he will be expelled from the house. For those wicked brothers who left the house and took their habits, and wore them among the taverns and prostitutes and in wicked places, and wagered them and sold them to wicked people, and brought to the house great shame and dishonour and great scandal: and for this reason the convent and worthy men of the house established that mantles are worth more than shoes or arming dagger or mace; because for each one of these things which he takes away, he will be expelled from the house.

559. But because of this they do not in any way transgress the first law, that whoever sleeps two nights outside as is said above, may recover his habit after a year and a day. Those who judge, if he comes after prime or sends his mantle, that he is expelled from the house, go against the first law which none may undermine unless the convent removes it; and also those who say after one day or after vespers. But it is our understanding that the one who keeps it for two nights and all the next day until the evening when it is past the hour of compline, henceforth, if he returns or sends back his mantle, then he may be sentenced to be expelled from the house; for then it could be said that he has kept it over two nights and one whole day. And his conscience may be saved and the first law not broken; but because this failing is not and never has been clarified, each one gives his own understanding of it. And I have not said ours, moreover I do not undertake another ruling for I have never heard it made clear;

taken several times by the Moslems, being rebuilt and repaired each time, but was finally lost in 1271. It still stands today, a single tower with chapel below and living quarters above. The chapel is still in use today and the town is predominantly Christian.

but I have heard the old men of the house recount what I have said above; but each one should save his own conscience.

560. It happened that one who was named Brother Hugh left the house in Acre, and returned all the things he should return, except his mantle which he kept for two nights, and the next day he returned it; shortly afterwards he repented and came to plead for mercy at the door as is established in the house, and the brothers sentenced him to be expelled from the house. And some brothers said again that it was not reasonable to be expelled from the house because of the mantle, if he had not kept it longer than he had kept it. But they did not say for certain for how long he could keep it. And he was in the wrong, because no-one knew for certain when he had returned it: and because of this the majority of the convent agreed that, because he had kept it longer than he should and two nights had passed, and they did not know when he had returned it, he could not re-enter the house. And let it be known that those who consider this and support it have often repented of their decisions. And if a change is made, it is not a law which should be adhered to, and it should not be adhered to; but if the Master and the convent establish something, that should be adhered to.

561. It happened that a brother left the house at Château Pèlerin and returned all his equipment, and then afterwards came to plead for mercy at the door; and the Master asked his question, and there were brothers who said that he had kept some things and that they knew it, and because they were not found he was expelled from the house. And every brother is believed against a brother, when he leaves the house, when he says he has lost his equipment through the fault of the brother who has left the house.

562. It happened that a brother left the house at Alba,[1] and went to Crac[2] and on his way he lost a longbow that he was carrying, and a sergeant found it and returned it to his commander; and the brother said that when he left he had left a sword in his place, and the commander did not find it; then the brother returned and pleaded for mercy and his sentence was deferred in front of the Master and the convent, and he came before the Chapter General and pleaded for mercy. And the brothers decided that because of the sword which was lost to the house and because of the longbow which was lost – for the house had not recovered it through him – for each of these he was sentenced to be expelled from the house.

563. It happened that a chaplain brother was coming from Tripoli by sea, and was stricken by illness, and died of it before he arrived at Beirut; and when the commander knew that he was in port, he went to look for him and had him buried. And the commander took some old clothing and dressed him in it, then

562.1 Château Blanc (see note 556.1).
562.2 The Hospitaller castle of Crac des Chevaliers, which held out to Saladin in 1188, but fell to the Mamluks in 1271.

he opened the bags of the chaplain brother and took some clothing in place of it; afterwards he sent all the clothes to the Master except one sword. Later, the brother was told that he could not do so, and he was a simple man, and pleaded for mercy for it before the Master. And because he knew little of the customs of the house and had done it in good faith, and no harm had come of it, the Master asked the worthy men who were there to take the thing upon themselves before it went any further. For if they took it further, the brother would be expelled from the house: for when a chaplain brother dies in regions this side of the sea, all his books and his clothing and all his jewels should come into the hands of the Master, except his day wear (robe de vestir) and nightwear and arms, which should go there where they should go; and if he dies in regions overseas, they should go into the hands of the commander whom he was under. And if any brother takes any of the above-mentioned things, he will be considered a thief.

564. If a brother breaks a key or lock which is not in his charge, and takes anything without the permission of the one in whose charge it is, and he is found guilty of having taken the things, he may be considered a thief.

565. If a brother puts his hand in another's bags and the brother to whom they belong says that he has lost what was inside, and he can have him convicted of having put his hand inside the bags and can prove that he has lost what he says from the bags, he will be considered a thief.

566. If a brother dies and either gold or silver is found in his bags or in his equipment, and he was a brother of the convent, or he had placed it outside the house or hidden it without the permission of the one who may give it, and did not confess it at his death to his commander or to another brother, he will not be put in the cemetery, but will be thrown outside to the dogs; and if he is already buried, he will be thrown outside, and this has been done to several others.

567. The fifth is conspiracy; for conspiracy is committed by two or more brothers. And if two brothers agree together and strike a brother or accuse him of anything which is a lie, and they are found guilty of having done it by agreement, this will be taken as conspiracy and they will be expelled from the house.

568. The sixth is, if a brother leaves the house and goes to the Saracens, he will be expelled from the house.

569. It happened that Brother Roger the German was taken at Gadre,[1] and the Saracens told him to recant, and made him raise his finger and swear the oath;[2] and he was put in prison with the other brothers, and pleaded for mercy before the brothers, and said that still he did not know what it was they had made him swear. And his sentence was deferred before the Master and the

569.1 The town of Gaza, which was held by the Templars between 1149 and 1187, when it was taken by Saladin.
569.2 'God is great and Mohammed is his prophet.'

convent, and when he was delivered up he pleaded for mercy in Chapter General, and was expelled from the house for this thing.

570. It happened at Saphet[1] that a brother who worked at the great forge left the castle with all his equipment with the intention of leaving the house, and went that night to a *casal* of the Germans[2] which was full of Saracens; and the next day he repented and went to Acre, the next day after prime, and came straight to our house, and at the first chapter which he attended he pleaded for mercy for this thing. And the brothers sentenced him to lose the habit, and some worthy men spoke of the fact that he had lodged one night with Saracens; and if the *casal* had not been under the command of Christians, and the *baillis* not been Christians, he would have been expelled from the house.

571. The seventh is if a brother is of bad faith and does not believe in the faith of Jesus Christ.

572. The eighth is if a brother does anything against nature and against the law of Our Lord, he will be expelled from the house.

573. At Château Pèlerin there were brothers who practised wicked sin and caressed each other in their chambers at night; so that those who knew of the deed and others who had suffered greatly by it, told this thing to the Master and to a group of the worthy men of the house. And the Master took the advice, that this thing should not come to chapter, because the deed was so offensive, but that the brothers should come to Acre; and when they had arrived, the Master put a worthy man in the chamber, and others in his company in the chamber where they were, and made them remove their habits and put them in heavy irons. And one of the brothers, who was named Brother Lucas, escaped by night and went to the Saracens. And the other two were sent to Château Pèlerin; and the one thought to escape, so he died, and the other remained in prison for a long time.

574. The ninth is, if a brother leaves his banner and flees for fear of the Saracens, he is expelled from the house. And our old men so say, if brothers are sent in the service of the house and the one who sends them gives them a commander of knights who does not carry a banner; and they say, if any brother leaves his commander and flees for fear of the Saracens, he will be expelled from the house because of it. And some other brothers say that although there is no banner, whoever leaves his commander in battle would indeed leave his banner; that is why it seems that he may reasonably be sentenced to be expelled from the house.

570.1 Saphet lies to the north of the Sea of Galilee. It was destroyed in 1219 and rebuilt under the mastership of Armand de Périgord with the support of Benedict, bishop of Marseilles. It was taken from the Order in 1266 by the Mamluk Sultan Baybars, who had all the defenders massacred.

570.2 The Teutonic Knights, the third great military order. They possessed several strongholds between Saphet and Acre, Montfort being the most important.

575. If brothers go in the service of the house and have no commander, and they see that they may be in danger from Saracens, they may elect one among them as commander, and then they should be obedient to him and keep near him in battle, just as if they had been given a commander.

576. For it happened that there were Tartars in this country;[1] and with the advice of the worthy men the Master sent twelve brothers to Jerusalem. And four of them left the town, and did not remain there. The Master heard of the danger in which the brothers were, so he sent a letter to the commander of knights and to the other brothers, that they should retreat as far as Jaffa,[2] so that they should not be assailed by the Tartars. The commander of knights did not wish to do so; on this, four brothers came to the commander and told him to do what the Master's letter commanded him, and he replied that he would not leave without the brothers of the Hospital who had joined his company. And the four brothers asked the commander to order them by command to remain in his company; and the commander said that he would not do so. On this, a brother who was the oldest man of the house among them all indicated that they could indeed go since the Master commanded them to go, and that they should not have fear of the justice of the house, for they could not be judged to have failed in this: these four returned, and when they were before the Master they pleaded for mercy for this thing of their free will.

577. And some said that they should have been expelled from the house because they had left their commander and their banner when in danger from Saracens. And the majority of them said that the Master's letter had gone to the commander and to all the brothers, that they should return, and the commander did not wish to order them to stay, and for this reason, that the oldest man of them all had indicated that they could return without harm coming to the house; for if the letter had not been sent in this way and the ruling not made, they may have been expelled from the house. And one of those four brothers said that he had permission to return when he wished, and the Master defended him, and the others were considered to have lost their habits, because they had not awaited their commander. And the one who made the ruling was put on one day.

578. If God summons one of the commanders of the provinces, the one who remains in his place should take all the equipment with the advice of a group of the worthy men of the house who are there around him, and seal the bags with the seals of the commanders who are there. And the seal of the commander who is dead should be put inside, for the bags should be sent to the Master, and all the

576.1 The Tartars, or Mongols, invaded in 1257. After having conquered Damascus, they made for Tiberias where they were defeated by the Sultan of Egypt in 1260. Jacques de Molay, last Grand Master of the Order, made an alliance with the Tartars against the Moslems, their common enemy.

576.2 Modern-day Tel Aviv, on the Israeli coast between Ascalon and Caesarea. It was finally lost in 1268.

other jewels, and the gold and silver, should be put in the commander's chest and sealed just as the bags; and he should inform the Master that he carries out his order, for all the above-mentioned things should come into the hands of the Master without removing anything. But the horses and day wear (*robe de vestir*) and nightwear and arms are at the will of the commander to do with as he pleases; and if he keeps anything else, he could be expelled from the house.

579. And if he was a Visitor on behalf of the Master and the convent, just as they ought to do, and God summons him [while he is] overseas, likewise should his bags be taken and his seal put inside, and all his small jewels that may be put there, and they should be well sealed with the seal of the commander and the other commanders, and sent to the Master. And all the other things, gold and silver or anything that may be in his portable altar, all should be put together and all should be sent to the Master in the land of Outremer, even the horses. For all the things briefly which are there, belong to the Master and the convent, except nightwear or day wear (*robe de vestir*), which should be given away for love of God.

580. It happened that Brother Martin Sanchez was Commander of Portugal and died before he arrived in his *baillie*. The one who was put in his place took some of the things he had sent there and gave them away willingly to the benefit of the Temple; and the brother had been in our house for a short while and did not know of the prohibition. And when the Master knew how it was, he sent for the brother and made him plead for mercy; and because he did not know the custom of the house, the Master took council with a large group of the worthy men of the house, and they did not wish to take the matter as far as it could be taken, for he did not know well the laws of the house.

581. And when God summons one of the commanders of the provinces, he may not put any brother in his place except while he is alive. And when God summons him, the one whom he has appointed in his place should send to the commander of the province and make known the death of their commander; and they should come, and elect one among them, whoever pleases them, when they are assembled in a suitable place which he will indicate to them on a given day. And the one who is in place of the commander should give proof of their old commander's wishes to the commanders and to the one who takes the place of the Grand Commander, until the Master has given his order; and the one who is put in place of the commander should inform the Master of the death of his commander and should send the things as is said above.

582. For it happened that Brother Guillaume Fouque was Commander of Spain and was ill: being in his illness he put Brother Adam in his place. And then some told him that he did wrong when he did not leave Brother Raymond de Lunel [in his place]; and he said, 'On behalf of God I leave him in my place,' upon which he died. And when he was dead Brother Adam said that he was in the place of the commander, and Brother Raymond de Lunel said that he had been before him, and they disputed about this; and the brothers of Castile and

Leon held with Brother Adam, and those of Portugal held with Brother Raymond de Lunel, and each one went to his party, and each one held chapter, and made *baillis*, and each one exercised as much authority as brothers who are in the place of a commander may exercise.

583. And they informed the Master of the facts as they were. And the Master sent a commander to Spain and sent for these two brothers to come to this country; and they came and pleaded for mercy for this thing before the Master and the convent. And the Master and the convent saw that the two brothers had been expelled from the house, and their sentence was deferred because they were two worthy men who led good and religious lives, and because the thing was new. Afterwards it happened that battle was to be waged at Gadre[1] between the Christians and Saracens, and our people were at Ascalon.[2] And the Master assembled the brothers after matins and asked them to take upon themselves the matter of these two worthy men; and they did so willingly and pardoned them their faults. But let it be known that they had been expelled from the house according to our laws, because they had exercised authority which they should not exercise, according to what is said above. And so the worthy men of the house said that this could be taken as conspiracy by all those who had supported the deed.

584. The tenth is, if a brother who has entered the house as a layman has himself ordained without the permission of the one who may give it, he may be expelled from the house. And if he was ordained as a sub-deacon or superior, and he concealed it at his promise and is found guilty of it, he may be expelled from the house.

585. For it happened that the Commander of France sent a brother this side of the sea, who was in his *baillie* and he had himself ordained as a sub-deacon, and came to the Chapter General which was at Caesarea. And there were there Brother Guirot de Braies and Brother Hugue de Monlo and many other old men, and he was sentenced to be expelled from the house for this reason that he had had himself ordained without permission.

586. For all these above-mentioned things one may be expelled from the house, and so there are others.

It happened that we had a knight brother, and there were brothers from his country who said that he was neither the son of a knight nor of knightly lineage, and the words were so serious for the house that it was fitting they should come before chapter.[1] And these same brothers said that if he were present he would be found guilty; so the brothers agreed to send for him, for he was in Antioch. And the Master sent for him, and when he had come to the first chapter he attended, he rose and said before the Master that he had heard the words which

583.1 Gaza (see note 569.1).

583.2 Ascalon lies on the Israeli coast north of Gaza. The town was captured by the Christians in 1153 and retaken by Saladin in 1187. He destroyed it in 1191.

586.1 This reflects the hardening of class attitudes which occurred in the thirteenth century.

were said about him. And the Master ordered those who had said the words to rise, and they rose, and he was found guilty of the fact that his father was neither a knight nor of knightly lineage: so his white mantle was taken from him and he was given a brown mantle, and became a chaplain brother. And the one who made him a brother was overseas, and when he had arrived this side of the sea he pleaded for mercy for what he had done, and said that he had done it at the command of his Commander of Poitou, who was dead, and this was found to be true. And if he had not found a witness that he had done it under orders, and this even that he had behaved well in his *baillie* and was a worthy man, the habit would have been taken from him, for none should give the habit to one who should not have it; for no sergeant should have a white mantle. And if such a thing happens to the Master, he may be treated just as has been done and said above.

These are the Things for which the Brothers Lose their Habits if they are Found Guilty, from which God Keep Them

587. The first is, if a brother refuses to carry out the commandment of the house and persists in the folly and does not wish to carry out the commandment which he has been given, the habit should be taken from him and he should be put in irons. But it would be severe to act in this way, thus he should be left to cool down from his wrath and someone should go to him quietly and say to him, 'Brother, carry out the commandment of the house'; it is closer to God. And if he does it and no harm has arisen, on behalf of God the habit is at the discretion of the brothers, whether to take it from him or let him keep it. To the commandment of the house no man should say, 'No,' but, 'On behalf of God,' and if he does not do so, the habit may be taken from him and he may be treated just as I have said above.

588. It happened at Tortosa[1] that the commander gave an order to a brother, and the brother said, 'Perhaps I will do it.' And the commander assembled the brothers and made him plead for mercy for this thing, and the brother said that he would carry out the command. And the brothers were all stopped from letting him keep the habit, because he had not consented to the order at the first word.

589. The second is if a brother lays hands on another brother in anger and wrath and makes him move his feet from the spot, or breaks the fastenings of his mantle, he may not keep the habit. And if the blow is very grave or serious, he may be put in irons because of it; and after a brother has been put in irons, he

588.1 Tortosa, north of Tripoli, lies on the Syrian coast. With its port it was a commercial town and the seat of a bishopric. It fell to the Moslems in 1291, and an unsuccessful attempt to recapture it was made in 1300 by Jacques de Molay and the Templars, the Hospitallers and king Amalric de Lusignan. The cathedral, a fine example of Gothic architecture, still stands today. It incorporates a shrine, said to be the site of the first church dedicated by St Peter to the Virgin Mary, which was a place of pilgrimage.

should not carry the piebald banner nor take part in the election of a Master. And before he is made to plead for mercy for his failing, he should be absolved of it. And also if he has struck a man of religion or cleric, he should be absolved before his failing is considered.

590. The third is, whoever strikes a Christian man or woman with a sharp weapon, or with a stone or staff, or anything a blow from which could kill or wound him, the habit is at the mercy of the brothers.

591. It happened in Acre that Brother Hermant was commander of the livestock, and two clerks took some *doreiz*[1] doves which belonged to the dovecote of the house. And the commander told them to do it no more, and they did not wish to stop it. And the commander had a brother who watched them when they took the doves, and the commander with the brothers beat them hard and wounded one on the head. And the clerks appealed to the legate, and the legate informed the Master; and the Master absolved them first, then made them plead for mercy in chapter, and their habits were taken from them, and they were put in irons and sent to Cyprus,[2] because the blow was very serious.

592. It happened that the convent was in Jaffa, and they were ordered to load their baggage at midnight; and some brothers who were in lodgings together heard the words, and one brother laid hands on the other by the hair and threw him to the ground, and there were brothers who saw it. And the next day the convent came by day to Arsuf,[1] and they heard mass and the hours. And Brother Hugue de Monlo was Marshal, and had heard this news; so he kept the brothers in the chapel and held chapter, and there were many brothers who marvelled, and he put forward the words he had heard. The brother rose and said that he was struck and that there were brothers who had seen it, and the Marshal thought that they should come forward.

593. And the brother who had done the deed rose and pleaded for mercy, and he sent him outside the chapter and the chaplain brother with him, who absolved him, for he had the authority; and after he had absolved him he returned to chapter and the chaplain brother said that he had absolved him. And he was made to plead for mercy again just as he had done before, and he was sent outside; and he was sentenced to lose his habit and be put in irons. And so there was a great debate among the old men of the house, because the blow was not apparent, nor was there any blood; and others maintained, since he had laid hands on the brother in anger and the matter had come to chapter, that it could indeed be done. And Brother Hugue de Monlo indicated that it could indeed be

591.1 I have been unable to ascertain what kind of dove this is.
591.2 The Templars bought Cyprus from Richard I in 1191, but had difficulties in governing the island. The next year Richard sold it to Guy de Lusignan. The Templars did not have large commanderies on the island, but rather smaller possessions such as *casals* and farms, warehouses and retreats for old and infirm brothers.
592.1 The fortress of Arsuf lay on the coast to the north of Jaffa. It belonged to the Hospitallers and fell to the Moslems in 1265.

done according to the customs of the house; and the majority agreed with this, and he [the offender] was put in irons and sent to Château Pèlerin.

594. The fourth is if a brother is found guilty of lying with a woman, and we hold guilty the brother who is found in a wicked place or in a wicked house with a wicked woman: he may not keep the habit and so he should be put in irons, nor should he ever carry the piebald banner or take part in the election of a Master; and it has been done to several.

595. The fifth is if a brother accuses another of something for which he could be expelled from the house if he were found guilty of it, and the brother who has accused him cannot have him convicted of it, he may not keep the habit; and after he has pleaded for mercy for it in chapter, and he has renounced it in chapter, the habit is at the discretion of the brothers, whether to take it from him or let him keep it.

The sixth is if a brother asks for permission to leave the house or to go to another order, and it is not wished to give it to him, and he says that he will leave the house, his habit is at the discretion of the brothers, whether to take it from him or let him keep it.

The seventh is if a brother falsely accuses himself in order to have leave of the house and is found guilty of it, he may not keep the habit.

596. The eighth is if a brother says that he will go to the Saracens, even if he says it in anger or wrath, the habit is at the mercy of the brothers, whether to take it from him or let him keep it.

The ninth is if a brother kills or loses or wounds an equine animal or mule through his own fault, the habit is at the discretion of the brothers, whether to take it from him or let him keep it.

The tenth is if a brother carries anything belonging to secular people or anyone other than of the Temple, and says that it belongs to the house and it is not true, and the lords of the lands or of the seas would lose their rights to it or their tolls, the habit is at the mercy of God and the brothers, whether to take it from him or let him keep it.

The eleventh failing is if a brother who does not have the authority gives away a live, four-legged animal, except a dog or cat, his habit is at the discretion of the brothers, whether to take it from him or let him keep it.

597. The twelfth is if a brother kills or wounds or loses a slave of the house through his own fault, the habit is at the mercy of the brothers, whether to take it from him or let him keep it.

The thirteenth is if a brother builds a new house of stone and lime without the permission of the Master or of his commander, the habit is at the discretion of the brothers, whether to take it from him or let him keep it; but other ruined houses he may indeed repair without permission.

The fourteenth is if a brother gives the habit of the house to a man to whom he should not, or who is not worthy of having it, he may not keep his habit.

598. The fifteenth is if a brother lends the alms of the house in a place where the house may lose them, he may not keep the habit.

The sixteenth is if a brother breaks the seal of the Master or of the one who is in his place without the permission of the one who may give it, he may not keep the habit.

The seventeenth is if a brother who does not have the authority gives the alms of the house to secular people or anywhere else outside the house, he may not keep the habit.

The eighteenth is if a brother keeps the income of secular people in a way in which he should not and says that it belongs to the house, and afterwards is found guilty that this is not true, he may not keep the habit.

The nineteenth is if a brother takes anything from secular people with the intention of helping them to become brothers of the Temple, he may not keep the habit, because this is simony.

599. The twentieth is if a brother refuses to another brother going or coming the bread and water of the house, so that he does not let him eat with the other brothers, he may not keep the habit, because when a man is made a brother he is promised the bread and water of the house, nor may any take it from him, unless his sin takes it from him.

The twenty-first is if a brother breaks a lock without the permission of the one who may give it, and no other harm comes of it, the habit is at the discretion of the brothers, whether to take it from him or let him keep it.

600. The twenty-second is if a brother lends his horse to another brother without permission, to take to any place where he may not go without permission, and the horse is lost or injured or dies, the habit is at the discretion of the brothers, whether to take it from him or let him keep it; but he may indeed lend it for pleasure in the town where he is.

The twenty-third is if a brother causes loss to the house knowingly or through his own fault of four deniers or more, the habit is at the mercy of the brothers, whether to take it from him or let him keep it, for all loss is forbidden us. And the loss may be so serious that he may be put in irons.

601. The twenty-fourth is if a brother hunts and harm comes of it, the habit is at the mercy of the brothers, whether to take it from him or let him keep it.

The twenty-fifth is if a brother tries out his arms and equipment and harm comes of it, the habit is at the discretion of the brothers, whether to take it from him or let him keep it.

602. The twenty-sixth failing is if a brother passes through the gate with the intention of leaving the house and then repents of it, he could forfeit the habit. And if he goes to the Hospital or anywhere else outside the house, the habit is at the discretion of the brothers; and if he sleeps one night outside, he should not keep the habit.

603. It happened that Brother George the mason left Acre and went to the Saracens; and the Master knew it, so he sent brothers after him, and he was

found guilty, and they found the clothing of a secular man under his own clothing; so he was sent to Château Pèlerin where he was put in prison and died.

604. It happened that Brother Hugh was a brother in the cobbler's at Saphet, and his commander was Brother Guillaume de Chartres,[1] and a sergeant came to ask for shoes from the cobbler's servant, and he did not wish to give them to him; and the brother told the servant to give him a pair of shoes or to give him the keys to the cupboard, and the servant said that he would not do so. And the brother broke open the cupboard and took a pair of shoes and gave them to the sergeant. And his commander took it badly and accused the brother, and the brother pleaded for mercy and admitted the thing just as he had done it, and came to chapter, and the brothers took the habit from him; and if he had taken out the things of the house which were under lock, he would have been expelled from the house, for he would have been a thief.

605. It happened that the convent was at Casal Brahim and the brothers went out walking for pleasure; and one brother took his mace and threw it after a bird which was on the bank of the water: the mace fell in and was lost. And the brother pleaded for mercy for this act, and the brothers said that he could lose the habit because of the harm which had come of it, and he was allowed to keep the habit for love of God.

606. It happened on Cyprus that a rich man had sent his horse which was sick to our house; and when it was cured, the commander rode it out and found a hare and chased after it, and the horse fell and was wounded so that it died of that wound. And the brother came to Acre and pleaded for mercy in Chapter General, and the brothers sentenced him to lose the habit; and there were some who thought to give it back, for they said that the horse did not belong to the house, and others said that that did not matter, for they had to heal the horse at the house and now it was dead: so one should not bring harm to another. And the brother lost his habit and some said that he could indeed have been put in irons because of the loss which was so great.

607. It happened that a brother tried out a sword at Montpellier, and the sword broke; and the brother came this side of the sea and pleaded for mercy for this thing, and the brothers sentenced him to lose the habit, then allowed him to keep it for love of God.

608. So it happened at Tyre that a brother had a mark of goblets and it fell from his hand:[1] so he broke one, and the brother to whom the others belonged took all the goblets and broke them, and then said that God and His mother were cursed; and then the brother pleaded for mercy for this thing. And the brothers sentenced him to lose the habit because he had done great harm to the house knowingly, and then they allowed him to keep it for love of God.

604.1 Grand Master 1210 to 1219.
608.1 These goblets were probably made of glass. They fitted one inside another and formed a game. The meaning of 'mark' is not clear.

609. It happened that the commander of the vault bought a ship laden with wheat, and ordered that it be put in the granary; and the brother in charge of the granary said that it was damp from the sea and that it should be spread on the drying terrace, for if he did not do so he would spoil it, and he would disclaim responsibility for it (*s'en descharroit*). And the commander ordered him to put it in the granary and he put it there; and after a short while the commander had the wheat carried to the drying terrace and a large part of it was spoilt; and he pleaded for mercy for this, and the habit was taken from him because he had done great harm knowingly.

610. It happened that Brother Jacques de Ravane was commander of the palace of Acre, and he took brothers and turcopoles and sergeants, ours and of the town, and made a raid on Casal Robert;[1] and the Saracens of the land responded to the alarm and defeated them and seized some of his men; and he pleaded for mercy for this, and the habit was taken from him and he was put in irons, because he had made a raid without permission.

611. The twenty-seventh is if a brother of the Temple carries a banner in battle and lowers it in order to engage and harm comes of it, the habit is at the discretion of the brothers. And whether he engages or not, and harm comes of it, he may not keep the habit; and the harm may be so great that it may be decided to put him in irons, nor may he ever carry the piebald banner, nor be a commander in battle, for it is a thing very much forbidden to the house, because of the great danger that is therein. For if the banner is lowered, those who are far off do not know why it is lowered, for good or ill, for a Turk could more easily take or seize it when it is lowered than when it is aloft; and men who lose their banner are very afraid, and may suffer a very great defeat, and because of this fear it is forbidden so strictly.

612. The twenty-eighth is if a brother who carries a banner charges without the permission of the one who may give it, unless he is surrounded or in a place where he cannot obtain permission as is given in the *retrait*,[1] the habit is at the discretion of the brothers, whether to take it from him or let him keep it. And the harm may be so great that he cannot keep the habit; and it may be decided to put him in irons, nor may he ever carry a banner or be a commander in battle, nor take part in the election of a Master, from the moment he is put in irons.

613. The twenty-ninth is if a brother who is in battle charges without permission and harm comes of it, the habit is at the mercy of the brothers; and the harm may be so great that he may not keep the habit. But if he sees a Christian in peril of death and his conscience tells him that he can help him without harm just as is said in the *retrais*,[1] he may do so; in no other way may any brother do so without putting his habit at risk.

610.1 Casal Robert lay between Château Pèlerin and Nazareth and was a possession of the Hospitallers.
612.1 See §242.
613.1 See §243.

614. It happened that the convent was lodged in Jaffa and the Turks advanced and then set two ambushes at Fontaine Barbe; and the Turcopolier came out first, and Brother Margot was delivered to all ten knight brothers who were to guard him; and the Turcopolier went forward between the two ambushes; and it seemed to the brothers who were guarding him that they wanted to attack the Turcopolier, and of the ten brothers who guarded him four brothers left without the permission of the commander – and one had no *chapeau de fer* – and they charged the ambushers. And two of these brothers lost two horses; and then the others who were left charged, with the permission of the commander, and defeated the ambushes, and the Turcopolier charged afterwards and defeated the others.

615. And when chapter was held, Brother Margot did not make peace with those who had charged without permission and he told the Marshal before all the brothers, and the brothers rose and pleaded for mercy; and for those two brothers who had not lost anything, it was decided that they could forfeit the habit, and for those two who lost their horses it was judged that they could not keep their habits. But because the thing turned out well, and the Turcopolier would have been at risk if that charge had not been made, those who lost their horses were allowed to keep their habits for love of God, and the other two were put on two days; and Brother Hugue de Monlo said that the failing had been well considered.

616. It happened in Acre that our[1] Master Brother Renaut de Vichier forbad any brother from the garden to eat or drink with another, unless it was water. And it happened shortly afterwards, that the brothers from the garden and from the large vineyard left Acre and agreed together to eat supper at the large vineyard; and they remained so long at supper that it was night, and the brother from the large vineyard accompanied them a little on their way. And then the two brothers went together and the brother in charge of money accompanied the one from La Chêne.[2] And when they had passed the river of Acre, they found Saracens who attacked them and killed one of the brothers and led away his *roncin*; the other was badly wounded.[3] And then the matter came to chapter and their sentence was deferred until Chapter General, and then they pleaded for mercy. And there was one old man who said that they were not found guilty because this harm had not come through them.

617. And when the request came to the Commander of the Land of Tripoli, he asked the Master if he had relaxed the prohibition that he had made to the brothers from the gardens against drinking and eating together, and the Master

---

616.1 This suggests that the writer may have been contemporary with the mastership of Renaut de Vichier, 1250 to 1265. Renaut de Vichier is often mentioned by the historian Joinville and in particular in connection with Louis IX's ransom.

616.2 A house dependent upon the main house at Acre.

616.3 This indicates a poor state of internal security in the Kingdom of Jerusalem in the mid-thirteenth century.

said no; then the Commander of the Land of Tripoli said that they were guilty of the harm which had arisen, because they had done what the Master had forbidden and for this reason harm had come of it. For if they had not eaten together and if each one had gone to his lodgings quietly and peacefully, the harm would not have arisen; and for this reason and for others that he said, the brothers were sentenced to lose their habits; and Brother Joffroi de Fos[1] supported this reason. And afterwards, because the brothers were ill and badly wounded as to death, so this kindness was shown to them that they were allowed to keep their habits for love of God.

618. It happened on Cyprus that brothers lost their habits; one was named John Harelip, and the other Brother Matthew. And Brother John was Commander of Paphos,[1] and he told his commander, who was named Brother Baudouin de Benrage, that he did not have the means to build his house. And he told him to sell some of his wheat to the value of six hundred silver besants, and to build his house with four hundred, and to keep the two hundred until he asked for them. After a while, he sent a brother who asked him for the two hundred besants, and Brother John said that he had put them towards the expenses of the house. And the commander sent for them and ordered the besants to be given to him, and he told him that he had spent them, and he could not say on what; and the commander became angry and accused him, and he came before the chapter at Recordane,[2] where another brother was sentenced to be expelled from the house according to the laws of the house. But because the brother had a good reputation, and the convent understood that he had not spent them in a wicked place, nor sent them outside the house, and because he did not deny ever having had the besants, [he was allowed to keep his habit]. And if any wickedness had been known of the brother, he would not have been able to keep his habit, and also if he had been under suspicion of wickedness.

619. The other brother who was named Brother Matthew happened to be at Gastria;[1] and the said Brother John Harelip was his commander, and he forbad him a light that the brother was burning, that it should be burnt no longer. And when the commander came from his office, he noticed that the light was still burning; and Brother John exacted justice from the sergeant, and accused the brother on the matter of the light which he was burning against his prohibition. And he did not wish to plead for mercy for his commander who held chapter with six brothers; and because he did not wish to plead for mercy in his chapter, he came before the convent and pleaded for mercy. And he was sentenced to lose the habit, and he lost it with Brother John Harelip in the same chapter of Recordane.

617.1 Marshal of the Order.
618.1 Paphos lies in the south-west of the island. It was one of the Order's largest casals.
618.2 Modern-day Shefar'am, Israel, lying between Nazareth and Haifa.
619.1 A castle and casal on Cyprus.

620. And for this reason said the Master, Brother Pierre de Montagu, and Brother Anselm the Burgundian, since the brother rebelled in his chapter, standing, the habit may be taken from him and he may be put in irons; and thus may be treated a brother who does not wish to plead for mercy in his chapter, just as it is established in the house. And this is to include if the one who holds chapter orders a brother to plead for mercy for whatever failing it may be. But if one brother of the convent accuses another, and he does not wish to plead for mercy, for this reason he will not lose his habit, for one brother is not under the command of the other, but his failing may be judged. And when one brother accuses another, he should plead for mercy according to the law of the house, and if he does not wish to do so the one who holds chapter should order him. And if he accuses another brother, he will never be believed against him unless he has witnesses, for they are both brothers; but if he names a brother, and he fails to defend him, for him neither a serious nor slight failing may be considered without the habit; but he may say, 'There were brothers . . . .'

621. The thirtieth failing is if a brother leaves the house and sleeps two nights outside the house, he loses his habit, and he may not recover it for a year and a day. And if he keeps the things which are forbidden, more than two nights, he is expelled from the house.

622. The thirty-first is if any brother tears his habit wilfully, or throws it to the ground out of anger and does not wish to pick it up despite the pleas and admonishments made to him, and another brother picks up his habit before he takes it, he should not recover it for a year and a day; but if he willingly takes it before, it will be at the discretion of the brothers, whether to take it from him or let him keep it. And if by chance he does not wish to pick it up, and any brother takes the habit and places it round the neck of the brother who has returned it, that brother will lose his own, for no brother should return the habit nor make a brother outside chapter; and the one to whom the habit is returned in this way will be at the mercy of the brothers, whether to take it from him or let him keep it.

623. And in all these things except the last two, the one who sleeps two nights outside the house and the one who wilfully gives back his habit, which are a year and a day as we have said above, the other faults of the habit are at the discretion of the brothers, according to the fault and the conduct of the brother, whether to take it from him or let him keep it.

624. If a brother of the Temple has his sentence deferred for a thing for which he may be expelled from the house or lose the habit, he should not be believed against another brother who may lose his own, nor bear witness by which he could be expelled from the house or lose his habit.

625. It happened that brothers were sleeping in lodgings, and the commander forbad them to enter the casal. And it happened that one brother entered the house of a woman, and thought to sleep with her that night secretly and had his pleasure of her. And he pleaded for mercy as I have said before, and he was

sentenced to lose the habit; and then they let him keep it for love of God, because he had hitherto a good reputation.

626. It happened that brothers were lodged in Ascalon and carried all their equipment to the saddlery, and one brother took another's saddle-cloth, and knew well that it was not his, and took it away. And it happened that the Marshal assembled the brothers and ordered them to look in their places, and return each other's equipment, whoever had it; and on this the brother kept it for three months, and pleaded for mercy just as I have said before. So the old men argued this point, and some said he was a thief and others said that he was not. And they agreed because they did not wish him to be expelled from the house, for he was a good brother, and they allowed him to keep the habit for love of God.

627. In whatever way a brother of the Temple passes through the gate with the intention of leaving the house, he has lost honour, so that he should never again carry the piebald banner nor take part in the election of a Master; and if he goes to the Hospital or anywhere else and returns the same day, the habit is at the mercy of God and the brothers; and if he sleeps one night, the habit should not remain round his neck; and if he sleeps two there, he should not recover it for a year and a day.

628. If a brother is on penance, so that his habit is at the mercy of God and the brothers, and he goes away and sleeps one night outside the house and comes back again to his penance, when he is raised he should be shown that he has left the house; and if he sleeps two nights, he should not recover it for a year and a day, and should plead for mercy at the gate. And of this none should indicate anything to him, because it is worth a year and a day; and he is quit of that penance and all others. And if he goes away while on penance of a year and a day and returns the same day, the Almoner should put him on his penance again, and he has lost nothing of what he has done; but he should indicate to him that he left the house, when he has recovered the habit after the year and a day and has been raised. And if he sleeps one night outside the house, the Almoner should not put him on penance, for he has lost what he had done before, and should start again from the beginning; and they should not indicate anything to him naturally, because he starts again from the beginning.

629. If a brother is in the infirmary and another brother is given his horses at the time he goes to prime, he is relieved of them.

And if a brother is on penance and he enters the infirmary because of illness, when he is recovered and goes to prime, he may eat if he wishes his three meals, before he returns to his penance, going everywhere on foot. And if a brother is in the infirmary he may eat his three meals, and if he wishes he may go out the same day without permission. If a brother has been considered put on penance elsewhere, he may be put [on penance] before the brothers without holding chapter.

630. If a brother goes outside the house and takes a woman as wife, or joins

another order, there will be no harm if he comes to ask for re-admission to the house; but he should not have taken anything he should not take, nor be bound to the woman in anything, nor to the order, nor to us either, for it has happened likewise.

If a commander who is made by chapter leaves the house, none may put him on penance except the Master and the convent.

If a brother is provided with another brother's horses and the brother finds his horses in battle, and nowhere else, he will take them as his own.

631. If a brother is in the place of a commander of knights, he does not have the authority to give sleeping space nor room for horses, but he may provide what is necessary for them.

If a brother is on penance he should come on Sundays to corporal punishment and should receive it before chapter has begun; and afterwards he should say, 'Good lords, pray to God that He advise us.'

And if a brother asks permission from his chapter to join another order somewhere else outside the house, he should never again carry the piebald banner, nor take part in the election of a Master.

632. If a man asks to be a brother, at death, the one who gives him the habit should not say anything, but put it over him, when he is convinced [of the man's worthiness]. He may take it back if he sees that he is sinful; and if he dies with all the habit, it is not required to say the paternosters that should be said for a brother.

633. The castellans of castles are under the command of the commander of knights in battle, where he has a banner; and inside the castles they are not, and may send a brother under their command, without [the permission of] the commander of knights, in their work and without permission.

If a brother goes to the land of Tripoli or Antioch, and he finds himself in Tyre or Tripoli, the commander of the house will give the orders. But in battle or if the alarm is raised outside the town, and they go, the commander of the house will be under the command of the commander of knights who governs those brothers.

634. And the commander who leads the brothers, if the Marshal appoints him and they find themselves in other houses, either in Tortosa or elsewhere, the brothers who have come from here and there with commanders for Chapter General, the commander of the house will henceforth give the orders. But if the commander of the province has said to the new commander of the house, 'You will be commander of the house,' the one who is there is relieved, and the one who comes gives the orders.

All *bailli* brothers, when they enter the infirmary, must present their seals and purses to the commander by chapter. And those who are [made] by the Master and by the convent are obliged only to the Master and the convent.

635. If the commander of knights of the convent and the commander of Château Pèlerin and of Saphet or of other houses find themselves together, each

one leading brothers, and the convent is not there, the one who has more brothers is commander over all the others.

636. If a chaplain brother sins, he should plead for mercy in his chapter, just like our other brothers, without kneeling, and should do what the other brothers sentence him to.

If a chaplain brother has left the house and then returns to plead for mercy at the gate, he should undress at the door of the chapter or in the nearest room to the chapter, and come to chapter before the brothers and plead for mercy without kneeling. And if he does nothing for which he should be expelled from the house, he should be put on penance, and the chaplain brother should give him his punishment, and he should be a year and a day without his habit; and he should eat at the household's table without a napkin, and should keep all the other fasts which the other brothers keep who are on penance, until the brothers release him.

637. And he should come on Sundays to corporal punishment privately to the chaplain brother, and may sing during the week privately without music. And when the other brothers who are on penance work with the slaves, the chaplain brother should say his psalter instead of working. And if there is a chaplain brother who leads a wicked life or who spreads discord among the brothers or who spreads discord and scandal within the Order, he may be more readily got rid of than another brother, for thus commanded the pope when he gave us chaplain brothers. And if he does penance with his habit, he should eat at the turcopoles' table without a napkin.

638. Those examples written above were put on record for two reasons: one so that the brothers who hear them may carry out the order which is given to them and which will be told to them, for from these two things comes almost all the harm which befalls the brothers. – For those who do not carry out the orders given to them and do not keep the prohibitions which are made to them, and on this harm comes of these two things, put their habits in jeopardy. – The other reason is so that those who consider the failings of their brothers know better how to consider them, so that they do not accuse their brothers more than they should, and so that they know how to keep the justice of the house.

639. For it customary among us to make a serious failing in a worthy man a slight one, and in one of foolish conduct a slight one serious, just as is said above. But if a worthy man of the house who has led a good and religious life makes a mistake in anything for which he could be expelled from the house or lose the habit, he may be spared in such a way that the justice of the house is not contravened; for whoever would consider the failing and say that in his opinion he has lost the house according to the customs of the house, should know that he may not then consider another failing. But if he is a worthy man as is said above, he may be spared before he is sentenced to be expelled from the house: that is to say that his sentence may be deferred and he may be sent privately somewhere else at the command of the house provided that he remains in the house. And

whoever does not wish at all to show him this kindness, before he is sentenced to be expelled from the house, may be sentenced to lose the habit, but many may say that in their opinion the failing could be taken further, so that the young people see the failing for what it is. And let it be known that whoever has deserved to be expelled from the house, has indeed deserved to lose the habit. And in any other way they may show him kindness without contravening too much the law of the house.

640. And so it happened at Château Pèlerin that Brother Baudoin de Borrages was commander of the knights and the Turks rushed before the castle. And when he was outside, he found the scouts who had discovered the Turks, and they asked him to turn back, for the Turks were so numerous that they could not resist them; and he did not wish to do so, so he went as far as Mirla,[1] and the Turks closed all round them. And when he was in their midst and he saw that they could not escape, he lowered the banner in order to charge in their midst and reached the shore and two brothers with him, and the others were all dead or taken, and all the equipment lost. And the said brother Baudoin had friends who sent him overseas, and he stayed until the things were forgotten; and one of the brothers also went overseas, and the other stayed in the country, and never again did he have authority in the Temple: thus it was.

641. And if a brother is sentenced to lose the habit, it is not customary to sentence him to anything else, but to let him keep the habit for God. If a brother is sentenced to two days and the third, he does not go on Wednesdays to the chaplain brother, but at least on one Friday and one day to the chaplain brother. And these things have we heard from our old men of former times.

642. And whoever wishes to take these things written above as an example may do so, and whoever does not wish to burdens his conscience, which each one is obliged to guard against. And may he not judge his brother out of hatred or wrath, nor for love that he has for him should he omit to uphold the justice of the house; but following our good ancestors who have upheld our good traditions and the fine customs which were established in the house, according to these should each one judge his brother. And in such a way they will save their consciences.

God is the beginning of all things.

This is How the Punishments of the House should be Meted Out

643. The first is to be expelled from the house, from which God keep each one.

The second, to lose the habit, from which God keep each one.

The third, when any brother is allowed to keep the habit for God, if he is on three whole days until God and the brothers release him and pardon him one of

640.1 Between Château Pèlerin and Caesarea. Traditionally the birthplace of St Andrew.

the days; and he should be put immediately on his penance, that is without deferment. And if he is taken ill, the Almoner may give him the broth of the infirmary. And if he is ill, and it is fitting for him to go to the infirmary, he should inform the Almoner of his illness, and he should inform the Master or the one who holds that office. And that one should ask the brothers, and if the brothers agree to raise him, let him be raised on behalf of God; and if they do not agree to raise him, he should ask them if they agree that he be put in the infirmary, and they should agree if the brother has need of it, and then he should enter the infirmary. And as soon as he is recovered, he should return to his penance without speaking to the brothers. And let it be known that just as the one who is on penance should be raised by the judgement of the brothers, so also should he enter the infirmary by the judgement of the brothers, if he is ill, for as long as he is on his penance, according to the customs of our house.

644. Let it be known that if the habit is taken from a brother in one chapter, and in that same chapter it is returned at the request of the brothers and because of his great repentance, since he has gone outside the chapter without his habit, he remains on two days, for he is pardoned the third because of the habit which is returned to him and because of the shame he has received before the brothers.

645. Yet the old men of our house say that when a brother's habit is considered and has been taken from him, and according to his true repentance and according to his good behaviour it is returned to him, because before he had eaten one day without his habit, he remains on one day and no more. For he is pardoned the two days because of the shame to which he has been put and which he has received before secular people. And that brother is quit of all those penances which he had to do according to the customs of our house. And the brothers who are on penance are not so soon raised from the ground when their habits are returned to them; but since he has eaten one meal on the ground in his habit, whoever wishes may raise him, if he has done his penance well; and if he has not done it well and peacefully, he may be kept there for a long time. – And let all the brothers of the Temple know that the brother who is on penance for a year and a day, and dies while doing it, should be treated just like any other brother.

646. The fourth is two days and the third during the first week if the third is named; and if it is not named, he remains on two days and no more, but if the third is named, he should fast on the day he committed the sin, whatever day it may be except Sunday; and if he did it on Sunday he should fast on the Monday, for the failing should be taken further. And this failing may be considered for brothers from whom everything is taken which may be taken from them except their habits, that is two days. And this may be considered for a brother for the slightest failing, when the commandment of the house is transgressed.

647. The fifth is two days and no more. And a brother who is on two days may be told, if he is a knight brother or sergeant brother of the convent, to take care of his equipment, and a craftsman brother to practise his craft. And a

brother who is on three days or on two should lead an ass and carry out one of the base duties of the house; and he should come on Sundays to corporal punishment at the beginning of chapter; and they should sit quietly and peacefully at daybreak in their places, and if they know carpentry or any other skill, they may do it. Thus all the brothers who are on penance of three days or on two or on four should behave; and they should not touch any arms, unless they are falling into disrepair somewhere and they cannot otherwise repair them.

648. The sixth is one day and no more, and the one who is on one day is not to lead an ass nor work, as is said above of those who are on three days or two.

The seventh is Fridays and corporal punishment, but if they are sentenced to Fridays in chapter, they should not fast during the octaves of Christmas or Easter or Pentecost, nor take punishment except from the chaplain brother. And if the brother is ill, the one who holds chapter should tell him to take his punishment from the chaplain brother.

649. The eighth failing is when judgement is deferred until the brother is brought before the Master and before any of the old men of the house for them to give a ruling on anything of which the brothers are not certain.

The ninth is when a brother is sent to the chaplain brother.

The tenth is acquittal.

650. Let all the brothers of the Temple know that no brother has the authority to remove the habit without the permission of the one who may give it. Neither the Master nor any other brother has the authority to raise a brother from penance without speaking to the brothers, and if they agree to the raising so let him be raised, and if they do not agree to it he will not be raised.

651. If the brother who has left the house wishes to return in order to regain entry to the house, he should go to the main gate of the house and should kneel to all the brothers who pass by, and ask them for love of God to have pity on him, and he should do this several times. And the Almoner should feed him at the door and house him and remember him to the one who holds chapter and who has the authority to put him on his penance. And he should say before all the brothers, 'So-and-so who was our brother is at the door and requests re-admission to the house which he left through his own fault, and awaits the mercy of the house.'

And the one who holds chapter should say, 'Good lord brothers, does any of you know if this man who was our brother' – and he should name him by his name – 'has done or taken anything for which he may not nor should re-enter the house?' And if he has not, he should regain entry just as is said above.

652. The one who wishes to regain entry to the house should undress naked to his breeches at the main door where he is, a rope round his neck, and thus should he come to chapter before the one who holds it, and kneel before him and before all the brothers. And the one who holds chapter should say, 'Good brother, you have behaved foolishly in that you have left the house and your Order.' And the one who wishes to regain entry to the house should say that he

is greatly distressed and vexed that he has acted foolishly, but that he will make amends willingly as is established in the house.

653. And if the brother is known to be of bad behaviour and will do his penance neither well nor peacefully, the one who holds chapter should speak in this way, 'Good brother, you know that you have to do a heavy and long penance, and if you asked leave to enter another order in order to save your soul I think and believe that you would be wise, and I would advise you to do so.' And if he asks for leave, the one who has the authority to put him on penance has the authority to give him leave with the advice of the brothers. And if he does not ask for it, he may not be given it because he has done nothing for which he should be expelled from the house; but before he comes to chapter to plead for mercy, his sentence should be long deferred and he should be made to wait for a long time, by which he may know his folly well.

654. And if the brother is known to be of good behaviour, then they should make him leave the chapter and dress in the clothing which befits him, and then he should return to chapter and should be put on his penance and dressed in a cope without a cross, for thus it is established in the house. And they should tell the Almoner to take care of him, and so he should make him sleep and lodge in his house as it is established. And from the moment he is on penance, the Almoner should teach him what he should do; and if the brother who is on penance is ill, the Almoner should give him what he needs for his recovery; and he should put in writing the day he began his penance, so that it may be remembered.

655. No brother who is on penance should be called to any council nor to any call of brothers which may be made for an assembly of brothers, but privately and apart he may be asked his advice if necessary.

Furthermore the old and worthy men of our house say that no failing for which a brother may lose the habit should be considered before any brother who does not have the authority to make a brother.

And they also say that for no failing, just as is said, should a brother be put on Fridays, for first he should be put on one day or more, and thus they say is the custom of the house.

656. If a brother is on penance with all his habit and the alarm is raised, he may be lent horses and arms in order to go to that task with the other brothers, and when he comes back he should return to his penance.

No brother who has left the house should take part in the election of a Master nor carry the piebald banner.

Reception into the Order

This is how a Brother should be Made and Received into the Temple

657. 'Good lord brothers, you see well that the majority is agreed to make this one a brother: if there is any among you who knows in him anything for which he should not be a brother directly, he should tell it; for it would be a better thing for him to say it beforehand, than after he has come before us.' And if no-one says anything, so he should send for him, and put him in a chamber near the chapter; and then he should send two worthy men or three of the oldest of the house, who best know how to indicate what is fitting.

658. And when he is before these, they should say to him, 'Brother, do you request the company of the house?' And if he says, 'Yes,' they should instruct him in the great sufferings of the house, and the charitable commandments therein, and also all the sufferings that they know how to indicate to him. And if he says that he will willingly suffer all for God, and that he wishes to be a serf and slave of the house for ever, all the days of his life, they should ask him if he has a woman as wife or fiancée; or if he has ever made a vow or promise to another order; or if he owes a debt to any secular man which he cannot pay; and if he is healthy in his body, and has no secret illness; or if he is the serf of any man.

659. And if he says, 'No,' that he is indeed free of all these things, the brothers should enter the chapter and say to the Master or the one who takes his place, 'Sire, we have spoken to this worthy man who is outside and have indicated to him the sufferings of the house as we were able and knew how to. And he says that he wishes to be a serf and slave of the house, and of all those things which we asked him he is quit and free; there is no hindrance which means he cannot and should not be a brother, if it please God and you and the brothers.'

660. And the Master should say again that if there is anyone who knows anything else, he should tell it, for it would be better now than later. And if no-one says anything, so he should say, 'Do you wish him to be brought on behalf of God?' And the worthy men will say, 'Bring him on behalf of God.' And then those who spoke to him should return, and should ask, 'Are you still willing?' And if he says, 'Yes,' they should tell and teach him how he should request the company of the house. That is that he should come to chapter, and should kneel before the one who holds it, hands joined, and should say, 'Sire, I am come before God and before you and before the brothers, and ask and request you for love of God and Our Lady, to welcome me into your company and the favours of the house, as one who wishes to be a serf and slave of the house for ever.'

661. And the one who holds chapter should say, 'Good brother, you ask a very great thing, for of our Order you see only the outer appearance. For the

appearance is that you see us having fine horses, and good equipment, and good food and drink, and fine robes, and thus it seems to you that you would be well at ease. But you do not know the harsh commandments which lie beneath: for it is a painful thing for you, who are your own master, to make yourself a serf to others. For with great difficulty will you ever do anything that you wish: for if you wish to be in the land this side of the sea, you will be sent the other side; or if you wish to be in Acre, you will be sent to the land of Tripoli or Antioch, or Armenia; or you will be sent to Apulia, or Sicily, or Lombardy, or France, or Burgundy, or England, or to several other lands where we have houses and possessions. And if you wish to sleep, you will be awoken; and if you sometimes wish to stay awake, you will be ordered to rest in your bed.'

662. And if he is a sergeant brother and he wishes to be a brother of the convent, he may be told to carry out one of the basest tasks that we have, perhaps at the oven, or the mill, or in the kitchen, or with the camels, or in the pigsty or several other duties that we have. – And 'often other harsh commandments you will be given: when you are at table and wish to eat, someone will order you to go wherever he wishes, and you will not know where. And many complaining words that you will hear many times you must suffer. Now decide, good gentle brother, if you could tolerate all these hardships.'

663. And if he says, 'Yes, I will tolerate them all if God pleases,' the Master or the one who takes his place should say, 'Good brother, you should not request the company of the house in order to have domains or riches, nor in order to have physical ease or honour. But you should request it for three reasons: one, to put aside and leave behind the sin of this world; the other, to do the work of Our Lord; the third is in order to be poor and do penance in this world, that is for the salvation of the soul; and such should be the thought by which you ask it.'

664. And so he should ask him, 'Do you wish to be, all the days of your life henceforth, a serf and slave of the house?' And he should say, 'Yes, if it please God, sire.' 'And do you wish to leave behind your own will all the remaining days of your life in order to do what your commander orders?' And he should say, 'Sire, yes, if it please God.'

665. And the Master will say, 'Now go outside, and pray to Our Lord that He advise you.' Then when he is outside, the one who holds chapter may say, 'Good lords, you see that this worthy man has great desire of the company of the house, and says that he wishes to be, all the days of his life henceforth, a serf and slave of the house, and I have said before that if there is any among you who knows anything in him for which he should not be a brother directly, he should tell it, for after he is a brother he will not be believed in anything.'

666. And if no-one says anything, the Master will say, 'Do you wish him to be brought on behalf of God?' And then a worthy man will say, 'Bring him on behalf of God.' Then one of the worthy men who spoke to him before should go and look for him, and he should instruct him again how he should request the company of the house as he requested before.

667. And when he has come to chapter, he should kneel with hands joined and should say, 'Sire, I come before God and before you and before the brothers, and ask and request you for love of God and Our Lady to welcome me into your company and into the favours of the house, spiritual and temporal, as one who wishes to be a serf and slave of the house all the remaining days of his life.' And the one who holds chapter should ask him, 'Have you considered well, good brother, that you wish to be a serf and slave of the Order and leave behind your own will for ever to do another's? And do you wish to suffer all the hardships which are established in the house and carry out all the orders you will be given?' He should say, 'Sire, yes, if it please God.'

668. And then the one who holds chapter should rise and should say, 'Good lords, rise and pray to Our Lord and Lady St Mary that he does it well.' And each one should say once the paternoster if it please them, and afterwards the chaplain brother should say a prayer to the Holy Spirit. And then the one who holds chapter should take the Gospels and should open them; and the one who is to be a brother should take them in both hands and kneel. And the one who holds chapter should say to him, 'Good brother, the worthy men who have spoken to you have asked you much, but whatever you have said to them and to us, all are vain and idle words, and neither you nor we could suffer great harm from anything you have said. But see here the holy words of Our Lord, and of the things we will ask you, you will tell us the truth, for if you lie you will be perjured and may be expelled from the house, from which God keep you.

669. 'But firstly we ask you if you have a woman as wife or fiancée, who may and should ask for you by the right of the Holy Church; for if you lie about it, and it happens tomorrow or some time later that she comes and she can prove that you are her husband and she can ask for you by the right of the Holy Church, the habit will be taken from you and you will be put in heavy irons, and so you will be made to work with the slaves. And when you have been put to shame enough, you will be taken by the hand and delivered over to the woman, and you will be expelled from the house for ever.

670. 'The second is if you have been in another order, or have made a vow or promise, for if you have made it and you can be found guilty of it, and the order asks for you as its brother, the habit will be taken from you and you will be returned to the order, and beforehand you will be put to much shame and will lose the company of the house for ever.

671. 'The third is if you owe any debt to any secular man which you cannot pay, either yourself or your friends, without taking anything from the alms of the house, the habit will be taken from you and you will be returned to the creditor, and then the house will be obliged to neither you nor the creditor for anything.

672. 'The fourth is if you are healthy in your body, that there is no secret illness in you except what we see outside; and if you are proven guilty of having had it in the world before being our brother, you could be expelled from the house, from which God keep you.

673. 'The fifth is if you have promised or given to a secular man or a brother of the Temple or to another, gold or silver or anything else for which he could help you enter this Order, for that would be simony, and you would not be able to save yourself in our house: if you were proven guilty of it, you would lose the company of the house.

'Or if you were the serf of any man and he asked for you, you would be returned to him and would be expelled from the house.' And if he is a knight brother do not ask him any of this, but he may be asked if he is the son of a knight and a lady, and if his father is of knightly lineage; and if he was born in legal wedlock.

674. Afterwards he should be asked, if he is a knight brother or sergeant brother, whether he is a priest or deacon or sub-deacon, for if he had any of these orders and concealed it, he could be expelled from the house. And if he is a sergeant brother, he should be asked if he is a knight. And they should be asked if they are excommunicated, both knight brothers and sergeant brothers.

And then the one who holds chapter may ask the old men of the house if there is anything else to ask, and if they say, 'No,' the one who holds chapter will say, 'Good brother, to all these questions that we have asked, take care that you have told us the truth, for if you have lied in any of these things, you may be expelled from the house, from which God keep you.

675. 'Now, good brother, now hear well what we will say to you: do you promise to God and Our Lady that henceforth all the days of your life you will be obedient to the Master of the Temple and whatever commander will be over you?' And he should say, 'Yes, sire, if it please God.'

'Do you also promise to God and to Lady St Mary that henceforth all the days of your life you will live chastely in your body?' And he should say, 'Yes, sire, if it please God.'

'Do you also promise to God and Our Lady St Mary that you, all the remaining days of your life, will live without property?' And he should say, 'Yes, sire, if it please God.'

'Do you also promise to God and to Lady St Mary that you, all the remaining days of your life, will keep the fine traditions and good customs of our house, those which are and those which the Master and the worthy men of the house will introduce?' And he should say, 'Yes, if it please God, sire.'

676. 'Do you also promise to God and to Lady St Mary that you, all the remaining days of your life, will help to conquer, with the strength and power that God has given you, the Holy Land of Jerusalem; and that which Christians hold you will help to keep and save within your power?' And he should say, 'Yes, sire, if it please God.'

'Do you also promise to God and to Lady St Mary that you will never leave this Order for stronger or weaker, nor for worse or better, unless you do so with the permission of the Master and of the convent who have the authority?' And he should say, 'Yes, sire, if it please God.'

'Do you also promise to God and to Lady St Mary that you will never be in a place where a Christian may be wrongfully or unreasonably deprived of his things either by your authority or your counsel?' And he should say, 'Yes, sire, if it please God.'

677. 'And we, on behalf of God and Our Lady St Mary, and on behalf of My Lord St Peter of Rome, and on behalf of our father, the pope and all the brothers of the Temple, we welcome you to all the favours of the house which have been done since the beginning and which will be done up to the end, and you and your father and mother and all those whom you will wish to welcome of your lineage. And you also welcome us to all the favours which you have done and will do. And so we promise you the bread and water and the poor clothing of the house and much pain and suffering.'

678. And then the one who holds chapter should take the mantle and should place it round his neck and fasten the laces. And the chaplain brother should say the psalm which is said, *Ecce quam bonum*,[1] and the prayer to the Holy Spirit, and each of the brothers should say the paternoster. And the one who makes him a brother should raise him up and kiss him on the mouth; and it is custom-ary for the chaplain brother to kiss him also.

And then the one who makes him a brother should make him sit before him and should say to him, 'Good brother, Our Lord has led you to your desire and has placed you in such a fine company as is the Knighthood of the Temple, because of which you should be at great pains to ensure that you never do anything for which it would be necessary to expel you from it, from which God keep you. And we will tell you some of those things which we remember of the failings of the house and the habit.

679. 'Now good brother, you have heard well the things for which you could be expelled from the house, and those of the habit, but not all: so learn them and take care if God pleases, and you should ask and enquire of the brothers about them. Now there are other things which are established, and if you do them other punishment will be given; that is that you should never strike any Chris-tian, nor touch him angrily or wrathfully either with your fist or the sole of your foot, nor pull him by the hair or kick (*villier*) him with your foot. And if you strike him with a stone, or staff, or a sharp weapon as I have told you before, with which you might kill or wound him with one blow, your habit will be at the mercy of the brothers, whether to take it from you or let you keep it. Nor should you swear to God or Our Lady, nor to any of the saints. Nor should you ever use the services of a woman, except for an illness of your body, or with the per-mission of the one who may give it to you; nor should you ever kiss a woman, neither mother nor sister nor any relative you may have, nor any other woman. Nor should you ever call a man a miser, stinking or a traitor, nor any other vile words, for all vile words are forbidden us, and all courtesies are permitted and good.

678.1 Psalm 133.

680. 'Now we will say how you should sleep: henceforth you should always sleep in a shirt and breeches and in woollen hose, and belted with a small belt;[1] and you should have on your bed three pieces of linen, that is to say a bag in which to put straw and two sheets, and in place of one sheet you may have a light blanket if the Draper wishes to give it to you; the rug is a favour if you find anyone to give it to you. Of clothing you should have only what the Draper gives you, and if you buy any other, harsh justice will be exacted.

681. 'Now we will tell you how you should come to table and how you should come to the hours. You should come whenever the bell sounds; when the bell rings for meals, you should come to the table and wait for the priests and clerks to say the blessing. And you should see if there is bread and water or whatever you should drink, and then say the blessing, and then you should sit and cut your bread. And if you are in a place where a priest may come, you should say one paternoster in silence, before you sit and cut your bread, and then you should eat your bread quietly and in silence, and whatever God has given you; and you should ask for nothing but bread and water, for you are promised nothing else; and if the brothers eat something else, you may ask for some of it privately. But if you eat meat or fish and it is raw, or bad, or discoloured, you may ask to change it, but it is a better thing for your companion to ask it than you; and if he has plenty he will change it, and if he does not, so he will give you something else instead, either from the household's food, or something of which there is plenty, and you should keep quiet and take it patiently.

682. 'And when you have eaten, you should go to the chapel after the priests and give thanks to Our Lord in silence, and you should not speak until you have said one paternoster, and the priests, grace. And if there is no priest, [you should say them] in the same place or in the most honourable place near here, and then you may go to your duties. And when you hear nones rung, you should come here: if there is a priest, you should hear them, and if there is no priest you should say fourteen paternosters, seven for Our Lady and seven for the day. – And also at vespers you should come to hear them, and if there is neither priest nor church, you should say eighteen paternosters, nine for Our Lady and nine for the day. And afterwards you should go to supper; and when you hear the bell for compline sound, you should come to take collation of what will be brought to you, for it is at the discretion of the Master whether he wishes wine or water; and then if any order is given you should hear it, and do what you are commanded. And then you should hear compline if there is a priest, and if there is not, you should say fourteen paternosters, seven for the day and seven for Our Lady. – And then go to lie down. And if you wish to give any orders to your household, you may command them privately whatever you wish. And when you have lain down you should say one paternoster.

683. 'And when you hear matins rung, you should get up if there is a priest and hear them, and if there is no priest you should say twenty-six paternosters,

680.1 See §54.

thirteen for Our Lady and thirteen for the day. And then you should say thirty paternosters for the dead and thirty for the living, before you drink or eat, except water. And you should not omit to say them except because of an illness of your body, for they are established for our *confrères*, and for our *consoeurs*, and for our benefactors, and for our benefactresses, so that Our Lord may lead them to a fine end and give them true forgiveness. And when you have heard matins if there is a priest – and if there is no priest [when you have] said them – you may go to lie down.

684. 'And when you hear prime and terce and sext rung, all one after the other, if there is a priest hear them, and if there is no priest you should say fourteen paternosters, seven for Our Lady and seven for the day; for terce as many; for sext as many; and you should say one after the other before you eat.

685. 'And all the things that I have told you, you should say; but you should say the hours of Our Lady first, and those of the day afterwards, because we were established in honour of Our Lady; and so say those of Our Lady standing and those of the day sitting. And if you sleep in a house of the Temple where a brother of the Temple dies, or you eat of the bread of that house where the brother dies, you should say one hundred paternosters for his soul: during the following seven days, when you are able, you should say them. And if God summons the Master, you should [say] two hundred paternosters in whatever place you may be, during the seven days. And you should never omit the paternosters for the dead, except because of an illness of your body, just as it is said above.

686. 'Now we have told you the things which you should do and what you should guard against, and those which lead to expulsion from the house, and those which lead to loss of the habit, and the other punishments; and we have not told you everything we should tell you, but you will ask it. – And may God let you say and do well.'

AMEN

APPENDIX

La Règle du Temple as a Military Manual
or
How to Deliver a Cavalry Charge

MATTHEW BENNETT

'In the charge against both cavalry and infantry each man will ride at his opponent at full speed with the fixed determination of running him through and killing him . . . In the mêlée, if both sides are equally determined, success depends on the handiness of the horse and the skill of the soldier as a man at arms.'
(Extract from Cavalry Training (Horsed) (1937))[1]

No one who has heard RAB lecture* could doubt that he was once a cavalry-man. In any display of slides, usually depicting castles, his Army sword is brought into play to point out important features.[2] Also, it has long been his contention that medieval soldiers were as professional as during any age.[3] This brief investi-gation of the Old French Rule of the Knights Templar is designed to show how a well-organised medieval cavalry regiment worked. For that is what the knights of the Order formed on campaign; up to 300 lance-armed heavy cavalrymen with all the additional personnel and logistical support such a body needs. La Règle du Temple provides a unique insight into medieval military professionalism.

It is exceptional because of its format, contents and date. As edited by Henri de Curzon the OF Rule is a compilation of the mid-thirteenth century. It pre-dates the first vernacular translations of Vegetius by a generation.[4] In addition, it

Acknowledgements I would like to thank Roy Boss for providing me with the idea for this paper, Prof. R. H. C. Davis for reading an earlier draft, Drs Malcolm Barber and Jinty Nelson for help with it, and RAB for inspiring my research in toto.
* This article was first published as a tribute to the late R. Allen Brown in Studies in Medieval History presented to R. Allen Brown, ed. Christopher Harper-Bill et al. (Wood-bridge 1989).

[1] See page 30: Fighting with the sword (22); The use of the sword in war (1 and 2). (HMSO 1937).
[2] RAB's love for his sword was such that he carried it strapped to the turret of his armoured car during active service in WWII. It is also worth noting that the 1909 pattern cavalry sword was designed to be used in exactly the same manner as the medieval knight's lance – that is to combine the impetus of man and horse behind its point!
[3] The Normans and the Norman Conquest, 1969, 49 'As soldiers, the Norman knights of 1066 were as professional as the age could make them.'
[4] Ed. H. de Curzon, SATF, Paris 1886, repr. 1976. L. Dailliez's edition, Dijon 1977, was

is probable that the military instructions it contains were drawn up at least a century earlier, when the Templars first took on their (self-imposed) task of protecting the Holy Land against the infidel.[5] It is important that it is composed in the spoken language of the brothers, because this brings us closer to their actual drills. But this is not a drill manual, although it reads like one in parts. Nor is it a military manual after the style of the *De re militari* or the *Strategikon* of Maurice, in the Roman and Byzantine tradition.[6] If it shares the pedantry of a modern training manual, in listing the equipment each brother must have, it is for a different reason. For the Templars were monks, living in communal poverty and so must give up the luxurious trappings of their knightly caste – except for the military essentials. Monastic rule and military instruction fit uneasily together. It is significant that the original Latin Rule contains (almost) nothing of use to the practical soldier. The OF Rule, on the other hand, is the empirical product of the largely French-speaking warrior class that made up the Order. There are none of the references to classical authority so beloved of military treatises.[7] This is its great value.

Of the *Règle*'s 686 articles the first seventy-two are translated from the Latin Rule adopted at the Order's official foundation at the Council of Troyes in 1128. There follows a series of seventy-five statutes describing, in great detail, the pieces of equipment, animals and retainers that accord to all the ranks down from the Master to the brother knight. The next twenty articles describe the organisation of a campaign and the rules for conduct in camp, on the march and on the battlefield.[8] Another thirteen statutes deal with the officers of the sergeants. There are further sections on meals, punishments and the ordering of the conventual life, before, barely half-way through, the work becomes a list of revisions or expansions of previous statutes (315*ff*.). The last articles deal with historical examples of infringements of the Rule and their punishments, and finally the ceremony for receiving a new brother into the Order.

It is worthwhile considering where the *Règle* fits into the tradition of military

consulted but is open to criticism. See K. Hiestand's review in *Deutsches Archiv* xxxiv, 1978, 641.

5   References to events in the Holy Land date the text to the 1260s. See Curzon, Intro, iv–v.

6   Vegetius ed. C. Lang, Leipzig 1885, rpr. Stuttgart 1967; G. Dennis (a) ed. *Das Strategikon des Maurikios*, Corpus fontium historiae byzantinae xvii, Vienna, 1981 Greek text/ German trans (b) *Maurice's Strategikon*, Pennsylvania UP, Philadelphia 1984, English trans.

7   See John Cruso, *Militarie Instructions for the Cavall'rie*, 1632 ed./facs. P. Young, Kineton 1972, for lavish references to Vegetius, Frontinus etc. to support his every assertion.

8   Much of this has been summarised by J. F. Verbruggen, *The Art of Warfare in Western Europe during the Middle Ages*, Oxford 1977. See also M. Jähns, *Geschichte der Kriegswissenschaften vornehmlich in Deutschland* (Geschichte der Wissenschaften in Deutschland xxi, Müchen u. Leipzig 1889) 3 vols., i, 212–16. The references in R. C. Smail, *Crusading Warfare 1097–1193*, Cambridge 1956, 129, to articles in the *Règle*, first encouraged me to study the source.

instruction manuals. Unlike every other book of advice for military men produced in the medieval West it contains no reference to Vegetius.[9] This late Roman commentator was the *vade mecum*, and more than that, a touchstone providing authority for any statement on warfare.[10] His general precepts and advice on strategy and tactics are excellent; but he says almost nothing about the use of cavalry.[11] This should have been a serious defect for an age where the horseman played such a great role in society and war. Certainly, in the mid-ninth century, Hrabanus Maurus was very selective in the excerpts he sent to King Lothar II.[12] The Carolingian scholar recognised that strictures on the qualities and skills of the young warriors were of more use than a dissertation on the long-gone Roman legion. It is not the size of the army that counts, he urged Lothar, but the skill and courage of its *milites*. He also anticipates the Crusaders' prejudice against soft southerners, whom he derides as 'wilier but lacking in spirit'.[13] In contrast to such an erudite and shrewd commentator, the earliest OF translations are but sad and slavish imitations of the original. Writing within half a century of our copy of the *Règle*, neither Jean de Meun nor Jean de Vignay make any attempt to adapt Vegetius to the world of the knights.[14]

This is exactly the ground that the Templar Rule occupies. In fact there are no references to the organisation or tactics of the infantry who made up a large part of Templar armies. The *Règle* is concerned with the socially élite world of the cavalryman; and how he is to be equipped, maintained and employed on campaign and on the battlefield. The number of horses each Templar is allowed is a sure guide to his status. The ordinary knight brother is entitled to have up to

9   Cf. Jähns i, 186–7, where he claims that medieval warfare exactly followed the late Roman pattern! Smail, 121 and fn. criticises H. Delpech, *La Tactique au XIIIième siècle*, 2 vols., Paris 1886, and other nineteenth-century writers, for the same reason. Another valuable military manual in the OF vernacular, *Les Enseignements de Théodore Paléologue*, is also ignorant of Vegetius, but then its author was a Greek writing in the Byzantine tradition. See Christine Knowles, ed., MHRA Texts and Dissertations xix, London 1973, 7, and a useful summary of the source by D. J. A. Ross, 'The Prince Answers Back: "Les Enseignements de Théodore Paliologue" ', in *The Ideals and Practice of Medieval Knighthood, Papers from the First and Second Strawberry Hill Conferences*, ed. C. Harper-Bill and R. Harvey, Woodbridge 1986.

10   E.g. John of Marmoutier's story of Geoffrey, count of Anjou, taking a castle in the Loire valley (1147), after referring to a Vegetius and using its recipe for Greek Fire (which it does not contain); see: *Historia Gaufredi*, in L. Halphen and R. Poupardin, eds. *Chroniques des comtes d'Anjou et des seigneurs d'Amboise*, Paris 1913, 218. The story is cited by A. Murray, *Reason and Society*, Oxford 1978, 127–30 and 446–7, as part of a discussion of Vegetius' medieval popularity, during which he emphasises that the text may well have been augmented in this way.

11   Nor is this surprising, since Vegetius is writing in praise of a return to the standards of the earlier Roman infantry legion. Cavalry is portrayed in a purely auxiliary role.

12   Ed. E. Dümmler, *Zeitschrift für deutsches Altertum* xv, 1872, 443–50.

13   *Ibid.* ch. 2. Hrabanus' actual words are: 'At contra qui septentrionem incolunt minus sapiunt sed fortiores sunt animo'. The idea comes from Vegetius i, 2.

14   New editions of both have been recently produced by L. Löfstadt, in *Suomalaison tiedeaktemian toimituksia*, Series B xx, 1977: de Meun; ccxiv, 1982: de Vignay.

four: one or two warhorses, one riding animal (a mule or a palfrey) and one packhorse. He has a squire to tend and ride each warhorse, and this small group of men and animals make up the basic military unit of the Templar host (138–40).[15] This increases in size up the hierarchy until the Master has a household of a dozen men and horses (74).

So much for those of knightly rank. In contrast, the ignoble sergeants have only one mount each, although their officers are entitled to two. In addition the sergeants are more lightly armoured than the knights. For example, their mail hose are to be without feet, enabling them to serve as infantry (141). One other group of combatants remains: the Turcopoles. These seem to have been troops equipped with the bow, capable of fighting in the Eastern manner. They occupy a position between the knights and sergeants, but are not subject to the Order's discipline, probably being recruited for each campaign.[16] Their chief officer, the Turcopolier, is a man of importance with four mounts, including a fine 'turcoman'. He may even command knights whilst on reconnaissance, which implies that the Turcopoles' main role may have been to act as scouts (169–173).[17]

The Hierarchy of the Order

A study of the command structure of the Order shows how carefully the Templars had thought about organising their cavalry regiment. The language is that of the professional military men who drew up the regulations. It may be significant that another vernacular work, the Anglo-Norman Hospitallers' *Riwle*, was also produced for a military Order. Only literate monks thought to write down what would normally have been transmitted verbally, in the vernacular military culture.[18]

The Templar hierarchy accurately reflects the secular military structure – with certain differences. The Master had overall control of strategy, but he was elected by Chapter and required its assent on occasion. These included declaring war or arranging a truce, alienating land or taking over the defence of a castle, appointing provincial commanders and chief officers and receiving a new brother into the Order (85, 87 and 97). Beneath him stood the Seneschal, whose duties were concerned with the administration of the lands, houses, food and pack train of the Order. He also held the 'confanon baucon' (Piebald Banner), both the symbol of the Templars and their battle standard (99–100). The

---

[15] The numbers of the 'retrais' cited are henceforward given in parentheses in the text.

[16] See, however, M. Melville's view, taken from the Catalan Rule, which allowed three bezants p.a., gifts of clothes and 'restor' of horses for such troops (*La Vie des Templiers*, Paris 1951, 98 n. 19). Smail, 111–12 describes their role on campaign and in battle.

[17] (170) limits his authority to groups of less than ten knights. A Commander of Ten, carrying a banner, was considered senior in rank.

[18] Ed. K. V. Sinclair, Anglo-Norman Text Society xlii, 1984. I am grateful to Prof. Ian Short for bringing this to my attention and for elucidating the need that many monks, not just military monks, had for instructional material in the vernacular.

description of his activities is very brief in the Rule, but he was a senior official who was sometimes elected Master on the incumbent's death.

In contrast, the 'retrais' concerning the Marshal's duties are long and detailed (101–9). He was responsible for the collection and distribution of all military equipment, not just for the knights, but also crossbows and 'Turkish arms' for the sergeants.[19] He also supervised the allocation of mounts, and received into his charge animals sent overseas by the houses in Europe. Brothers were forbidden to request particular horses from him, and if they did so were given the worst animal. If they had trouble with their mounts (the Rule describes 'pullers', 'stoppers' and 'throwers') they could appeal to the Marshal for a replacement. Once he had agreed to the deficiency the brother received another mount and the trouble-maker was returned to the 'caravanne' or train. The same applied when horses were lost in battle.[20]

The Commander of the City of Jerusalem fulfilled the duty of the original Templars: that of guarding pilgrims on the route to the Jordan. To assist him in this task he was assigned ten knights. In war-time they formed his bodyguard 'never leaving him by night or day'.[21] He was also responsible for collecting the secular 'confrères', who rode under his banner when on campaign, and all brother knights resident in Jerusalem, in the Marshal's absence (120–4).

The Commander of the Kingdom of Jerusalem acted as treasurer, and had authority over the goods of the Order. He was also responsible for the supervision of horses and herds and flocks of livestock, which he handed over to the Marshalcy, as required. This included horse breeding, for there is a reference to the 'polains' (foals) cared for on the 'casals', or farms. He took charge of all livestock and pack animals gained in war, but handed saddle horses over to the Marshal. Finally, he distributed the brothers between the Temple in Jerusalem and houses and castles in the countryside, so that they might best be supported in time of peace (110–19).[22] The Commanders of the Lands of Tripoli and of

[19] This equipment included anything bought, received in alms or won as booty (102). Turkish arms may mean powerful composite bows, although maces are referred to with this adjective in the Knight's 'retrais' (139). Note also that the Marshalcy kept a store of crossbows (103).

[20] The emphasis here is probably on the destriers. Cf. a nineteenth-century Prussian manual which warns the cavalryman to be wary of various types of horses: those who stretch their necks, keep their noses in the air or too low and stumblers (Maj. Gen. Carl von Schmidt, *Intructions for the training, employment and leading of cavalry*, trans. Capt. C. W. Bowdler Bell, HMSO London 1875, 16). See also, *Manual of Horsemastership, Equitation and Animal Transport*, HMSO London 1937, Ch. 3, sections 77–86, for how such vices were corrected in RAB's day.

[21] The Commander of the City of Jerusalem has this bodyguard because it is alleged in the Rule that he carried the True Cross in battle (122).

[22] Another important logistical duty was control of the ships of the Order at Acre (119). Also in his role as Quartermaster, the Commander of the Kingdom had the Drapier, responsible for all matters of dress, under his command (112). For an idea of what the Templars were capable of, as regards the construction and maintenance of castles, see R. B. C. Huygens ed., *De constructione castri Saphet*, Amsterdam 1981.

Antioch had similar responsibilities. Special reference is made to their obligation to equip the castles of their commands. They were to ensure that these were provided with wheat, wine, iron, steel, leather and leather equipment and 'sergeants to guard the door' (125–9). Below them in the provincial structure came the Commanders of Houses, and finally the Commanders of Knights. The duties of these last included acting as officers on the battlefield (132–5, 137). Together with all higher ranks they were permitted to carry standards, both as marks of status and rallying points in battle.

Then came the knight brothers. By the mid-thirteenth century, only a man whose father and grandfather were knights was eligible for the honour, and anyone born outside marriage was automatically disbarred (337). They were distinguished from ignoble brothers by their white robes, while the sergeants were allowed only black or brown; and the Rule makes several references to the importance of the distinction.[23] The officers of the sergeants were headed by the Turcoplier, whose role had already been reviewed. He commanded all the sergeants when they were 'under arms' (171). Beneath him the Undermarshal was responsible for 'le menu hernois' (the lesser gear). This included the repair and distribution of horses' harnesses, the padding for saddles and various arms (173–6). He was also responsible for distributing barrels to hold, and buckets to draw, water. He was the subordinate of the Marshal in matters concerning the equipment of the brothers, and all serving brothers of the Marshalcy were at his command.

The office of Confanonier (Standard Bearer) was an important one (177–9). He directed the activities of the squires, who played a crucial role in caring for the Order's horses and assisting their masters on campaign and in battle. He was their paymaster for their term of service, directed their chapter and was responsible for disciplining and punishing them.[24] When they were required to do their duties communally, whether working with the pack train, or watering, feeding or grooming their masters' mounts, the Confanonier was to lead them, carrying the banner at their head. This he also did on the battlefield.

Here we have evidence of an impressively comprehensive military structure. It was a disciplined body, the warrior monks having given up their free will in the same way as a modern soldier. Even those of lower social rank were expected to obey detailed rules of behaviour whilst on campaign and in battle. I shall return to examine these activities later. First though, what were a knight brother's duties in peacetime? The Rule has little to say on this. As a monk he was obliged to observe the daily Hours (e.g. 146–7). It is likely that most knights were illiterate, however, and chaplains were appointed, with special privileges, to conduct the services (268–78). In any case, a brother was excused attendance

---

[23] (17), (68), (337) and (586), which cites the case of a brother who wrongly claimed the mantle of knighthood.

[24] For the paid nature of the squires' work see (67) and (177), and my article, 'The Status of the Squire: the Northern Evidence', in *Ideals and Practice*, (cited n. 10) 1–11.

at Nones or Vespers for a number of reasons. One, which shows that he had personal responsibility for maintaining his mounts, was if he had taken a horse for re-shoeing (300). There is unfortunately little evidence as to how he spent the rest of his spare time. Before meals in morning and afternoon he was expected to repair his gear, or failing that, and following the adage that 'The devil makes work for idle hands', he was to carve tent pegs (285). The ordinary pursuits of secular knights were largely forbidden. No hunting, except of the lion, was permitted, and shooting with crossbows was to be restricted to target practice. In such contests wagering was to be strictly curtailed (317). Horse racing was allowed only with the express permission of the Master, and riding anywhere too impetuously was condemned. There were the same restrictions on practice jousts ('bouhorder'), which were only permitted in the Master's presence (95, 126 and 315).[25]

Now this raises a real problem. A glance at other cavalry manuals, from Maurice's *Strategikon* up to modern times, shows how much importance is laid upon practice with weapons and movement in troops and squadrons. 'A troop should only execute before the enemy such manoeuvres as it has been accustomed to in times of peace', affirms an influential Prussian treatise of the last century.[26] How did the Templars learn to do this? The *Règle* is mute on this point although the description of how to deliver a charge implies that some such training must have taken place. Certainly detailed regulations are laid down for behaviour on campaign: on the ordering of the march, the making and striking of camp, foraging, and responding to attack. These will be considered next.[27]

The Templars on Campaign and in Battle

At the beginning of a campaign the brothers were mustered from their various quarters, bringing with them horses, pack animals and livestock which were organised into a caravan, or possibly separate caravans, by the Marshal. His permission was required for their distribution, but when fed or grazed communally they were under the charge of the Confanonier, as commander of the squires (178).

Each brother knight had a tent and in camp these were set up around the chapel, but only after the Marshal's order: 'Herbergés vos, seignors frères, de par Dieu!' (148).[28] The knight chose a place outside the guy-ropes of the chapel,

---

[25] Much useful training in tactics and fighting technique came through the sort of continual skirmishing described by Usamah ibn Munqhid, an Arab nobleman. See *The Autobiography of Ousama*, ed./trans. G. R. Potter, London 1929, and, as *Memoirs of an Arab-Syrian Gentleman*, P. K. Hitti, Beirut 1964. I am grateful to Dr Richard Barber for pointing out that *bouhorder* was only a training exercise, not as dangerous as the real thing. This limitation further supports the strictness of Templar discipline and their desire not to risk a limited manpower.

[26] Von Schmidt, *Instructions*, 10.

[27] See also Verbruggen, *Art of Warfare*, 76–9.

[28] Those allowed to establish themselves before the Chapel were the Marshal, the

with enough space for himself and his retainers, and, putting all his gear within it, pitched his tent. The order was then given for the squires to go out foraging, taking a horse and saddle, and to collect water and firewood. It was forbidden to set off without permission, and at no time should anyone stray out of earshot of the camp bell. The crier (of orders) and the 'granatier', or distributer of fodder were to camp with the Confanonier, who organised the squires in feeding and caring for the horses (149).[29] Rations for the men were distributed communally, but graded according to status and the brother knights ate apart from the sergeants, in pairs (150–3). It was forbidden to buy food, and any given or found had to be handed over for distribution, as did fodder.[30]

If the alarm was raised for an attack on the camp, those nearby were instructed to take up shield and lance and rush to repel it; while others were to go to the chapel to await the Master's orders (155). An example of Templar discipline in practice took place on the Fifth Crusade. When the Egyptians attacked the Crusader camp on 31 July 1219, their swift response saved the day.[31] Camp was to be struck quietly and in an orderly manner. No one was to mount or load his gear until the order was given. If a brother wanted to speak to the Marshal he had to go to him on foot, and then return quietly to his place. On the order, the knights mounted, and at the walk or amble took up positions to form a line of march, their squires following behind with the baggage. It is not clear if they formed up behind the Commanders of Houses and Commanders of Ten Knights, although this seems likely. Once in position they set their squires before them with their lance, shield and led horses. This matches descriptions in the 'chansons de geste', where the boys are depicted as bowed down under the weight of all this equipment.[32] On the march they were instructed to go quietly and in good order, keeping silence at night-time, until Prime (157).[33] Any

Commander of the Kingdom and the provisions tent. This was only practical and sensible, as are the orders, which on few occasions they are reported are in French. Contrast this with the detached, textbook style of Maurice's *Strategikon*, where they are in Latin!

[29] Additional instructions include that the saddle should be covered with a rug to protect it, that the war-saddle should be used with special permission, and that only one squire should be allowed to go out foraging.

[30] Rations and status were also closely connected. (150) and (319) deal with their distribution, (336) states that this should be under the supervision of an older Brother, (386) that this should also happen in every house, and (372) that he was to ensure equal portions and equal quality of food. In (319) we discover that the ration of wine on fast days was scarcely less than normal!

[31] Oliver of Paderborn, *Historia Damiatina* ch. 28, trans. J. J. Gavigan, as *The Capture of Damietta*, Philadelphia 1948, repr. Oxford 1980, 39–40.

[32] See, e.g. *Le Couronnement de Louis*, ed. E. Langlois, CFMA 1925, ll. 277–8. I use the word 'boys' advisedly, in the sense of a servant of any age, a usage now largely confined to 'houseboy' etc. of our old colonies.

[33] This almost casual reference to marching at night is a striking example of what medieval armies could achieve. For the difficulties inherent in such a manoeuvre see: *Cavalry Training (Horsed)* iv, 91, 109–11 (problems of pace, navigation, contact and alarms) esp. 91.3 on the need for training in night movement.

movement by individuals along the line of march had to be made downwind, so as not to discomfort the others with their dust. Groups were forbidden to travel away from the column, and all must keep to their places (158). Also, despite the tradition of the poverty of the Order's founders, it was expressly forbidden that two brothers should ride on one horse (379). During peacetime the brothers might water their horses at a running stream, without permission, but in war, or when scouting ('en terre de regart'), only when the gonfanon at their head halted. If the alarm was raised, they acted as in camp. Those nearby were permitted to mount their destriers and take up shield and lance to await the Marshal's commands, while the rest rode up to him for orders (159).

The impression of a well-organised force, where every man knew his station, is striking. It is not surprising to find this good order carried onto the battlefield. A first principle of the Rule was that a brother should obey any other set above him. The section on riding 'en eschielles' – in squadrons – talks of 'nominated' leaders, each with a gonfanon and ten knights to guard him. It is difficult not to believe that he was their superior in peacetime, and that the brothers fought alongside those with whom they normally lived (166).[34]

When the knights were armed they took up their position in line, placing their squires with their lances and shields before them. They were expressly forbidden to break ranks or charge without permission, and even turning their horses' heads to the rear in order to fight, or in response to an alarm, was not allowed (161). For two reasons only could a brother leave the ranks. He might ride his horse a little way to check that it was sound, and whether his saddle or harness needed adjusting, and then return to his place. With permission he could take his lance and shield. Or, if he saw a Christian straggler attacked by a Muslim and in peril of death, he could, 'if his conscience reproached him', ride out to save him and then return to the ranks (162). If he should charge or break ranks for any other reason he suffered the humiliating punishment – for a *chevalier* – of being made to go on foot on the march and in camp (163).

The Confanonier was to arrange the squires also in squadrons. When the Marshal led the knight brothers in the charge, the squires who rode the spare destriers were to charge after them. This animal provided a remount if their master's charger was wounded or blown. Meanwhile, those with the palfreys or mules which the knights rode to battle, were to follow the Confanonier's banner, well-ordered and at the amble.[35] (This supposes, of course, four mounts and two squires.) The Turcopolier, who commanded the sergeants when under arms,

---

[34] The military value of knowing the men around you, and trusting them is timeless. The modern British Army lays great weight on the 'buddy, buddy' system whereby (infantry) men are taught to operate in pairs, just as the Templar knights did.

[35] Mounting from riding animals is described in the *Chanson de Roland*, ed. F. White-head, Oxford 1978, ll. 1000–1:

laissent muls e tuz les palefreiz

Es destrers muntent, si chevalchent estreiz.

Cf. Maurice's *Strategikon* v, 2, doubting the ability of 'boys' to handle warhorses in battle.

drew them up too. Sometimes each group had a knight assigned to lead them, 'in closely ordered ranks', behind the knights, in case they had need of assistance or rescue (172).[36] Armoured sergeants were expected to fight like the brother knights. Those 'unarmoured' could join in 'for the love of God and their brothers' but if they were wounded, or could not resist the attacks of the enemy, might retire without permission (172).[37]

Every precaution was taken to ensure that the charge was delivered under the Marshal's orders. When he took the Piebald Banner from the hands of the Undermarshal he appointed a guard of ten knights, under a commander, to protect him. This commander carried a rolled banner, so that if, 'God forbid', the Marshal's banner should fall, he could unfurl it and the knights could rally to him. He led the charge if the Marshal was wounded or forced to retire (165).

Delivering the Knights' Charge

'The real sphere of action for cavalry, its decisive influence on the enemy, in short the very life and soul of our army, is the charge.' Von Schmidt.[38]

At this point, just before the charge is released, I feel I must explain something about cavalry. I turn to George Bernard Shaw to do this for me. In his play *Arms and the Man*, the heroine, Raina, learns about war in conversation with the enemy soldier she discovers in her room.

> *The Man:* 'You never saw a cavalry charge, did you?'
>
> *Raina:* 'How could I?'
>
> *The Man:* 'Ah, perhaps not – of course! Well it's a funny sight. It's like slinging a handful of peas against a window pane: first one comes, then two or three close behind him, then all the rest in a lump.'
>
> *Raina:* (*her eyes dilating as she raises her clasped hands ecstatically*) 'Yes, first One! – the bravest of the brave!'
>
> *The Man:* (*prosaically*) 'Hm! you should see the poor devil pulling at his horse.'
>
> *Raina:* 'Why should he pull at his horse?'
>
> *The Man:* (*impatient at so stupid a question*) 'It's running away with him, of course; do you suppose the fellow wants to get there first and be killed. . . ? Then they all come. You can tell the young ones by their wildness and their slashing. The old ones come bunched up under number one guard; they know they're mere projectiles, and that it's no use trying to fight. The wounds are mostly broken knees from horses coming together.'[39]

---

[36] (172): 'Se l'en met frères por garder les sergens d'armes . . . il doivent mener les sergens serrés et rengiés après, a plus beau qu'il porront, que se les frères auront mestier d'aye, que les sergens les puissent rescorre'. The passage does not say whether the sergeants should be mounted, although this seems to be assumed.

[37] This with the proviso that no Christian should be endangered.

[38] *Instructions* ch. 4, 71.

[39] *The Works of Bernard Shaw* viii, *Plays Pleasant and Unpleasant* ii, 1931, 15.

This marvellous piece of debunking nevertheless makes the point clear: the impetuosity of cavalry can be its downfall.

Every cavalry manual from Maurice's *Strategikon* onwards supports Shaw's view

> A charge, even on good ground, is seldom executed by the whole line at once; the enemy is reached in succession by different points in the line more advanced than others. It is therefore of the greatest consequence that those detachments which reach the enemy first shall be compact, and go at him as one man, to burst through.

So said Louis Edward Nolan in 1853. He is chiefly known for his part in the Charge of the Light Brigade (not the most notably successful cavalry action) in which he carried the disastrously misunderstood order, but his treatise on *Cavalry Tactics* is valuable for its concise lucidity.[40]

> No distance can be laid down at which to charge, it depends on so many different circumstances. When the ground is favourable and your horses in good condition you can strike into a gallop sooner; but the burst, the charge itself, must always be reserved till within 50 yards, for in that distance no horse, however bad, can be left behind, nor is there time to scatter, and they fall on the enemy with the greatest effect.[41]

Hence the emphasis in the *Règle* on the Marshal, the most experienced knight in the line, choosing the exact moment to charge home. Hence, also, the ten knights, 'all around the Banner, and as close to it as they may, and they are not to leave it or move away'. The other Templar knights were instructed to ride to right and left, before and behind, so they might do most harm to the enemy and come to the Banner's aid if need be (164).

---

[40] Maurice's *Strategikon* urges cavalry to: 'ride on in good order, not too fast but at a trot, to avoid having the impetus of their charge break up their ranks before coming to blows with the enemy, which is a real risk' (iii, 5). An Austrian training manual of the late eighteenth century, cited by G. E. Rothenburg, *Napoleon's Greatest Adversaries: Arch-duke Charles and the Austrian Army 1792–1814*, 1982, 107, stresses the same point, suggesting an 80 yard 'burst'. Finally, in modern times: *Cavalry Training (Mounted)*:

3. The object (of a mounted attack) is to strike an irresistible blow with the maximum impetus. The line therefore, should be well closed up and in good order. . . 4. The tactical formation must be of the simplest, and be capable of rapid alteration to suit any change of situation. Manoeuvring for position will probably result in the opportunity being lost. 5. In order to retain cohesion and to keep the horses fresh for the actual shock, the attacking troops will remain as long as possible at the trot. . . 6. The commander will give the command 'Line will attack', usually when about 300 to 50 yards from the enemy. . . 7. The shorter the distance over which the charge is made, the greater will be the cohesion, and the fresher will be the horses for the actual shock. The charge should not be ordered, therefore, until the line is about 50 yards from the enemy.

[41] Nolan, *Cavalry Tactics*, 182–3, 281–2.

Nolan also draws attention to what should be done after the charge.

> If you succeeded in overthrowing the enemy's line, your own will be in
> disorder. The *mêlée* which ensues, soon, however, turns into a pursuit, and
> this affords the opportunity of destroying those who have turned; for the
> charge and the *mêlée* do not last long enough to inflict or sustain heavy loss
> in men or horses . . . The pursuit must be kept up with vigour . . . This is
> not the time to stay the slaughter, but watch over the safety of the pursuers
> with your cavalry reserves till the flying enemy is entirely dispersed. . . .
> Then rally.
> Reserves must always be at hand to follow up steadily any success
> achieved, or, in case the first line is brought back. . . . The reserves should
> follow closely and be ready to act whenever and wherever their action is
> required. . . . Innumerable reverses are attributable to the neglect of these
> rules about reserves.[42]

These instructions explain the duties of the sergeants, outlined above. That
is, to hold back a victorious enemy with their 'closely ordered ranks' and give the
knights time to recover, or to follow a pursuit in good order in case of an
unexpected reverse. The squires with the fresh horses add another dimension, as
they enable the better-equipped knights to return to the *mêlée* if their first
destrier was wounded or blown.

Once the charge was launched, and the *mêlée* begun, no brother could leave
his squadron for rest or because of his wounds without permission (though he
might send another to seek it) (166). Should he be unable to return to his
banner, he was to rally to one of the Hospital, or, failing that, any Christian
banner (167). The importance of banners on the battlefield cannot be over-
stated. In the *geste* of *Girart de Roussillon* a divine thunderbolt destroys the
gonfanons of both the rebel and Charlemagne; the battle is immediately brought
to an end in confusion.[43] So, each Templar commander carried a banner to lead
the way and form a rallying point. As Nolan explains: 'Once a line of cavalry is
hurled against the enemy, all orders from the commanding-officer must necessarily cease for a time. The men of each troop look to their leader . . .' and after the
charge: 'Each troop rallies for itself, and, when formed, is led into line'.[44]

What better way of signifying this than a banner waving above the dust of
battle? At no time was it permitted to lower a banner in order to strike a blow at
an opponent. Any Templar guilty of this offence, if any harm came of it, was
open to the severest punishment. That is, to be banished from the Order. It was
one of the nine great crimes, on a par with heresy, killing a Christian, desertion
to the Saracens, or sexual offences. The punishment might include life imprisonment (232, 241–2). Should the Marshal's banner fall, and the Christians be
thrown back – 'which God guard against!' – a brother was to rally to another

---

42 *Ibid.*, 282 and 283.
43 Ed. P. Meyer, 3 vols, SATF, Paris, 1941–46, ll. 2862–9.
44 Nolan, *Cavalry Tactics*, 280: *Cavalry Training (Mounted)*, which stresses that 'No
attempt will be made by the men to take up their original places in the ranks', 133.

banner. If all banners turned in flight he might escape to a garrison, wherever he thought best (168). It only remains then to show the Templars as successful on the battlefield by following their Rule. In truth this is difficult to do in the same sort of detail that the 'retrais' give us. One might mention the defeat of Nur al-Din in 1163 and Saladin in 1177, where Templar knights provided an important proportion of the Christian host.[45] In Egypt, the episode at Damietta in 1219, already mentioned, or at Mansourah in 1250, showed Templar discipline as most effective in battle, though often at great cost to themselves.[46] Perhaps the most famous example of the value of Templar expertise was on the Second Crusade. Only when an inept Louis VII allowed the Templar Master to re-organise his column of march, were the undisciplined French Crusaders saved from certain annihilation.[47] But then chroniclers pay less attention to victories, which were God-given, than to defeats, where someone was to blame.

The Christian defeat at Gaza in 1244 is a fine example of what could go wrong if the Rule's precepts were not followed. According to the *Estoire d'Eracles*, written in OF, like the *Règle*: 'The Christians began to hurl themselves after (the enemy). The squires and footsoldiers became mixed up with the squadrons, and the knights were unable to charge or come against the Turks . . . Folly, greed and pride,' as they rushed after booty, were the Christians' downfall. If we may believe the figures the Patriarch of Jerusalem gave in a letter, the losses amongst the Military Orders were especially heavy as a result of this disaster.[48]

It is impossible to talk about Crusader defeats without mentioning Gerard de Ridefort. At the Springs of Cresson in 1187, he led ninety Templars, ten Hospitallers, including their Master, Roger de Moulins, and forty secular knights against 7,000 Saracens. When his Marshal, Jaques de Mailli demurred, Gerard is supposed to have accused him of being too fond of his blond head to risk it. Only Gerard and two other brothers survived this encounter. As a happy postscript, however, the squires who guarded the gear, when they saw their masters disappearing into the massed ranks of the enemy, turned and fled. Now, it is a commonplace that after a battle the defeated side loses all its gear. The squires, who must have been following at a moderate pace, as the Rule dictates, were able to make off in safety: – 'and of the Christian gear, none was lost.'[49]

---

[45] See Smail, 96 and William of Tyre, *Historia rerum in partibus transmarinis gestarum*, RHC Hist. Occ. i, Paris xix, xxi, repr. 1969, vol. i, 2, 895, 1038.

[46] Jean, Sire de Joinville, *Histoire de St Louis*, ed. N. de Wailly, Paris 1874, ch. 7.

[47] Odo of Deuil, *De profectione Ludovici VII in orientem*, ed./trans. V. G. Berry, New York 1948, 126–7. Everard de Barres, the Templar Master, instituted companies of knights 50 strong, under orders not to pursue harassing Turks, to charge and retire as instructed and to stand as required, and to maintain an agreed order of march, which was to be strictly kept to. Essentially he was applying the Rule's practice to the secular Crusaders.

[48] *Histoire d'Éracles*, RHC Hist. Occ. ii, Paris, 1859, 429 (Rothelin, 564).

[49] *Histoire d'Éracles*, 40. Gerard de Ridefort has had a universally bad press for his rashness and impetuosity, and this has influenced historians when thinking about Templar military capabilities in general. Two recent essays attempting to reinterpret

Gerard de Rideford has come down to us as a notoriously proud and head-strong character. To him, also, is accorded the responsibility for persuading King Guy to march across waterless lands to the Horns of Hattin, the battle that lost the Kingdom. Once more Gerard escaped, spared by Saladin, who personally ordered the execution of all the other knights of the Temple and Hospital, as his most dangerous opponents. Like Lord Cardigan, de Ridefort was a survivor. But he had not followed the guidelines laid down in the *Règle* for the proper conduct of warfare. No set of regulations, however thorough, can entirely dictate human behaviour, least of all in the confusion of battle. As Captain Nolan was to discover at Balaclava – there can be a fatal gap between theory and practice.

the actions of previously criticised Crusader leaders suggest that it may be time to reassess de Ridefort as well. See: R. C. Smail, 'The predicament of Guy de Lusignan, 1183–87', in *Outremer: Studies in the history of the Crusading Kingdom of Jerusalem*, 159–76; B. Hamilton, 'The Elephant of Christ, Reynald de Chatillon', in *Studies in Church History*, Oxford 1978. For an explanation of what Gerard may have been attempting at the Springs of Cresson, on 1 May, 1187, see, *Cavalry Training (Mounted)* 131: '8. If small bodies (of cavalry) show resolute determination to attack whenever possible, they will establish a moral ascendancy over the enemy, which will prove of inestimable value', although this is in relation to other scouting forces. There was, of course, the complicating factor that de Ridefort's enemy, Count Raymond of Tripoli, had given the Muslim force safe conduct and freedom to take water; which makes the Templar Master's conduct both reprehensible and understandable.

Bibliography

PRIMARY SOURCES

Manuscript
Dijon, Arch. Depart. H.III (French Rule, ends at Clause 197)
Rome, Acad. des Lincei, cod. 44 A 44 (French Rule)
Paris, Bibliothèque Nationale, fonds français 1977 (French Rule)
Barcelona, Archivos de la Corona de Aragón, Cartas Reales ms 344 (Catalan Rule)

Printed
Albon, Marquis d', ed. *Cartulaire Général de l'Ordre du Temple, 1119?–1150*, Paris 1913.
Bernard of Clairvaux 'Liber ad Milites Templi de laude Novae Militiae', *Sancti Bernardi Opera*, ed. J. Leclercq, Rome 1963. Tr. C. Greenia, Cistercian Fathers Series: 19, Michigan 1977.
Curzon, H. de, ed. *La Règle du Temple*, Paris 1886.
Daillez, L. *La Règle du Temple*, Nice 1977.
Delaville Le Roulx, J., ed. *Cartulaire Général de l'Ordre des Hospitaliers de St. Jean de Jérusalem*, 4 vols., Paris 1894–1904.
Dubois, Pierre *The Recovery of the Holy Land*, tr. W.I. Brandt, New York 1956.
Gabrieli, F., ed. *Arab Historians of the Crusade*, tr. E.J. Costello, London 1969.
Garmondsway, G.N., tr. *The Anglo-Saxon Chronicle*, London 1953.
James, B.S., tr. *The Letters of Bernard of Clairvaux*, London 1953.
John of Jaffa 'Livre des Assises de la Haute Cour', *Recueil des Historiens des Croisades, Lois*, vol. I.
Manrique, A., ed. *Annales Cistercienses*, Lyons 1642.
McCann, J., ed. & tr. *The Rule of St. Benedict*, London 1952.
Odo of Deuil *The Journey of Louis VII to the East*, tr. & ed. V.G. Berry, New York 1948.
Philip of Novara 'Livre de Forme de Plait', *Recueil des Historiens des Croisades, Lois*, vol. I.
Scheffer-Boichorst, ed. 'Chronica Albrici Monachi Trium Fontium', *Monumenta Germaniae Historica*, vol. XXIII.
Wilkinson, J., ed. with J. Hill and W.F. Ryan, *Jerusalem Pilgrimage 1099–1185*, The Hakluyt Society, vol. 167, London 1988.
William of Tyre 'Chronicon', ed. R.B.C. Huygens, *Corpus Christianorum*, vols. LXIII & LXIIIA, Brepols 1986. Tr. A.E. Babcock & A.C. Krey, *A History of Deeds Done Beyond the Sea*, New York 1976.

SECONDARY SOURCES

Baldwin, J.W. *The Government of Philip Augustus*, University of California Press 1986.
Barber, M.C. 'The Origins of the Order of the Temple', *Studia Monastica*, 1970, vol. XII, pp. 219–40.

Barber, M.C. *The Trial of the Templars*, Cambridge 1978.

Bordonove, G. *La Vie Quotidienne des Templiers au XIIIe Siècle*, Paris 1975.

Brundage, J.A. *Medieval Canon Law and the Crusader*, Madison 1969.

Burman, E. *The Templars Knights of God*, Crucible 1986.

Carrière, V. 'Les Débuts de l'Ordre du Temple en France', *Moyen Age*, 1914, vol. 18, pp. 308–35.

Cousin, Dom P. 'Les Débuts de l'Ordre des Templiers et Saint Bernard', *Mélanges S. Bernard, XXIVe Congrès de l'Association Bourguignonne des Sociétés Savantes*, Dijon 1953, pp. 41–52.

Demurger, A. *Vie et Mort de l'Ordre du Temple*, Paris 1985.

Forey, A.J. *The Templars in the Corona de Aragón*, London 1973.

Forey, A.J. 'The Military Orders in the Crusading Proposals of the Late-Thirteenth and Early-Fourteenth Centuries', *Traditio*, 1980, vol. 36, pp. 317–45.

Forey, A.J. 'Women and the Military Orders in the Twelfth and Thirteenth Centuries', *Studia Monastica*, 1987, pp. 63–92.

Hefele, C.-J. *Histoire des Conciles*, tr. H. Leclercq, vol. 5, 2, Paris 1912.

Hiestand, R. 'Kardinalbischof Matthäus von Albano, das Konzil von Troyes und die Entstehung des Templerordens', *Zeitschrift für Kirchengeschichte*, 1988, vol. 99, pp. 295–325.

Housley, N. *The Avignon Papacy and the Crusades 1305–1378*, Oxford 1986.

Knowles, D. *The Monastic Order in England*, Cambridge 1963.

La Monte, J.L. *Feudal Monarchy in the Latin Kingdom of Jerusalem*, New York 1970.

Leclercq, J. 'Un Document sur les Débuts des Templiers', *Revue d'Histoire Ecclésiastique*, 1957, vol. 52, pp. 81–91.

Leclercq, J. 'Saint Bernard's Attitude toward War', *Studies in Medieval Cistercian History*, vol. II, ed. J.R. Sommerfeldt, Kalamazoo (Michigan) 1976.

Lekai, L.J. *The Cistercians*, Kent State University Press 1977.

Little, L.K. *Religious Poverty and the Profit Economy in Medieval Europe*, London 1978.

Lizerand, G. *Clément V et Philippe IV le Bel*, Paris 1910.

Loiseleur, J. *La Doctrine Secrète des Templiers*, Orléans 1872.

Lourie, E. 'The Will of Alfonso I, *El Batallador*, King of Aragon and Navarre: A Reassessment', *Speculum*, 1975, vol. 50, pp. 635–51.

Lynch, J.H. *Simoniacal Entry into Religious Life*, Columbus 1976.

Magnou, E. 'Oblature, Classe Chevaleresque et Servage dans les Maisons Méridionales du Temple au XIIe Siècle', *Annales du Midi*, 1961, vol. 73, pp. 377–97.

Melville, M. *La Vie des Templiers*, Paris 1951.

Nicolle, E. *Arms and Armour of the Crusading Era 1050–1350*, 2 vols., New York 1988.

Parker, T.W. *The Knights Templars in England*, Tucson, Arizona 1963.

Partner, P. *The Murdered Magicians*, Crucible 1987.

Prawer, J. *The Latin Kingdom of Jerusalem*, London 1972.

Prawer, J. 'Military Orders and Crusader Politics in the Second Half of the XIIIth Century', *Vorträge und Forschungen – Die Geistlichen Ritterorden Europas*, vol. XXVI, eds. J. Fleckenstein & M. Hellman, Sigmaringen 1980.

Reinach, S. 'La Tête Magique des Templiers', *Revue de l'Histoire des Religions*, 1911, vol. 63, pp. 25–39.

Richard, J. *The Latin Kingdom of Jerusalem*, tr. J. Shirley, Oxford 1979.

Riley-Smith, J. *The Knights of St. John in Jerusalem and Cyprus 1050–1310*, London 1967.

Riley-Smith, J. 'The Templars and the Castle of Tortosa in Syria: An Unknown

Document concerning the Acquisition of the Fortress', *English Historical Review*, 1969, vol. 84, pp. 278–88.

Riley-Smith, J. *The Feudal Nobility and the Latin Kingdom of Jerusalem 1174–1277*, London 1973.

Riley-Smith. J. 'Peace Never Established: The Case of the Kingdom of Jerusalem', *Transactions of the Royal Historical Society*, 1978, vol. 28.

Riley-Smith, J. 'Crusading as an Act of Love', *History*, 1980, vol. 65, pp. 177–92.

Robinson, I.S. 'Gregory VII and the Soldiers of Christ', *History*, 1973, vol. 58, No. 193, pp. 169–92.

Rovik, S.S. *The Templars in the Holy Land during the Twelfth Century*, Oxford (D.Phil. thesis) 1986.

Schnürer, D. *Die Ursprüngliche Templeregel*, Freiburg 1903.

Seward, D. *The Monks of War*, London 1972.

Valous, G. de 'Quelques Observations sur la toute Primitive Observance des Templiers', *Mélanges S. Bernard, XXIVe Congrès de l'Association Bourguignonne des Sociétés Savantes*, Dijon 1953, pp. 32–40.

Warner, M. *Alone of All Her Sex*, London 1976.

Some of the most recent work carried out on the Templars

Bramato, F. *Storia dell'Ordine dei Templari in Italia*, 2 vols, Rome 1991 and 1994.

Barber, M.C. *The New Knighthood. A History of the Order of the Temple*, Cambridge 1994.

Barber, M.C., ed. *The Military Orders: Fighting for the Faith and Caring for the Sick*, Aldershot 1994.

Benvenisti, M. *The Crusaders in the Holy Land*, Jerusalem 1970.

Cardini, F. *Poveri Cavalieri del Cristo. San Bernardo e la Fondazione dell'Ordine Templare*, Rimini 1992.

Cerrini, S. 'La Tradition Manuscrite de la Règle du Temple', in *Autour de la Première Croisade. Actes du Colloque de la Society for the Study of the Crusades and the Latin East (Clement-Ferrand, 22–25 juin 1995)*, ed. M. Balard, Paris 1996 (Publications de la Sorbonne, Série Byzantina Sorbonensia, 14), pp. 203–19.

Cerrini, S. 'La Nouvelle Edition de la Règle du Temple, Latine et Française', in *Welfare and Warfare*, ed. H. Nicholson, Aldershot (forthcoming).

Forey, A.J. *The Military Orders. From the Twelfth to the Early Fourteenth Centuries*, London 1992.

Kennedy, H. *Crusader Castles*, Cambridge 1994.

Minnucci, G. and Sardi, F., eds. *I Templari: Mito e Storia. Atti del Convegno Internazionale di Studi alla Magione Templare di Poggibonsi-Siena, 29–31 Maggio, 1987*, Siena 1989.

Nicholson, H. 'Templar Attitudes towards Women', *Medieval History*, 1991, vol. 1, part 3, pp. 74–80.

Nicholson, H. *Templars, Hospitallers and Teutonic Knights. Images of the Military Orders, 1128–1291*, London 1993.

Pringle, D. *The Churches of the Crusader Kingdom of Jerusalem*, vol. 1, Cambridge 1993.

Riley-Smith, J., ed. *Atlas of the Crusades*, London 1991.

Tommasi, F., ed. *Acri 1291. La fine della presenza degli ordini militari in Terra Santa e i nuovi orientamenti nel XIV secolo*, Biblioteca di Militia Sacra, vol. 1, Perugia 1996.

Glossary

Arming jacket	a padded jerkin worn under armour
Bailli	a provincial commander, who could be a knight brother or sergeant brother
Baillie	the territory under the command of a bailli
Brunete	a fine woollen cloth worn by men of rank
Casal	a farm or village dependent upon a house or castle
Casalier	an officer commissioned to guard one of the Order's casals or farms
Castellan	an officer commissioned to guard one of the Order's castles
Chapeau de fer	a wide-brimmed helmet
Coif	formerly an integral part of the hauberk, in the thirteenth century it became a separate hood of mail
Confrère	an associate brother who served in the Order for a short time and did not take the monastic vows
Consoeur	the female equivalent of a confrère
Cope	a heavy, hooded cloak covering the whole body and fastened by string or hook
Convent	the brothers who made up the fighting force of the Order, i.e. the knight and sergeant brothers
Garnache	a sleeveless cloak
Guarelle	a sort of bag
Hauberk	a coat of mail with coif enveloping the head and leaving just the face uncovered
Helmet	this was probably conical in shape
Palace	originally the headquarters in Jerusalem, and by extension the main hall, which was used as the refectory
Roncin	an entire horse, little better than a pack animal
Scarlet	a cloth of superior quality in a variety of colours
Surcoat	an overgarment of some kind
Tunic	this had short sleeves and was worn over the shirt; short at first, it became longer in the twelfth and thirteenth centuries
Turcoman	an élite riding horse
Turcopole	a fighter of native Middle Eastern or mixed race, a light cavalryman with special skills

Index

References to the Introduction and Appendix are by page number and are at the beginning of each entry; all other references are to clause numbers.